IMAGES
of America

THE JEWISH COMMUNITY UNDER THE FRANKFORD EL

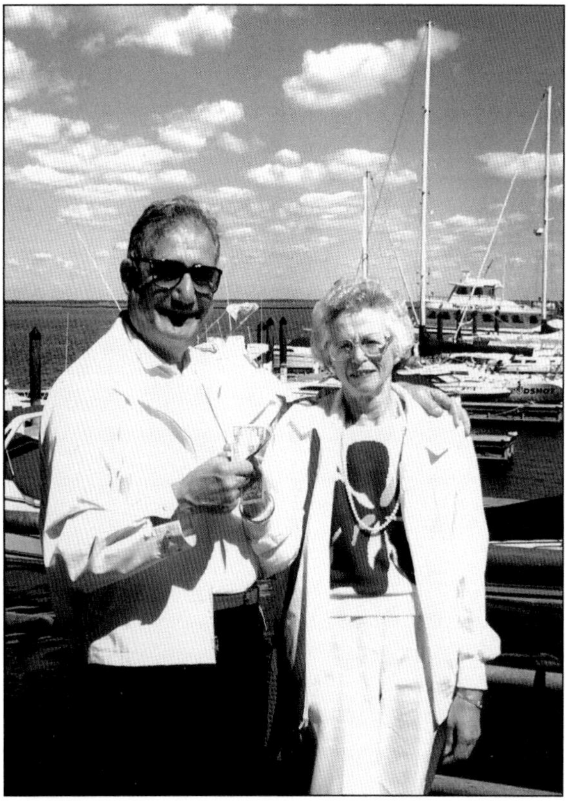

Sidney and Florence Padlasky Nathans instilled a great sense of family into their two children, Carl and Eileen, as youngsters growing up in Philadelphia. Sidney's parents, Morris and Ida Nathans, along with Florence's parents, Rae and Harry, instilled a strong sense of community through Jewish traditions. Carl and his father were discussing Jewtown in the home of his grandfather (Morris Nathans) during a family function in the late 1970s. Florence, along with her mother, overheard the conversation, and she chimed in "We are from Jewtown too!"

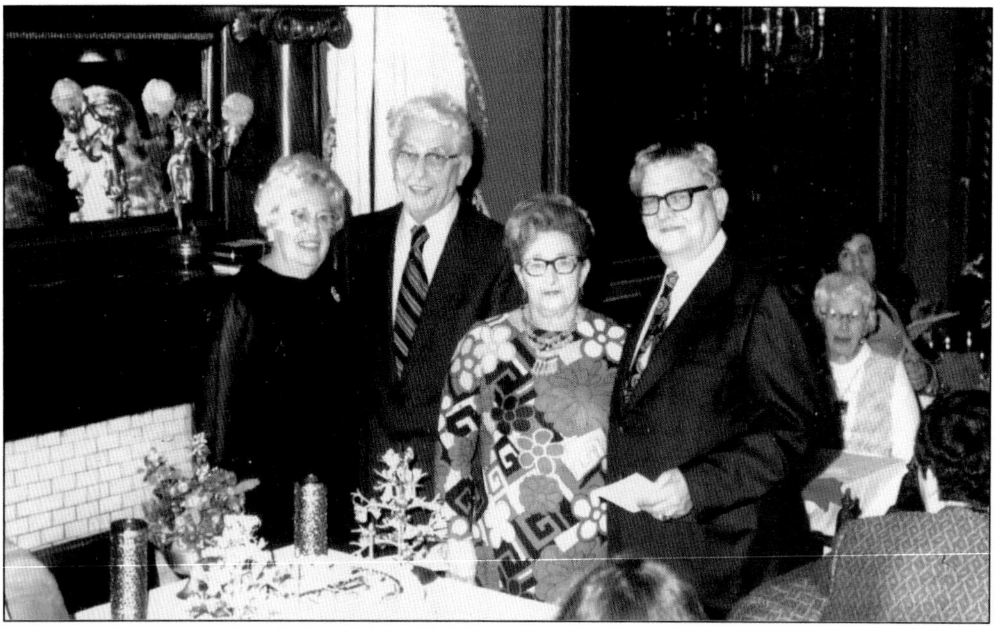

Morris and his second wife, Madeline (left), are pictured with his brother and sister-in-law Barney and Thilda Nathans. The start of an extended family tree became the focus for Carl Nathans that wonderful day during Chanukah in 1978.

IMAGES
of America

The Jewish Community under the Frankford El

Allen Meyers with Carl Nathans

ARCADIA
PUBLISHING

ISBN 978-0-7385-1221-1

Published by Arcadia Publishing
Charleston, South Carolina

Printed in the United States of America

Library of Congress Catalog Card Number: 2003104391

For all general information contact Arcadia Publishing at:
Telephone 843-853-2070
Fax 843-853-0044
E-mail sales@arcadiapublishing.com
For customer service and orders:
Toll-Free 1-888-313-2665

Visit us on the Internet at www.arcadiapublishing.com

This book is dedicated to the memory of Sidney and Florence, who passed away in February 1999 and February 2001, respectively.

On the Cover: The completion of the Frankford El in 1922 allowed residents to commute downtown in less than 15 minutes via a railroad built above Front Street, and Kensington and Frankford Avenues. The Jewish community flocked to Kensington, sought private residences, and converted them into storefront businesses directly under the length of the Frankford El at key locations. The large intersection of Kensington and Lehigh Avenues and the coal train yard was easily spanned by an arched superstructure that carried the Frankford El north and southbound, *c.* 1962. (Courtesy of Dick Short.)

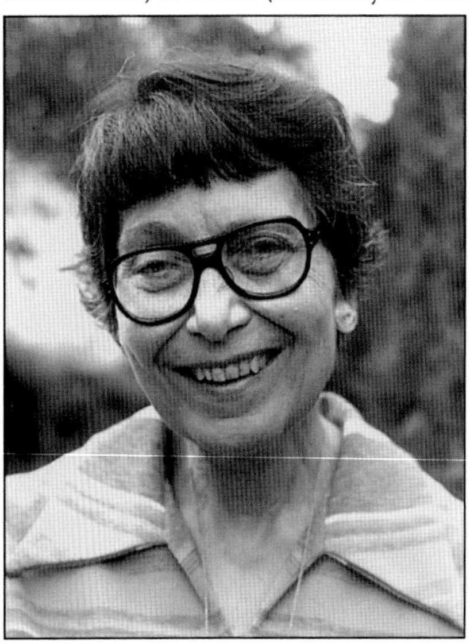

This book is a tribute to Nora Levin, a history professor at Gratz Hebrew College, who in 1978 suggested to Allen Meyers a unique way to honor the passing of his grandparents Rose and Louis Ponnock. The resulting oral history project documented ordinary Jewish people who grew up in Philadelphia. Nora Levin passed away in 1989. She is recalled by all as a kind person. The Hebrew translates as "Nelka [Nora's Hebrew name] the daughter of Yehuda and Baylah, her memory should be blessed."

Contents

PREFACE

This book is a tale of two young men, Allen Meyers and Carl Nathans, who paralleled each other during the late 1970s in their quest to recall the heritage, culture, and history of Jewish people in Philadelphia but never met until more than 20 years later. Meyers started a community history project under the direction of Gratz Hebrew College professors Nora Levin, Dr. Rela Geffin, and Dr. David Passow to recall the history of the Jewish population vis-à-vis the neighborhood experiences in the 20th century. With a tape recorder in one hand and a camera in the other, he documented the rich culture of Jewish life in Philadelphia and expanded his audience by his inclusion in the Jewish Federation of Philadelphia's Jewish Speaker's Bureau under the auspices of the Jewish Community Relations Council. His thesis is entitled "From One Neighborhood to Another—The History of Jewish Philadelphia."

The methodology used to collect this vast mine of community treasures included oral history interviews and public discussions with several major pictorial exhibits that concentrated on specific sections of the city, such as South, West, and North Philadelphia. The neighborhood exhibits were hosted by the National Jewish Museum (Fifth and Market Streets), the Philadelphia Jewish Archives Center (Seventh and Market Streets), and the main Jewish Community Center (Broad and Pine Streets).

Carl Nathans, along with his father, Sidney, toured one of Meyers's exhibits and came away with a great appreciation of the history of Philadelphia's Jewry. However, they yearned for a section of Philadelphia known as "Jewtown"—located in the Richmond-Kensington section of Philadelphia, which ran along the Delaware River only several miles north of South Philadelphia—and wondered why it was not included in the portrayal of neighborhoods.

Shortly thereafter, Nathans created a history project of his own to tell what Meyers left out in his overall picture of Jewish neighborhoods. Even though Nathans grew up in southwest Philadelphia, he often took rides to where his father grew up in the 3500 block of Frankford Avenue. He went to the expense of an placing an advertisement in the *Philadelphia Jewish Exponent* to search and seek out former "Jewtowners." The response was great, and many people invited him over for coffee and a couple hours of schmoozing about the old neighborhood. The result yielded dozens of oral history tapes and hundreds of photographs of many families who lived off Lehigh and Aramingo Avenues near Tulip and Auburn Streets dating back to the centennial celebration of America in 1876.

Meanwhile, Meyers, a longtime McDonald's restaurant manager, visited Jewtown in 1978 while checking on a management prospect for his store in northeast Philadelphia. Upon driving up Tulip Street, he was enamored by what he thought was a building that had markings of a synagogue at Tulip and Auburn Streets, and he circled around the block to investigate it more thoroughly. To his surprise and delight, the building on the northeast corner indeed had the Star of David over the front door even though it was being utilized as a warehouse. Exasperated, he then thought long and hard to imagine how and when Jews had lived in this section of the city. He went to the opposite corner (southwest) of Tulip and Auburn Streets and to his amazement discovered a cornerstone on the side of a church with Hebrew writing—another synagogue.

Meyers and Nathans came in contact with each other more than 20 years later by coincidence. The two historians finally met at a book signing organized at Nathans's brother-in-law and sister's bookstore for Meyers's third publication on Philadelphia's Jewish neighborhoods, entitled *The Jewish Community of West Philadelphia*.

Introduction

More than 120 years ago, a third wave of Jewish immigrants fled central Europe due to economic and religious persecution in hope of settling in a place they could call home. Many Lithuanian and Hungarian Jews migrated across the Atlantic Ocean on freight ships that allowed for people to come to America in the hulls or steerage compartments for the two-to-three-week voyage. Upon landing in Philadelphia, these hardy souls stepped off the White and Red Star Lines ships and found refuge in the then northeast section of Philadelphia directly along the Delaware River districts in several distinctive communities and neighborhoods: Richmond, Kensington, Fishtown, Port Richmond, Frankford, and later Juanita Park and the Tacony section.

The days of the pioneer immigrants were filled with hope and survival. Itinerant peddlers created weekly routes along the banks of the Delaware River and traveled as far north as Trenton, New Jersey, several years before America celebrated her 100th birthday in 1876. Orthodox Jews faithfully returned to usher in the Sabbath as the head of their households every Thursday afternoon. Jewtown, named by the surrounding Gentile population, became home to hundreds of Jewish people who called it "Little Jerusalem."

Separate from the German-Jewish community, the new immigrants created new Jewish colonies, which later gave way to permanent residences and businesses along such thoroughfares as the King's Highway (locally known as Frankford Avenue), Kensington Avenue, Front Street, and Torresdale Avenue. Late-19th-century row houses made wonderful residences for the successful entrepreneurs, as they lived above or behind their business and raised their children for several decades according to Jewish tradition.

Additional waves of Russian and Polish immigrants in the early 20th century added to the bulging Jewish population that totaled more than 40,000 in a narrow path carved in the Delaware River corridor districts, which stretched 10 miles north of Delaware Avenue. New synagogues, communal institutions, bakeries, delicatessens, and kosher butchers stayed the course as the Market Street Elevated was extended northeastward to the end of the Frankford district in the early 1920s. Real estate property values soared in anticipation of the high-speed, overhead transportation system, which quickly and conveniently connected the masses to the downtown area in the post–World War I era, and Jewish life flourished for a second and third generation into the 1960s.

The postindustrial era in late-20th-century Philadelphia ushered in a large loss of manufacturing jobs throughout the city. Coupled with the Jewish people's desire to encourage their children to better themselves, future Jewish generations moved away from Jewtown as they became professionals with college degrees.

Today, the vacant buildings and residences hold tales of a bygone era when little voices could echo and be heard for some distance under the superstructure where the sun rarely shined into business owners' display windows. New immigrant groups occupy some businesses and eke out a daily living. The federal government has invested millions of dollars to repair and rebuild the El for future generations to use, and new special service districts have been set up to assist economic growth in the shadows of the Frankford El.

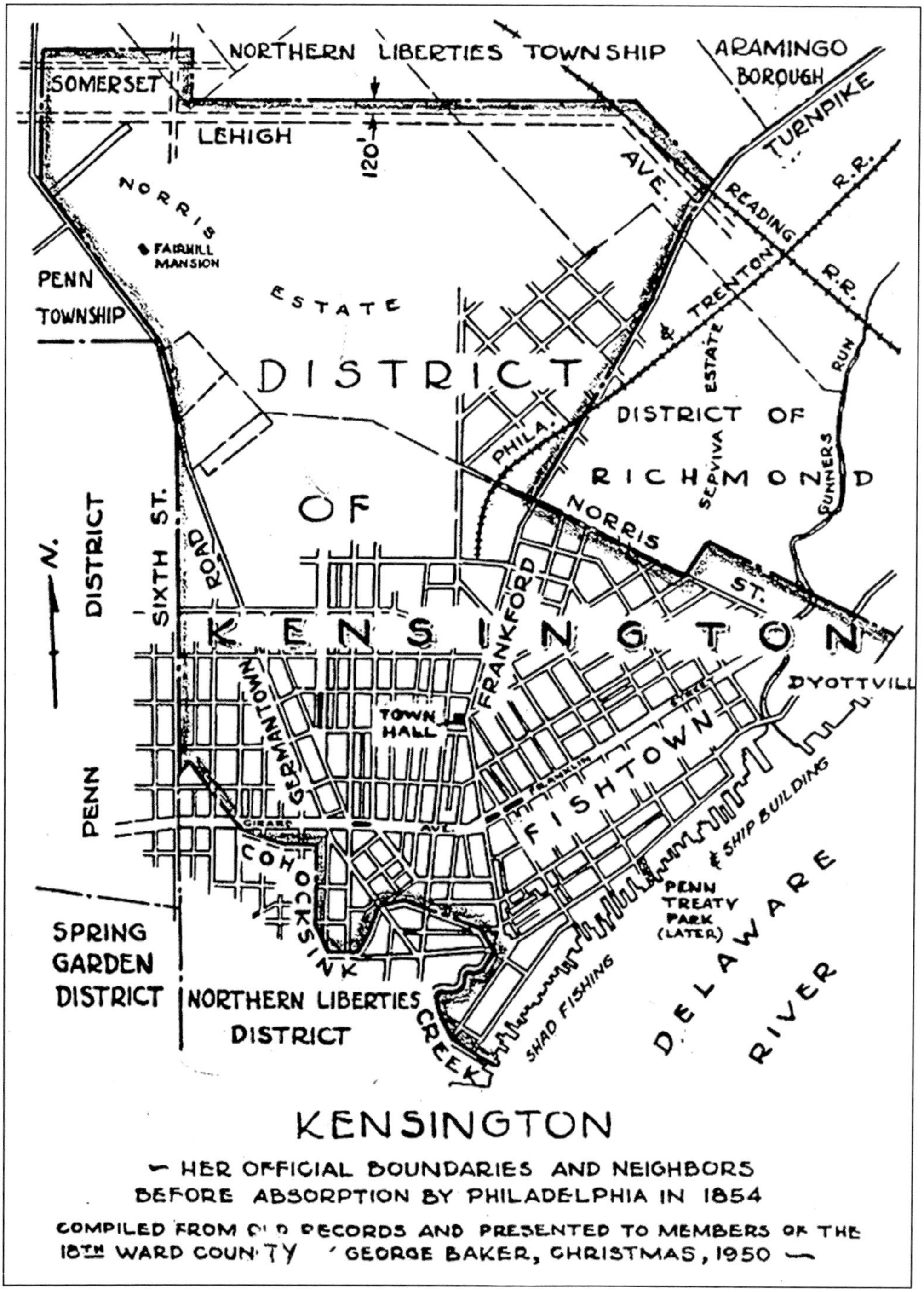

Separate districts made up the city of Philadelphia in the mid-1800s. Kensington, Richmond, and Frankford became part of Philadelphia County via the Incorporation Act of 1854. Transportation, industry, and private homes helped unify the community, which attracted a wide array of ethnic groups that included Irish, German, Polish, Italian, Russian, and Jews in a cooperative economy. (Courtesy of Ken Milano.)

One

Community Landmarks

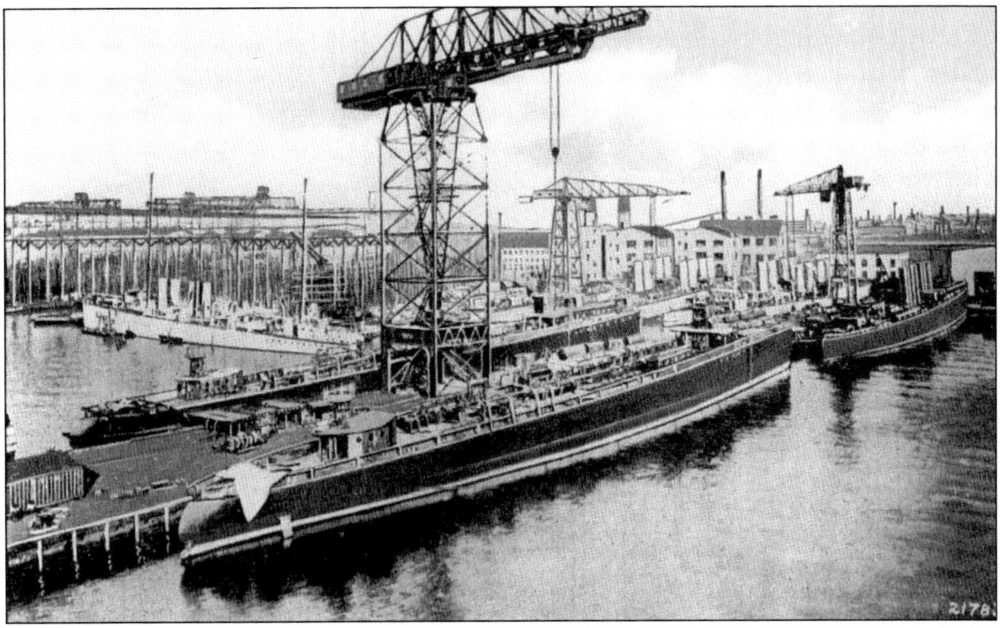

Development of northeastern Philadelphia focused on the Delaware River. Commerce included fishing, trading, and shipbuilding that dated back to the 1600s, when Philadelphia was founded by William Penn. Community landmarks identified specific areas of the city as centers for continuous development and regional trade. The William Cramp Shipyard opened in 1830 and employed during its peak more than 25,000 workers, who built seaworthy ships for peace and war. Many of the ships used to transport Eastern European Jews to America were built along the Delaware River at the Cramp Shipyard in the late 19th century. (Courtesy of the Gus Spector postcard collection.)

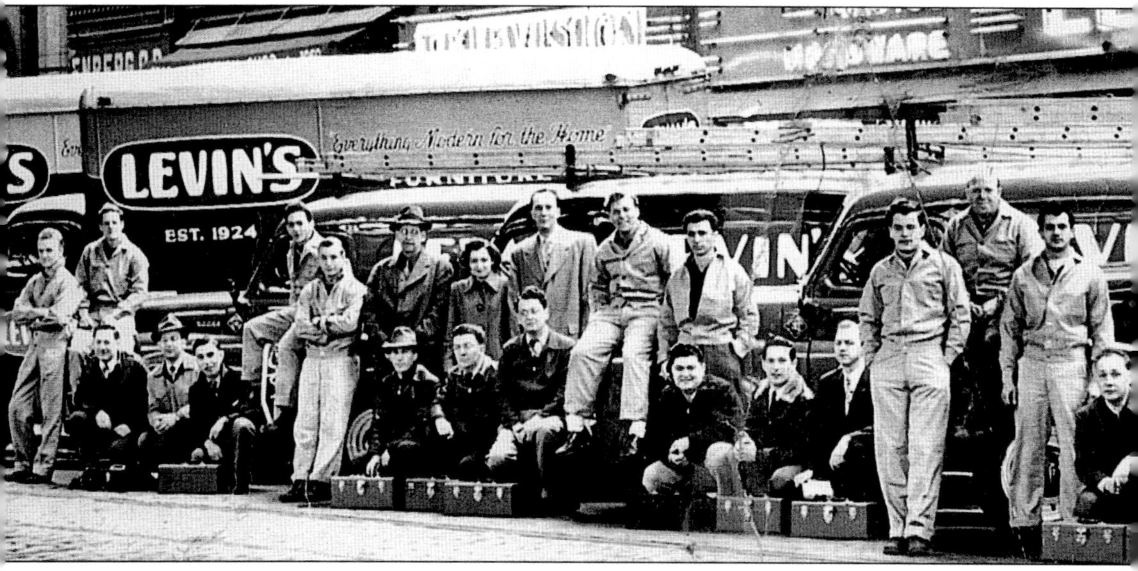

Family-run businesses were popular under the Frankford El. Many businesses had several locations at strategic intersections up and down the line. As good trade developed, Levin's, a multi-store concept, grew on the same block (3000 Kensington Avenue) in response to a changing economy and a spirited man named Harry Levin, who came to Kensington in search of his own business as prerequisite to marriage to his wife. The original hardware business grew to include radios, television, major appliances, and a furniture showroom, stretching along 14 individual storefronts.

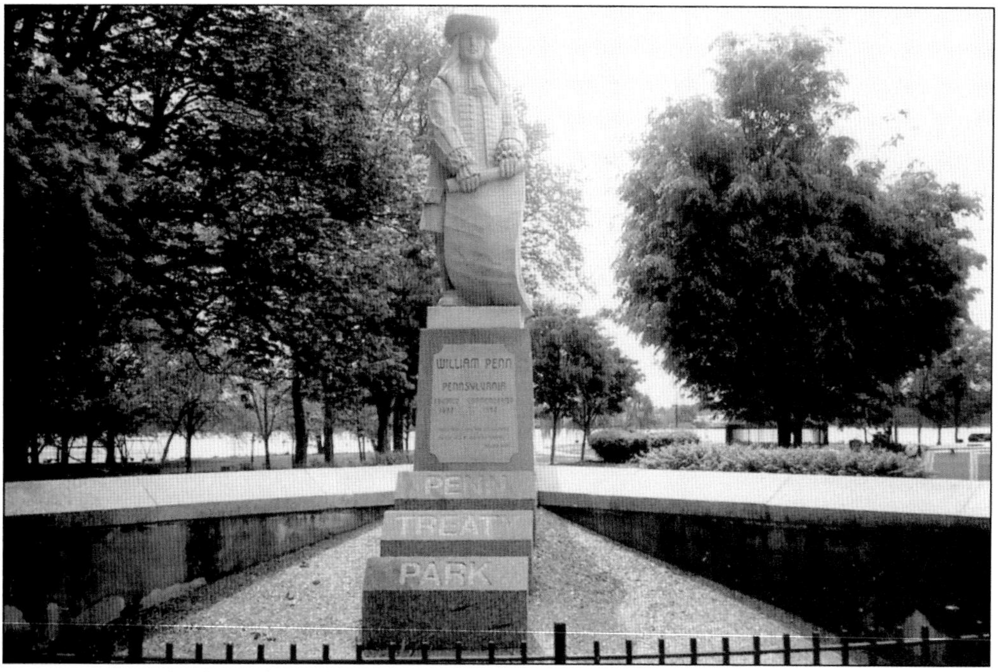

Penn Treaty Park, along the Delaware Avenue above Frankford Avenue, is a great family retreat within the city. Originally, William Penn bargained with Native Americans c.1682 to obtain access to the interior land for hunting and trading. Today, the park offers residents access to the Delaware River for boating, fishing, and recreation.

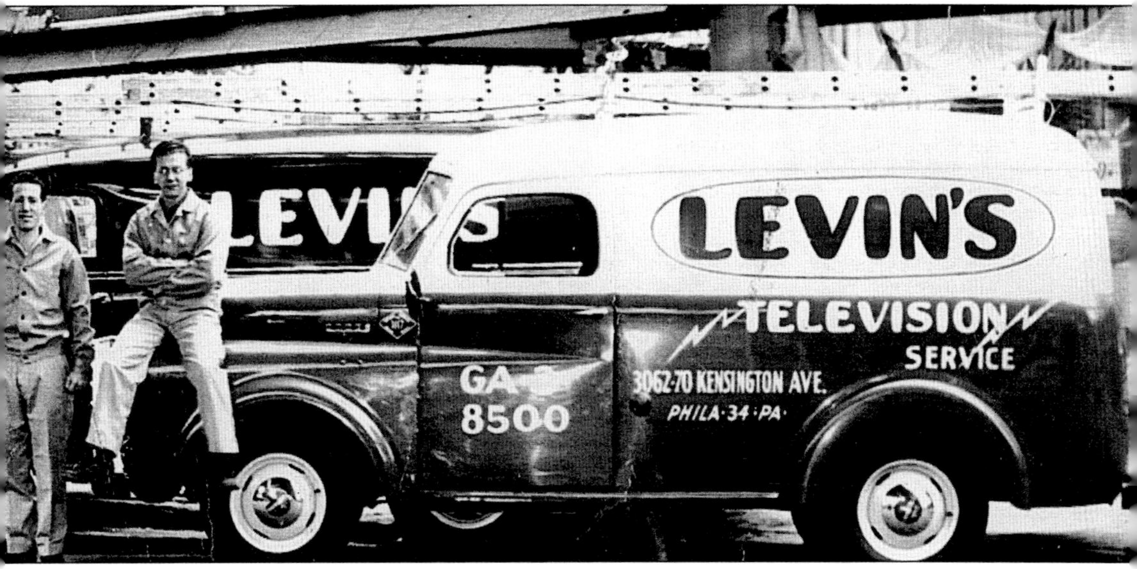

The real estate acquisitions were made possible by a $2,000 loan granted by the Kensington Corn Exchange bank on only a handshake with Levin in the late 1930s. Levin's grew into a multimillion dollar business after World War II. (Courtesy of Marvin Levin.)

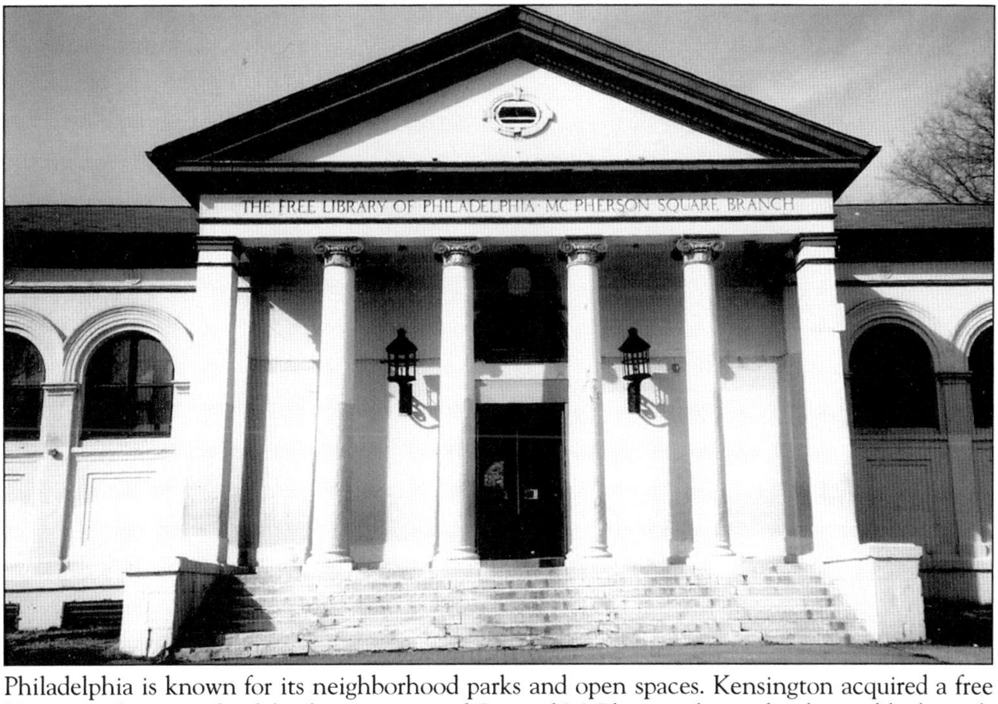

Philadelphia is known for its neighborhood parks and open spaces. Kensington acquired a free library on the grounds of the former estate of General McPherson, located only one block south of Kensington and Allegheny Avenues in the early 1900s. This Greek architectural wonder attracted many children and adults to its reading rooms. The surrounding park grounds were perfect for all outdoor activities and included areas to ride bikes, walk, or place a folding chair.

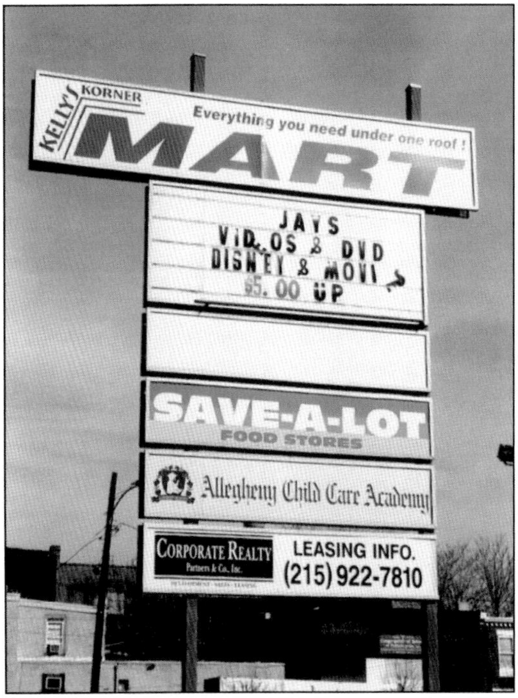

Kelly's Korner, a familiar landmark in the lower end of Kensington, attracted thousands of people every week for best buys on irregular merchandise. The concept of a large department store under one roof appealed to the residents of the community. With its wide aisles and deals, the store attracted whole families who came in to outfit their children, especially for Christmas and Easter.

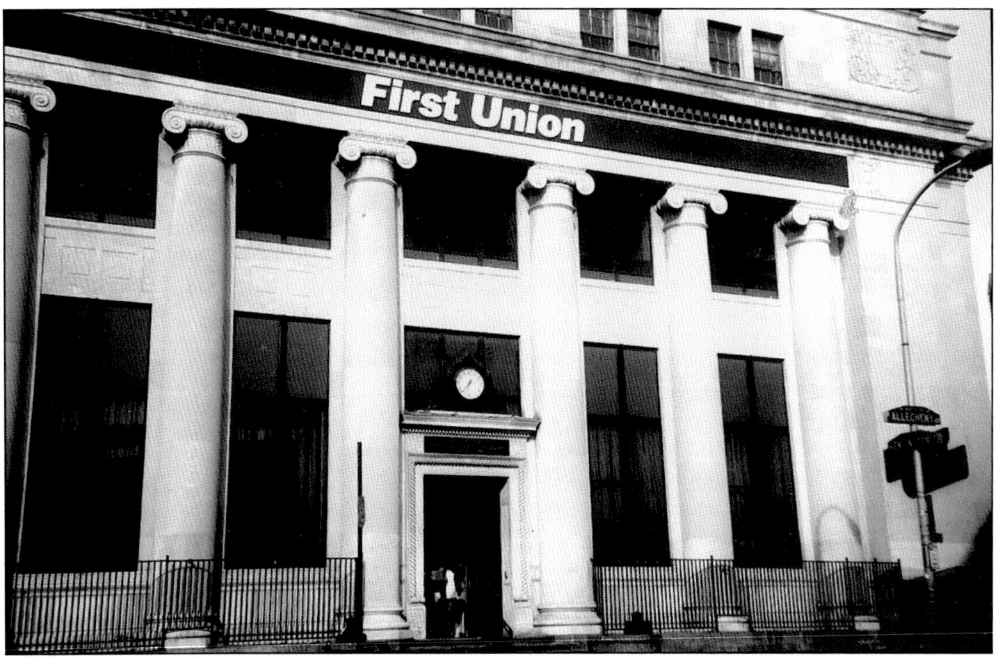

With the arrival of the El train in the 1920s, the intersection of Kensington and Allegheny Avenues (K&A) became a crossroads for commerce and travel. The Corn Exchange Bank of the early 1900s, located on the northwest corner of K&A, became a well-known lending bank and was acquired by the Pennsylvania Bank, then the First Pennsylvania Bank. The familiar landmark became a branch of the large First Union Bank in the late 1980s.

Familiar landmarks give a person from any generation a grand sense of direction. The Harbison Dairy plant with its tall milk bottle is one of those unforgettable landmarks. Situated along the Frankford El line before the York-Dauphin station is a water tower cleverly hidden with some fancy artwork. The rusting icon is still a landmark, helping those riding the Frankford El know what part of the city they are in.

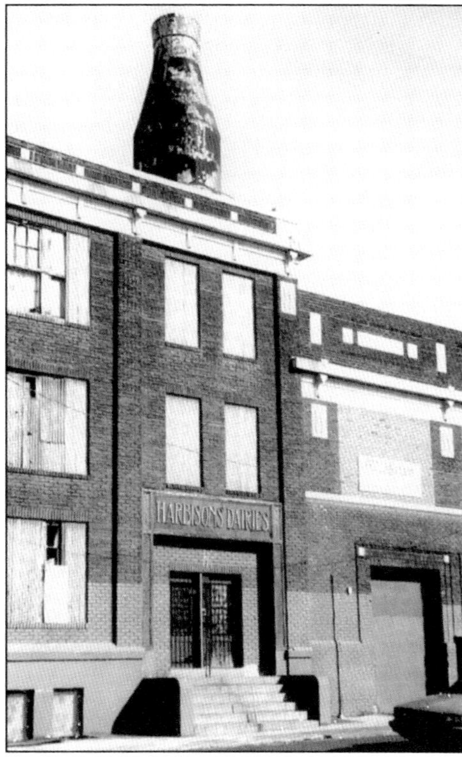

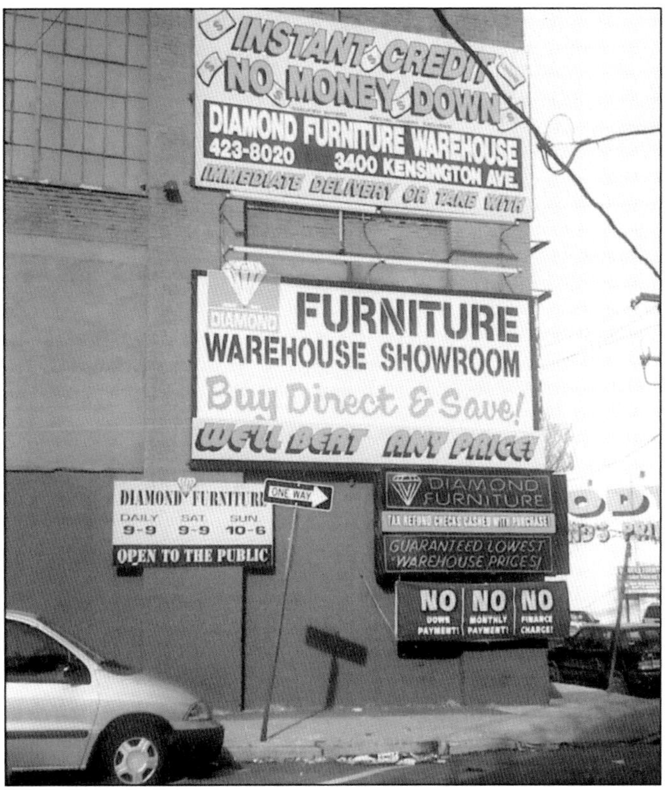

Diamond Furniture store is best known for its advertisements on television and radio and in the newspapers of the day. Founded in 1927, the family-owned-and-operated furniture outlet offers good value on home furnishing items, from rocking chairs to living room sets. Advertisement is a great asset of this company, which also painted its main warehouse overlooking Interstate 95—affectionately known as the Diamond Hill landmark—and erected a lighted sign to alert commuters of impending traffic tie-ups.

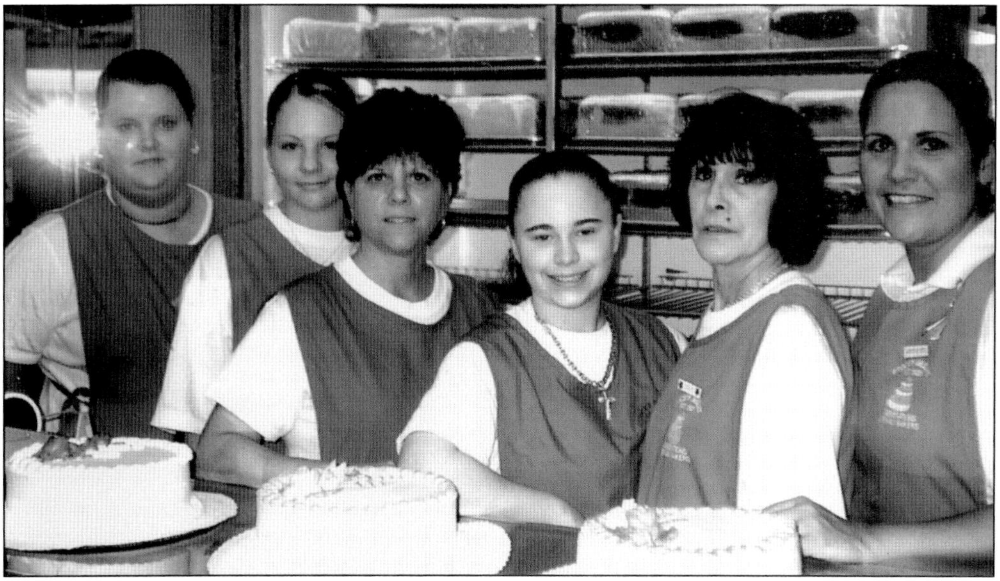

German and Jewish baking tastes still abound in Philadelphia, with loyal customers refusing to choose some preservative-laden, mechanically produced sweet cake. The key ingredient in both German and Jewish baking is cinnamon. The Stock family opened up its store at Lehigh and Mercer near Richmond Street in the 1910s. The flagship product of the bakery remains the pound cake, created for various occasions and good old-fashioned eating.

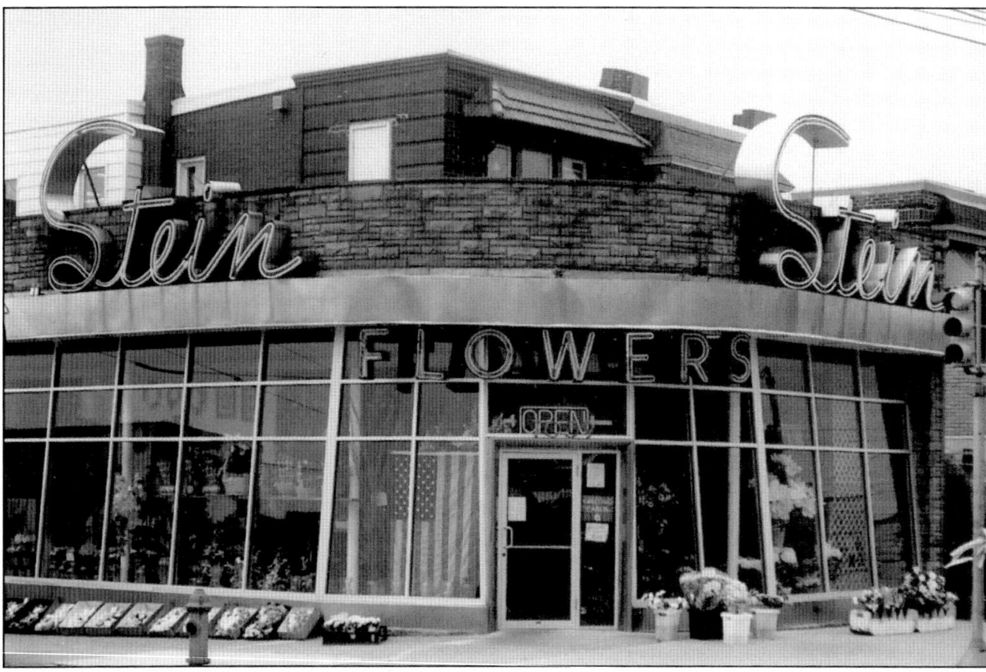

A well-respected name in the world of flowers is Stein florist of Fishtown and Kensington. Now more than 100 years old, Stein creates floral settings for weddings, bar mitzvahs, baby showers, and sweet-16 parties. The business began on Front Street in Kensington under the Frankford El. Today, the grandson of the founder has reopened Stein Flowers in the Mayfair section of northeast Philadelphia at Frankford and Princeton.

Two

Early Jewtowners

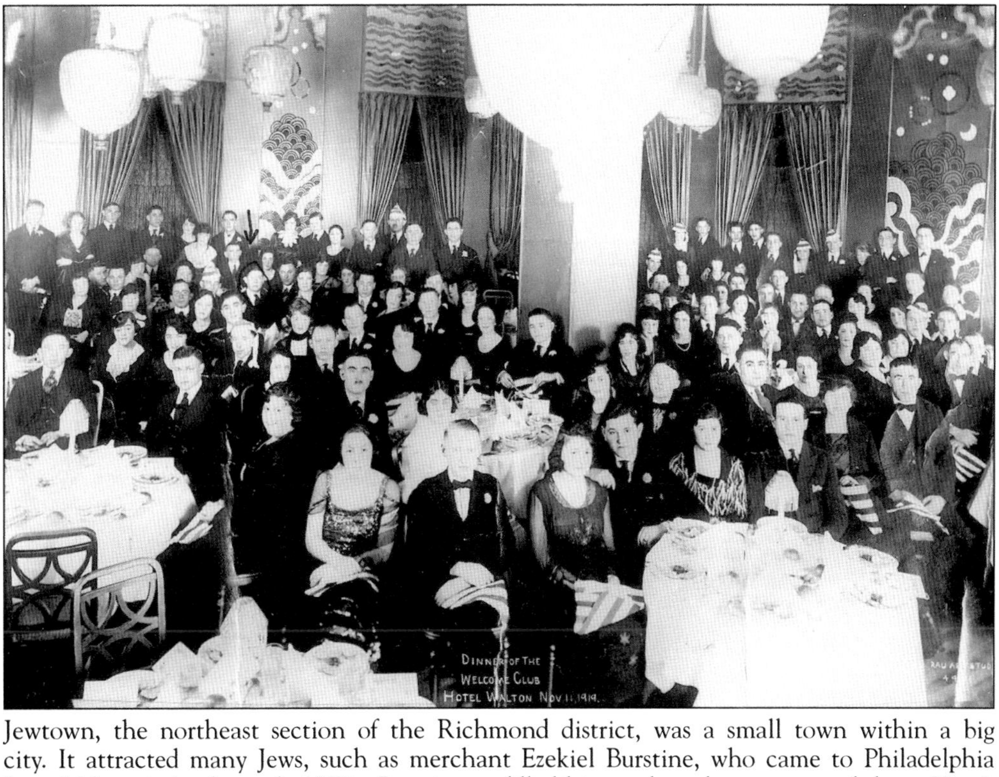

Jewtown, the northeast section of the Richmond district, was a small town within a big city. It attracted many Jews, such as merchant Ezekiel Burstine, who came to Philadelphia from Lithuania in the early 1870s. Burstine peddled his goods and wares up and down King's Highway, better known as Frankford Avenue, all the way to Trenton, New Jersey. He traveled a full week before coming home each Thursday night to prepare for the Sabbath. Although native Philadelphians named the area Jewtown, the Jewish people themselves identified with the name and were proud to tell others where they lived. The community celebrated the end of World War I at the Walton Hotel with a dinner. The northeast Jewish community expanded as peddlers settled down to neighborhood huckstering and then onto a permanent location to do business in the community. (Courtesy of Paul Sokolof.)

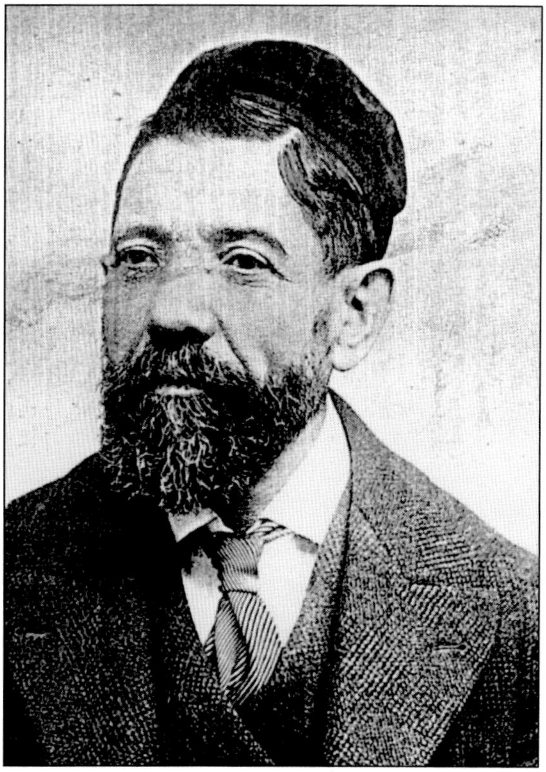

Asher Silverman, one of the five founding members of Jewtown in 1870, had the support of his wife, Rebecca Goldfarb. The other four member of the first Russian-Jewish colony in Philadelphia included Ezekiel Burstine, Pinchas Levy, Samuel Natan (the ritual slaughterer and cantor), and Morris Gorman. The five men organized the synagogue B'nai Israel, which attracted more friends of the original five men and developed into a full community during the late 19th century. (Courtesy of Joan Gross.)

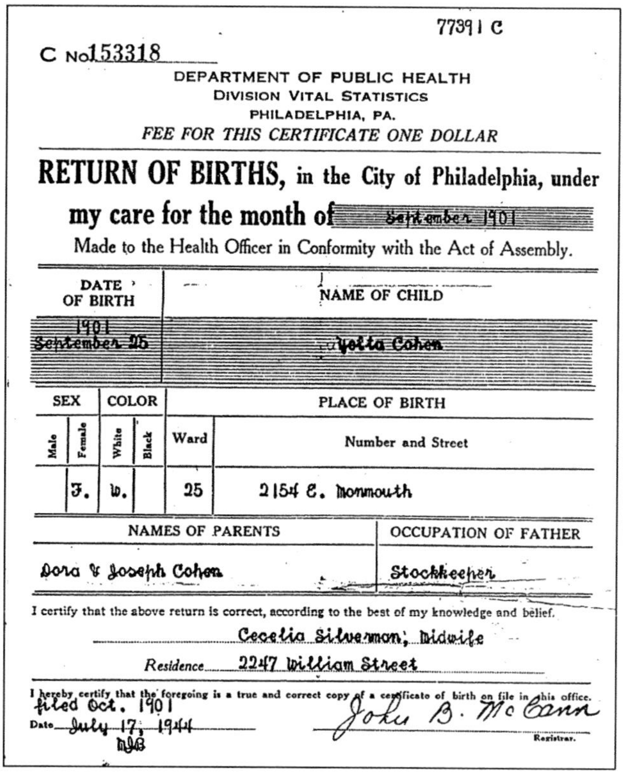

77391 C

C No. 153318

DEPARTMENT OF PUBLIC HEALTH
DIVISION VITAL STATISTICS
PHILADELPHIA, PA.

FEE FOR THIS CERTIFICATE ONE DOLLAR

RETURN OF BIRTHS, in the City of Philadelphia, under my care for the month of September 1901

Made to the Health Officer in Conformity with the Act of Assembly.

DATE OF BIRTH	NAME OF CHILD
1901 September 25	Yetta Cohen

SEX: Male	SEX: Female	COLOR: White	COLOR: Black	PLACE OF BIRTH: Ward	PLACE OF BIRTH: Number and Street
	F.	W.		25	2154 E. Monmouth

NAMES OF PARENTS	OCCUPATION OF FATHER
Dora & Joseph Cohen	Stockkeeper

I certify that the above return is correct, according to the best of my knowledge and belief.

Cecelia Silverman, Midwife

Residence 2247 William Street

I hereby certify that the foregoing is a true and correct copy of a certificate of birth on file in this office.

filed Oct. 1901

Date July 17, 1944

MJB

John B. McCann
Registrar.

Many Jewish women served as midwives in Philadelphia. Cecelia Goldsmith, born in Lithuania in 1862, immigrated to America with her family and settled in Baltimore, Maryland. She married Isaac Silverman, the son of Asher Silverman. She delivered babies up and down the east coast as a midwife. A close bond in the community existed, which accounted for the delivery of a family member of Ed Schweriner's mother, Yetta Cohen. Sadly, one year later, in 1902, Cecelia Silverman succumbed to tuberculosis. (Courtesy of Joan Gross.)

Rabbi Benjamin Block poses with his wife, who came from Kovna Gurbernia in Lithuania during the 1880s along with 40,000 other Jews who arrived in Philadelphia. Rea Abrams watched her grandfather, Rabbi Block, preside over services from the *beama* (pulpit) and recalled a feeling of deep reverence and pride. (Courtesy of Rea Abrams.)

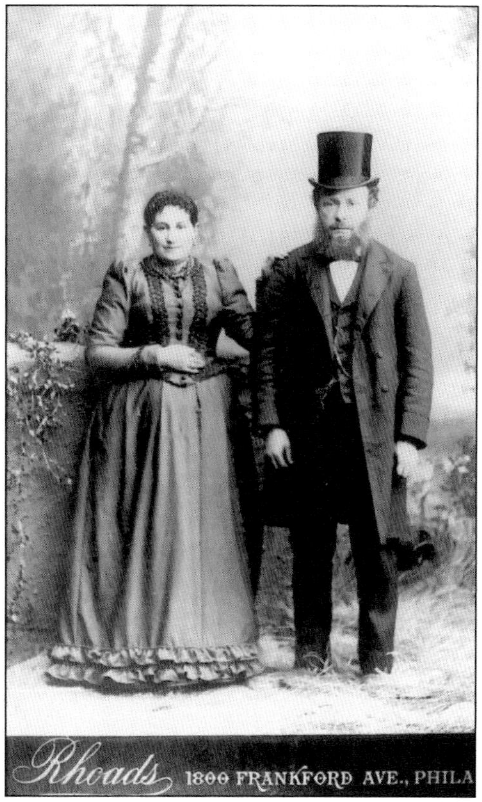

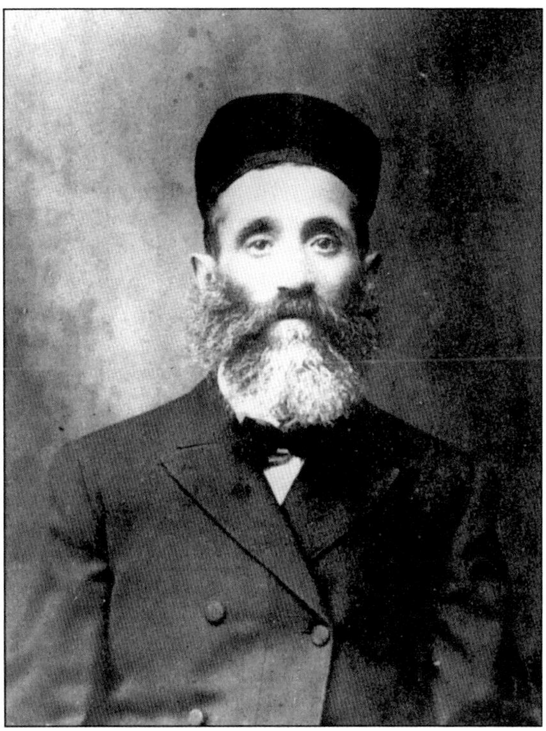

Reverend Arkowitz lived at 2259 Jenny Street. He was a *melmad* (very knowledgeable teacher) of Jewish customs. He taught children throughout the neighborhood, usually in their homes for a small fee. The subjects he focused on were Jewish history, customs, and holidays. (Courtesy of Rea Abrams.)

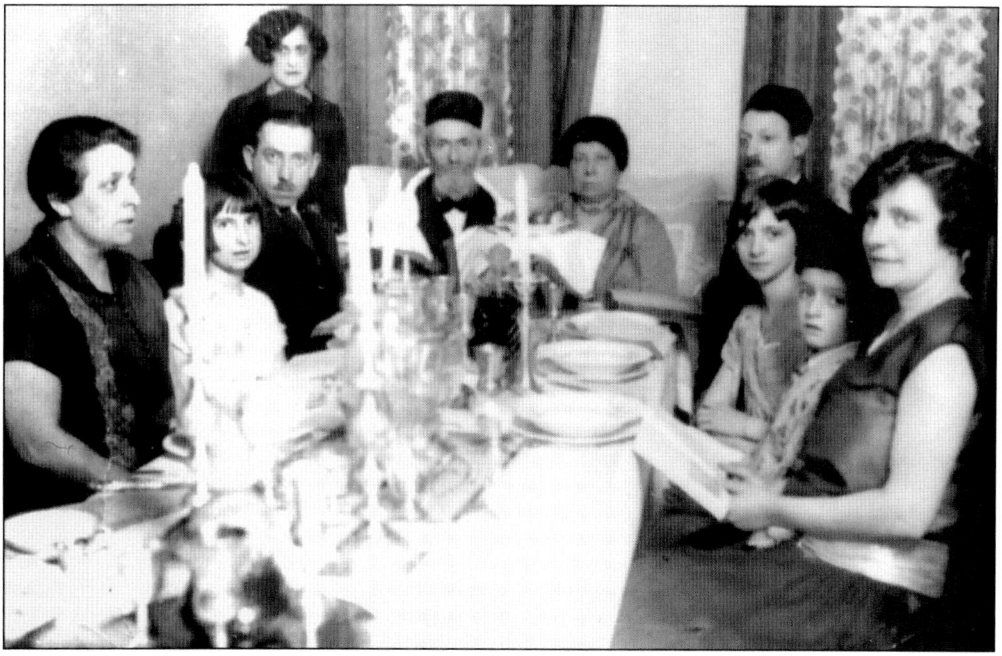

Rabbi Nahum Brenner had a large extended family in Philadelphia, with relatives in Jewtown and South Philadelphia. Jewish holidays presented an opportunity to gather the entire family in one location. In 1924, the Brenners sat down to a Passover Seder with Esther, Nessie, Nisson, Joe, Natalie, Marvin, and Sarah. The closeness of the family defined the larger community, which was transported in whole from Eastern Europe. (Courtesy of Lou Brenner.)

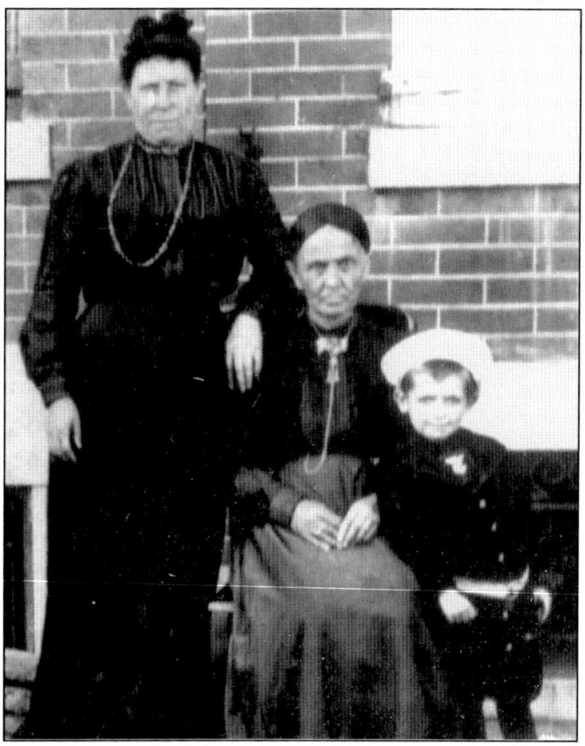

Family portraits were taken in front of homes throughout Jewtown on a regular basis. The wife of Rabbi Benjamin Brenner (left) commanded the respect of the entire community, without people uttering her first name. She was affectionately addressed as *rebbetzen*, Yiddish for "the wife of a rabbi." The rebbetzen is pictured proudly with Rachel Pershonsky and Jay Gerson Brenner. (Courtesy of Louis Brenner.)

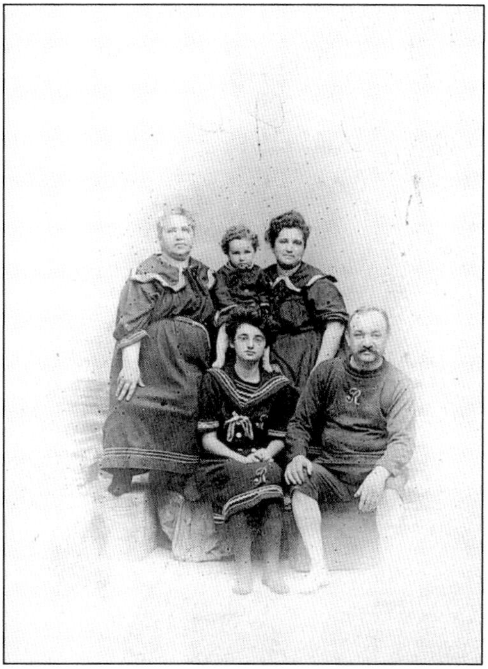

Large families abounded in Jewtown during the 1880s. Bernard Finklestein and his wife, the former Sofie Roeshman, had 13 children who came to reside at 622 Wayne Street, later known as Williams Street and the heart of Jewtown. Finklestein and his wife are photographed with three of their children: Esther, Ralph, and a little boy. (Courtesy of Guy Davis.)

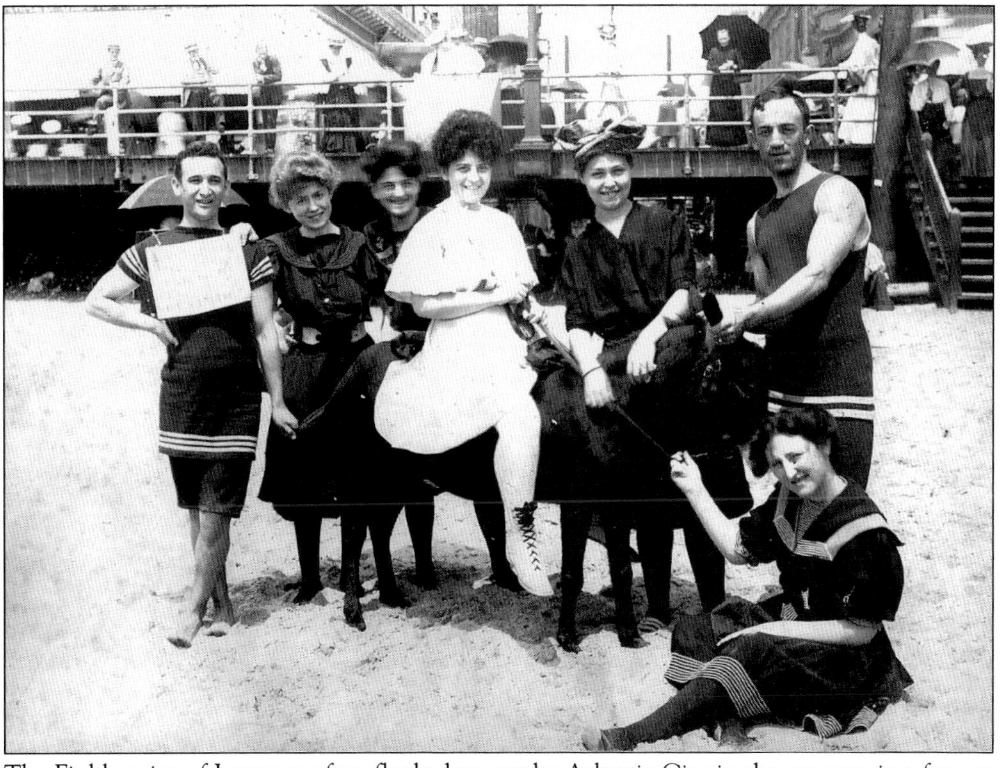

The Finklesteins of Jewtown often flocked to nearby Atlantic City in the summertime for sun and recreation. The 10 surviving children out of 13 were Harry, David, Jake, William, Moe, Annie, Esther, Lena, Sara, and Goldie. William, born in 1883, received his name in the same year that Wayne Street changed to Williams Street. (Courtesy of Guy Davis.)

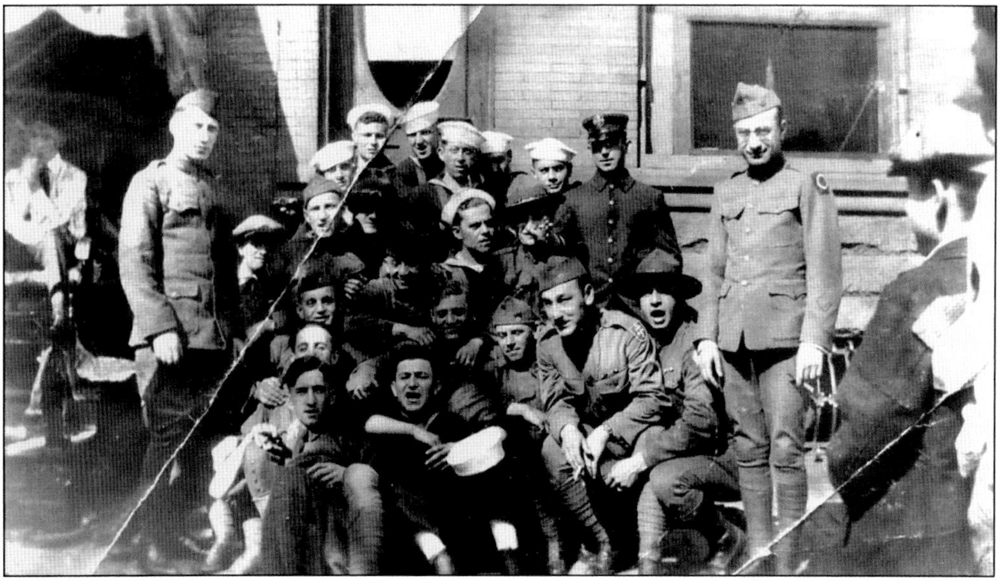

Jewish soldiers inducted into the military service during World War I stand in front of Louis and Temma Finesinger's home on Williams Street in 1918. Harry Finesinger adjusted to army life. Only one generation earlier, his father escaped to America, fleeing from the 25 years of mandatory conscription into the czar's army in Russia. He knew that he could return to civilian life after serving his country, and he posed with his fellow Jewtowners as a proud American Jew. (Courtesy of Anita Berman.)

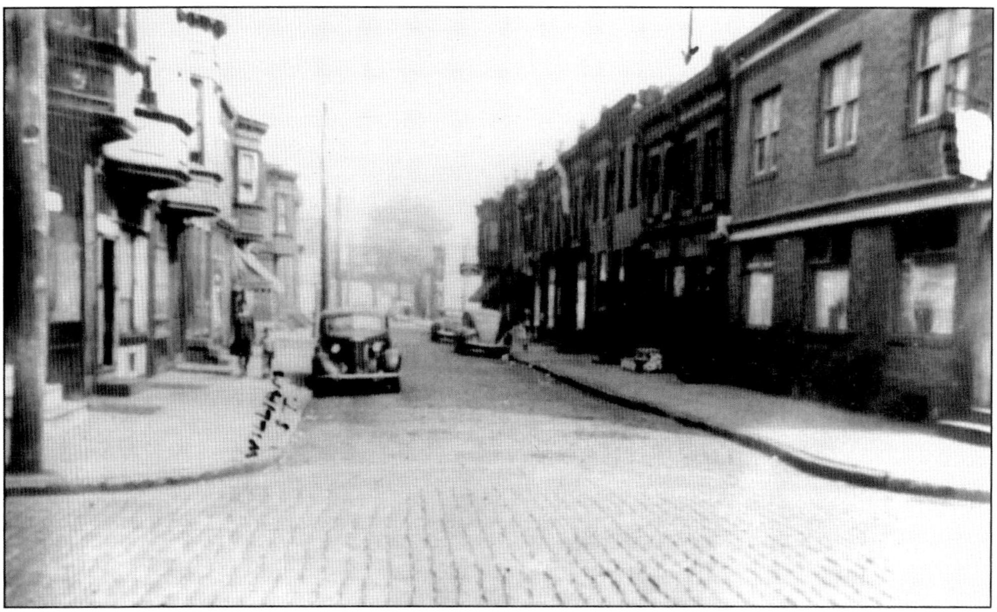

Williams Street at Tulip Street, the heart of Jewtown, contained shops and residences only one block away from the two synagogues. The enclave of streets north of Lehigh and east of Frankford Avenue had natural and physical boundaries that included the railroad yards and a small creek. In the late 19th century, the area experienced the changing of its street names and the addition of electricity and adequate plumbing indoors. The streets in the community were upgraded with cobblestone paving for health and safety concerns. (Courtesy of Izzy Yanus.)

Jeannie Berman Berger, descendant of the Berman family from Jewtown, sits in an old-fashioned highchair as a toddler. The daughter of Berty Berman, she was later known to the whole family as "Cuz." She married Irv Berger of South Philadelphia. The couple had two children, Iris and Jeff. (Courtesy of Carl Nathans.)

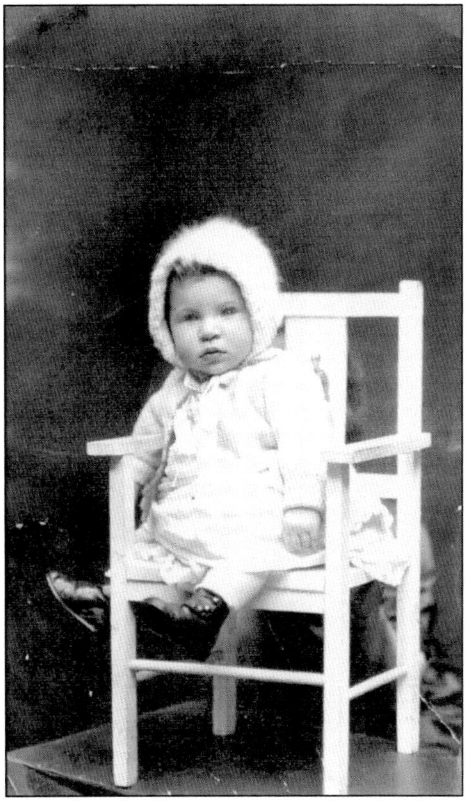

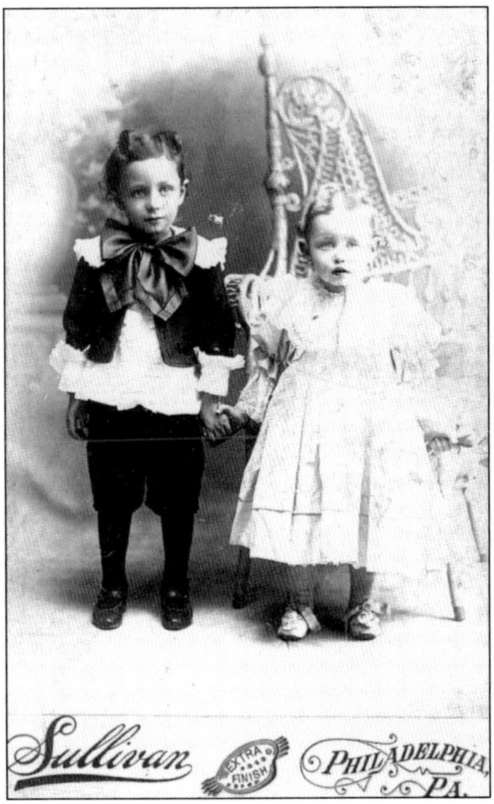

As always, brother and sister Harry and Rae Wolf are dressed up for the Jewish High Holidays c. 1895. Rae took a job downtown at Wanamaker's department store as a skip locator, responsible for finding deadbeat accounts by using various speech dialects. The grandmother of Carl Nathans, she never forgot her roots and often traveled with her mother, Esther Wolf, from their Passyunk Avenue shoe store in South Philadelphia to visit her Bubbe Temma Berman in Jewtown. (Courtesy of Carl Nathans.)

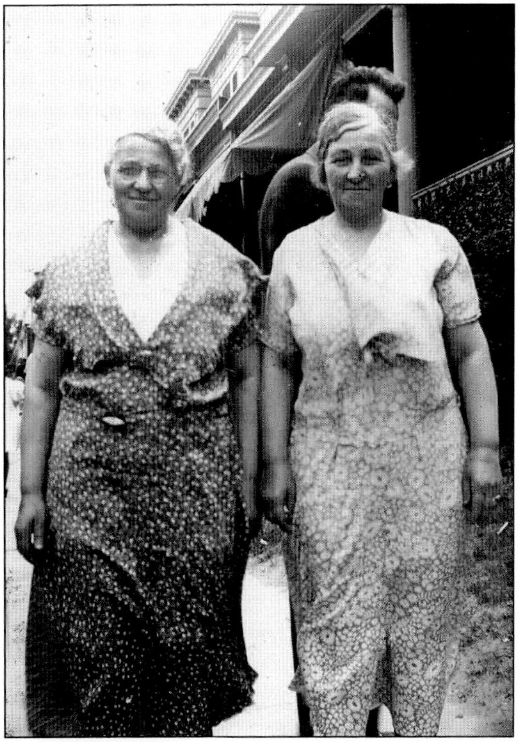

Esther Wolf and her sister Jenny were inseparable as a pair well into their old age. Both were born in Jewtown, traveled all around the city, and lived into their 90s. Esther married and settled in South Philadelphia. Later, she lived with her daughter Rae in southwest Philadelphia. Jenny went to live in Trenton, New Jersey, at the end of the train line that once ran in back of Jewtown to the west of the community over an elevated structure. (Courtesy of Carl Nathans.)

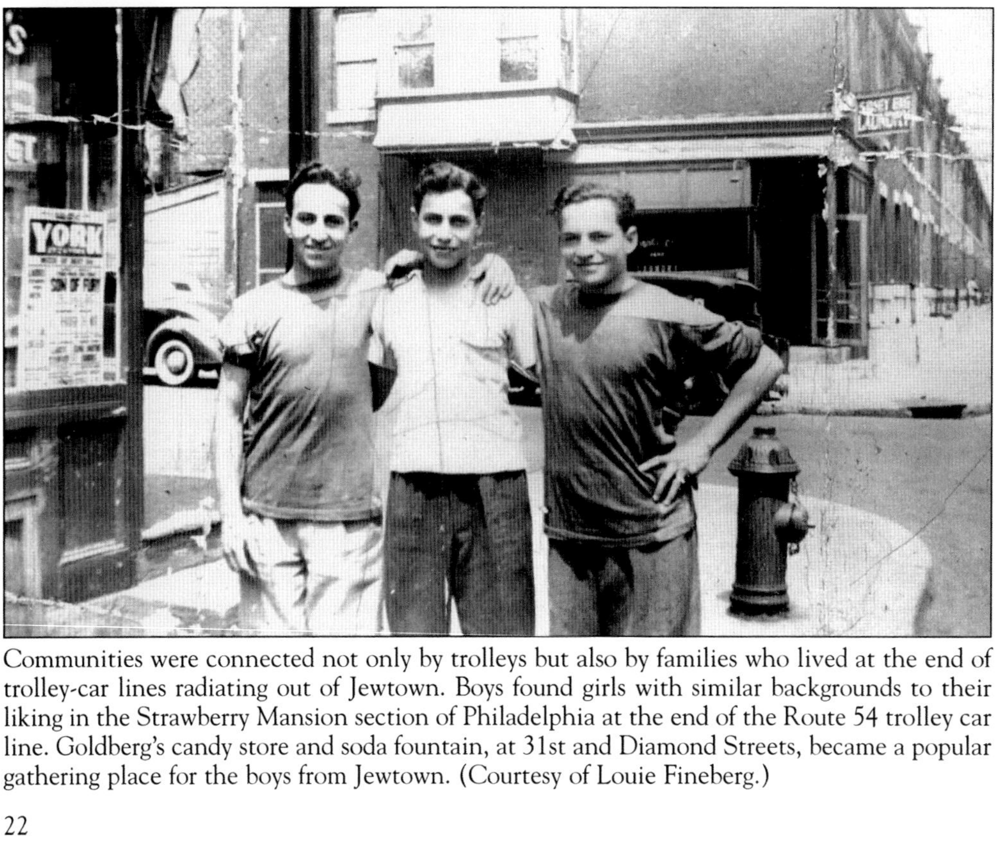

Communities were connected not only by trolleys but also by families who lived at the end of trolley-car lines radiating out of Jewtown. Boys found girls with similar backgrounds to their liking in the Strawberry Mansion section of Philadelphia at the end of the Route 54 trolley car line. Goldberg's candy store and soda fountain, at 31st and Diamond Streets, became a popular gathering place for the boys from Jewtown. (Courtesy of Louie Fineberg.)

Shimon Feinberg lived in the heart of Jewtown on Jenny Street parallel to Auburn Street. Sadie Nagel recalled riding with her grandfather Shimon on a horse and wagon to Booth's soda water company to pick up ice for his customers. During the wintertime, Shimon hung wallpaper and worked as a glazier. (Courtesy of Sadie Nagel.)

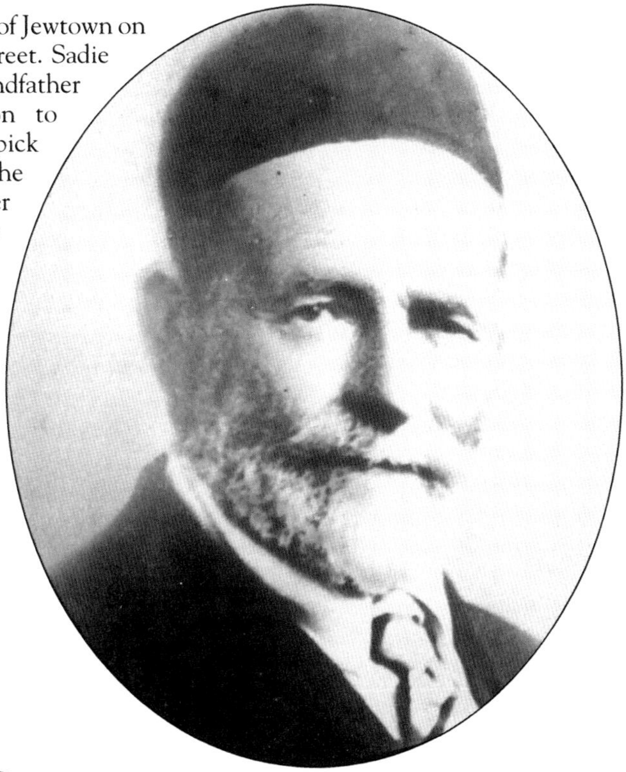

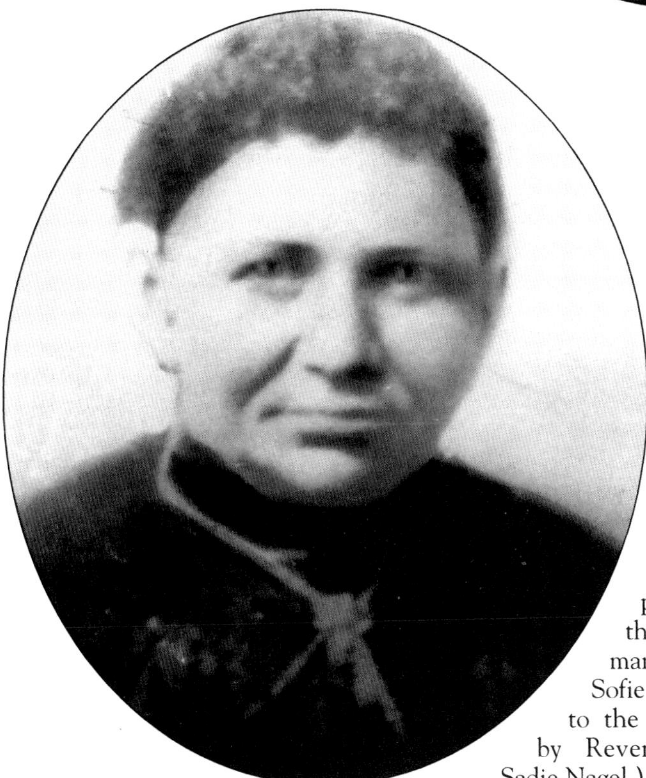

Sofie Feinberg lived with her husband, Shimon, and raised six children: Sarah, Yetta, Ida, Irene, Jake, and Henry. In America, the responsibility of passing along Jewish traditions to the children transferred from the man to the women in households. Sofie ensured that her children all went to the *cheder* (elementary school), run by Reverend Arkowitz. (Courtesy of Sadie Nagel.)

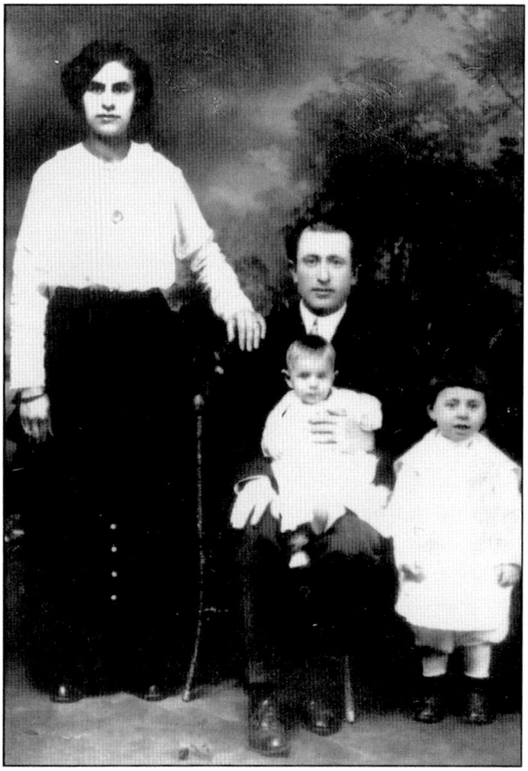

Eva and Morris Jaffe arrived in Jewtown from Lithuania in 1906. The couple settled at 2700 East Cambria, where they ran a grocery store and had two children, Dave and William. The family came to the area to be near their parents and a brother, who had immigrated earlier: Jonah, working as a shingle maker, and his wife, Hatti, lived in the 2800 block of Jenny Street, and the brother lived nearby in the 2900 block of Richmond Street, a location known as Cheap John's remnants and goods. (Courtesy of William Jaffe.)

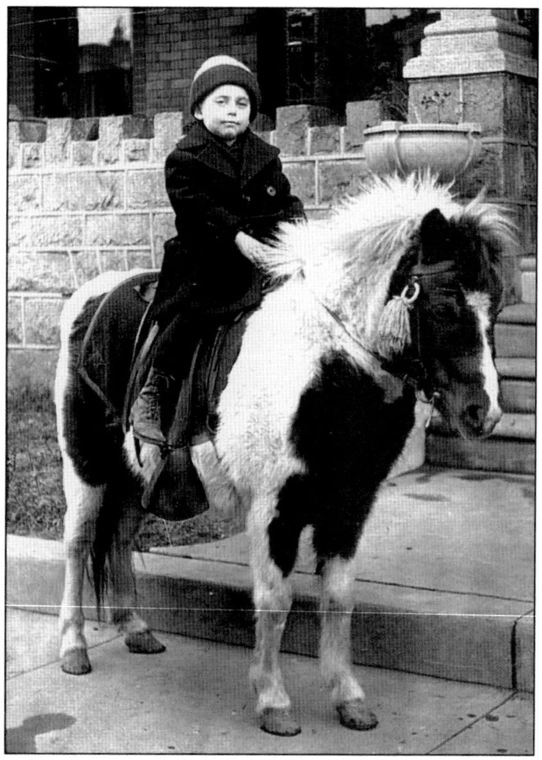

Isadore Gordon, the son of a kosher butcher, grew up in Jewtown. One of his favorite hucksters in Jewtown was the community photographer who brought around a pony on which the children posed outside their home. The children would then ask their mother for a quarter to pay for the photograph. (Courtesy of Dr. Isadore Gordon.)

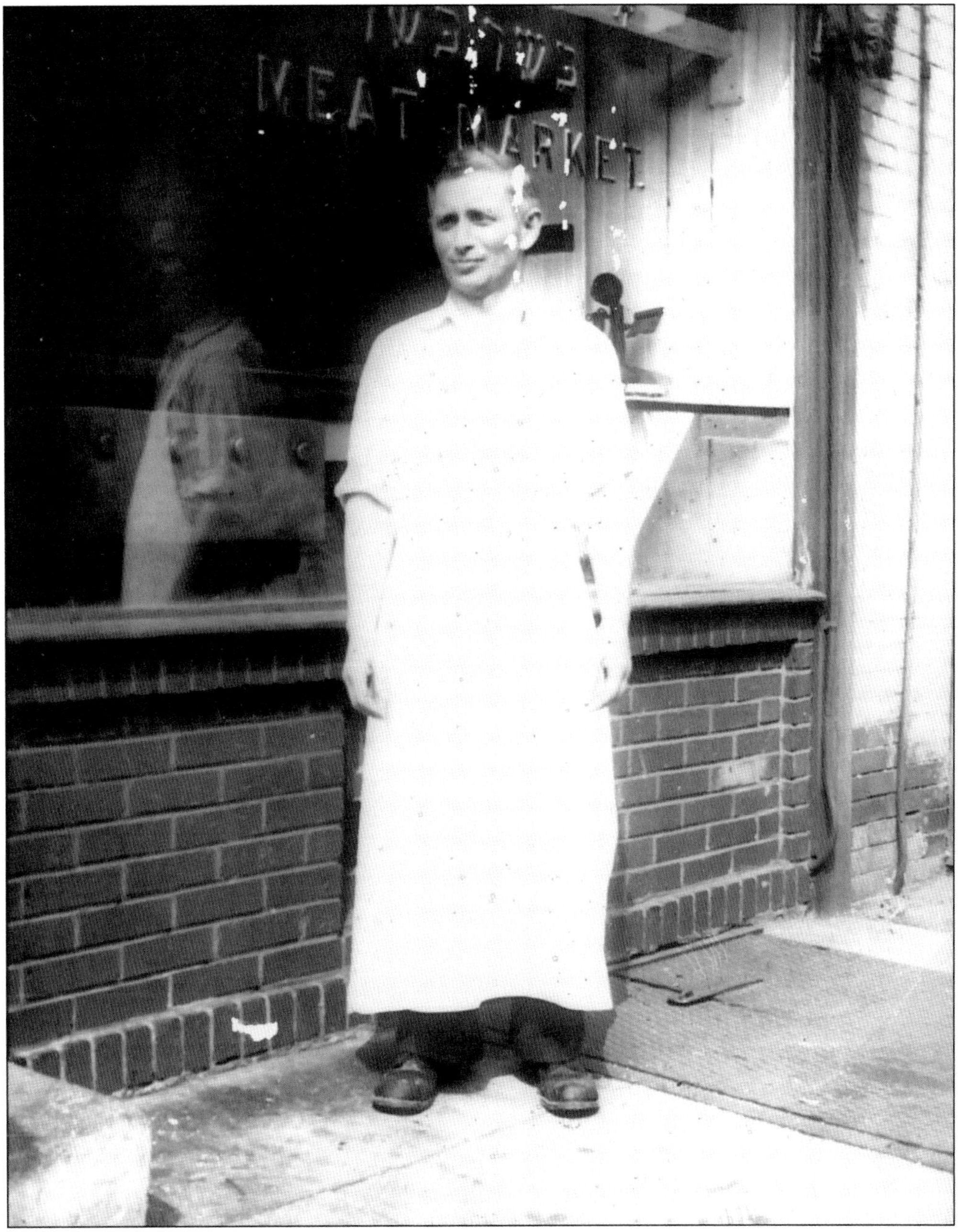

Mr. Gordon, along with partner Mr. Ressler, took over the kosher meat shop from the Satinskys and served the community well into the 1940s. In those days, cold cuts were popular ends of meats made into tasty snacks for Sunday morning brunch, which included knockwurst and salami—kosher, of course. Jewish people came here from other areas to purchase their provisions. (Courtesy of Dr. Isadore Gordon.)

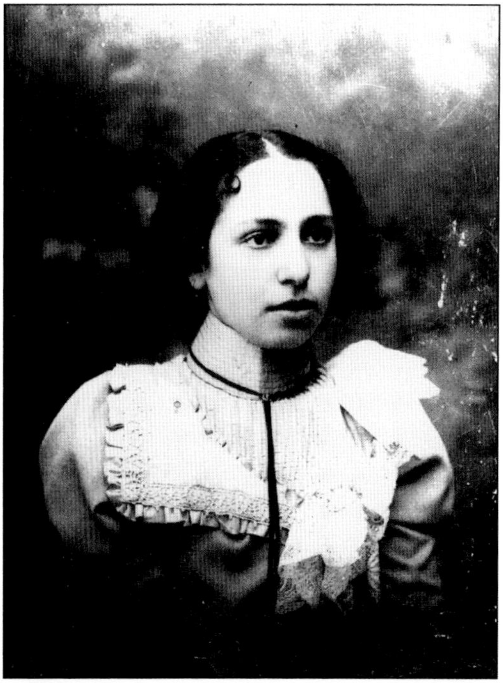

Flarrie Lyons supported her husband in the grocery business that also sold fresh chickens and fish. Bill Lyons recalls seeing his mother on cold, snowy days outside with a shawl over her head, scraping and cleaning the fish, chopping it for the customers to take home. (Courtesy of Bill Lyons.)

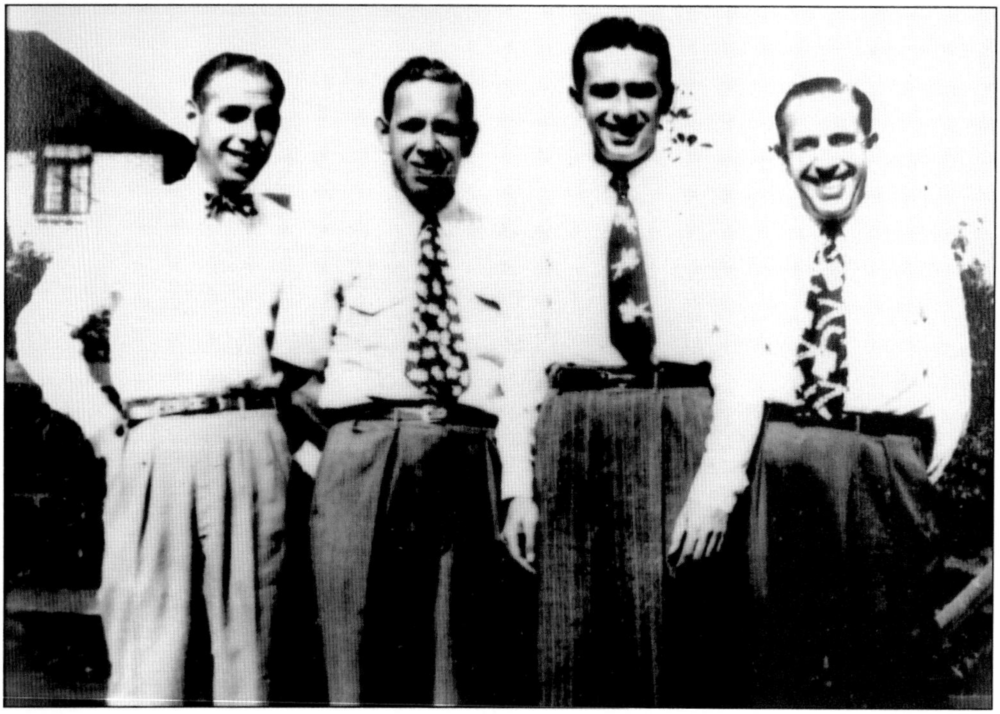

Charles and Flarrie Lyons had four sons: Bill, Shalazer, Hershall, and Kalman. The family lived at 2259 East Williams Street. Lyons advertised his fresh provisions and grocery business on the side of his horse-drawn wagon. Business was especially brisk during the Passover season, and he kept a lot of fresh carp in large tin tubs for all the mavens in the neighborhood to purchase. (Courtesy of Bill Lyons.)

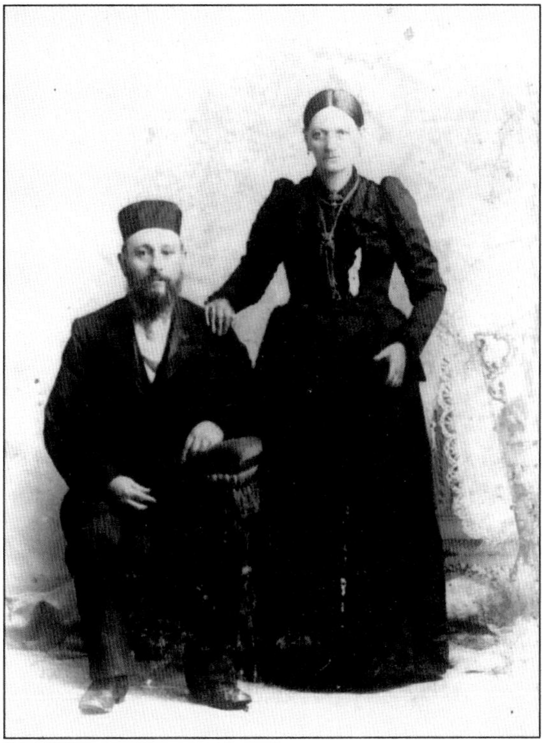

Isaac and Dora Satinsky ran a kosher butcher shop at 2258 Wayne Street, which became Williams Street in the 1890s. Their descendants included Sol, a president of the Jewish Federation in Philadelphia; Morris, a donator of the Lucien Moss Rehab Center; and Phil, who started the Organization for the Jewish Blind. Among the women in the family was Sylvia Satinsky, who led the Hebrew Sunday School Society. (Courtesy of Rhea Abrams.)

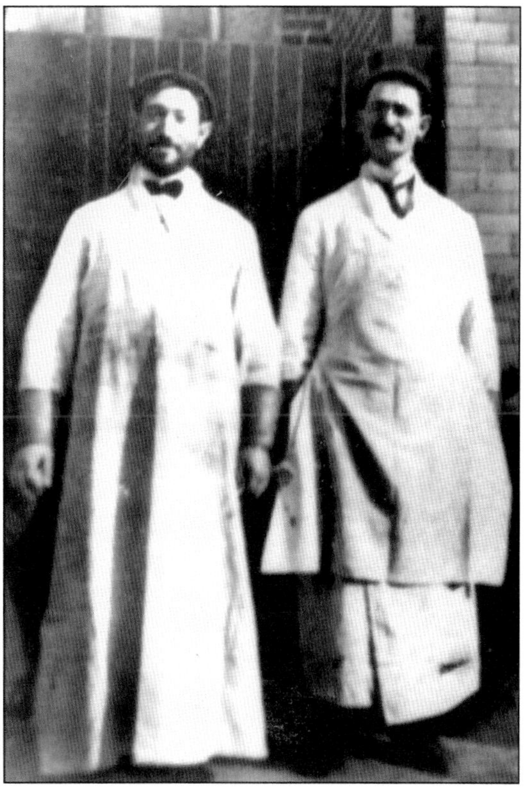

The next generation of children followed in their parents' footsteps and continued the family businesses. Max and David Satinsky are pictured in their long work clothes of the day. The brothers sold the butcher shop to two former workers, Mr. Gordon and Mr. Ressler. The Satinsky brothers purchased a textile business in the Frankford section at Adams Avenue and Church Street in the 1920s. (Courtesy of Minnie Glazier.)

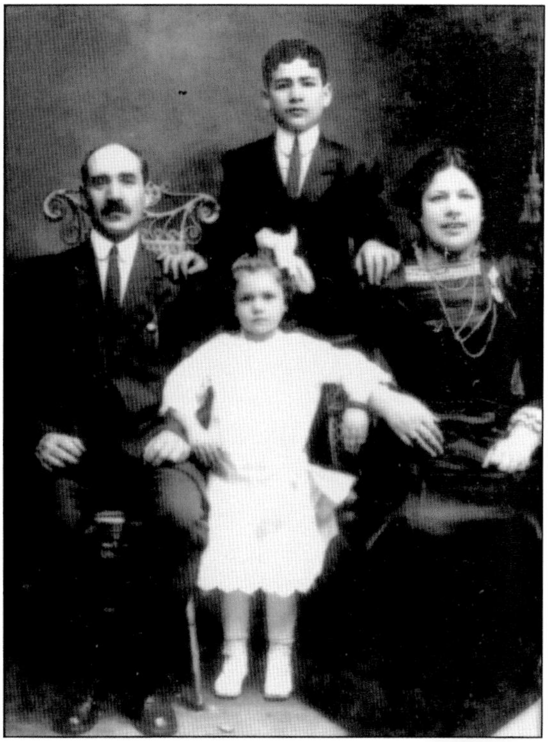

George Katz and his wife, Sofie, resided at 2254 East Williams Street with their children, Joe and Rose. Katz migrated to Jewtown in 1907 from Russia and became a wallpaper hanger. He remained on his street as the last surviving Jewish resident of Jewtown. His African American neighbors looking out for his well-being until he passed away at the age of 93. (Courtesy of Joe Katz.)

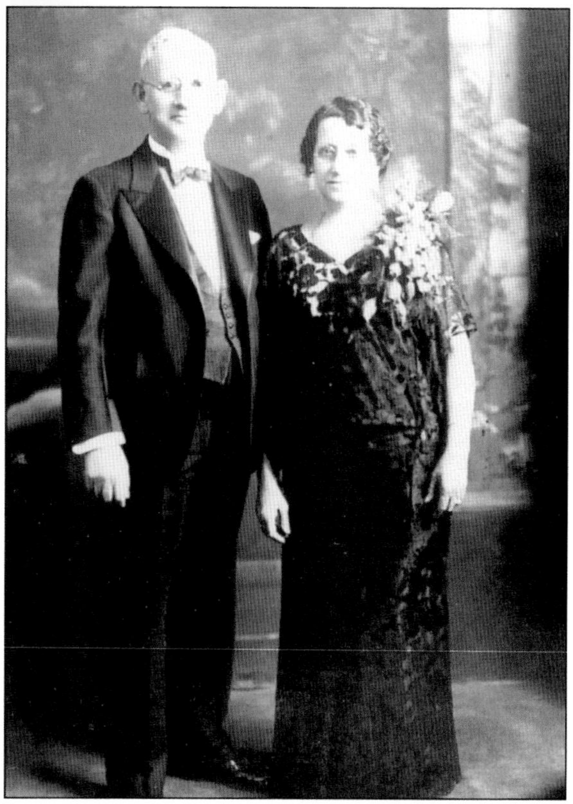

Harris Leavy and his wife, Sarah, lived at 2850 Tulip Street with their son, Sam. Originally from England, they migrated to Jewtown in the late 1890s. Leavy worked in the city comptroller's office and kept the books for the judicial magistrates. He later went into the printing business. In the 1940s, he moved to the Logan section of Philadelphia. Sam Leavy married and moved to 2000 East Birch Street. (Courtesy of Sam Leavy.)

Abraham Movitz taught hundreds of Jewish children trades at the Richmond Manual Training School at 2854–2858 Weichel Street in the late 19th century. Founded by the Hebrew Education Society, with branches in Eastern European Jewish enclaves, the school strived to bridge the cultural gap between German and Eastern European Jews by assimilation into American society. Cyrus Adler, Moses Deford, Jay Solis-Cohen Jr., and Dr. Charles Spivak were early teachers at this location. A sewing school for girls complemented the facility. (Courtesy of Sam Leavy.)

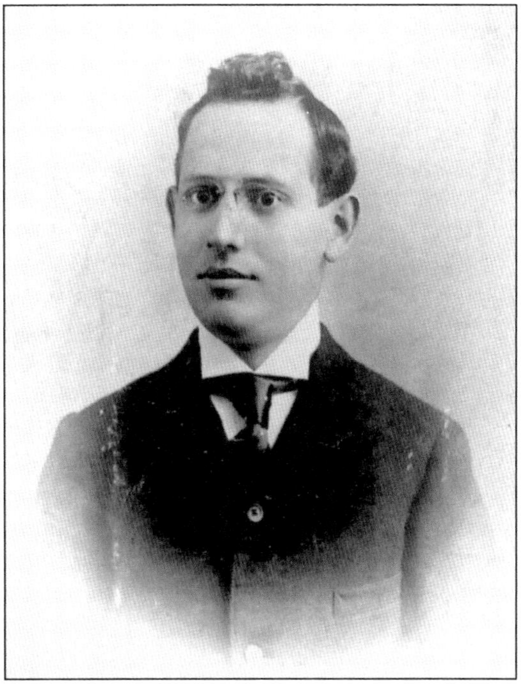

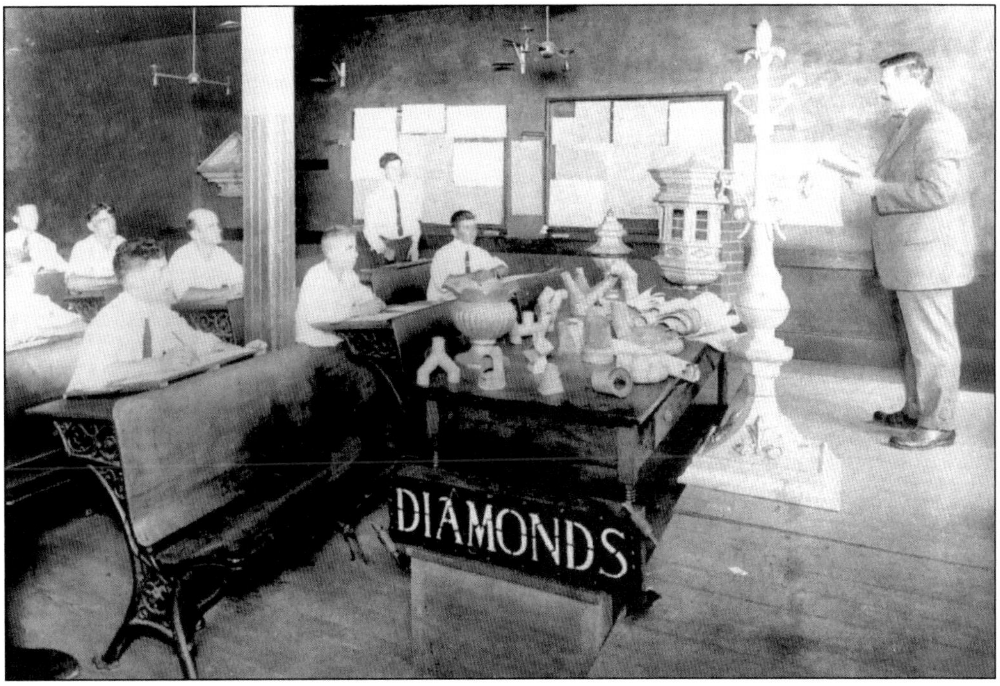

The Weichel Street Trade School served the Jewtowners and their children in a variety of ways. Founded in the early 1880s, the school taught children three trades: carpentry, cigar making, and drafting. It existed until World War I. Sam Leavy, age 12, is pictured on the far left with his childhood friends Sol Rosenberg, Morris Somenarsky, Morris Tishler, and Billy Silverman. In the evening, classes for people learning English were held at the school. (Courtesy of Sam Leavy.)

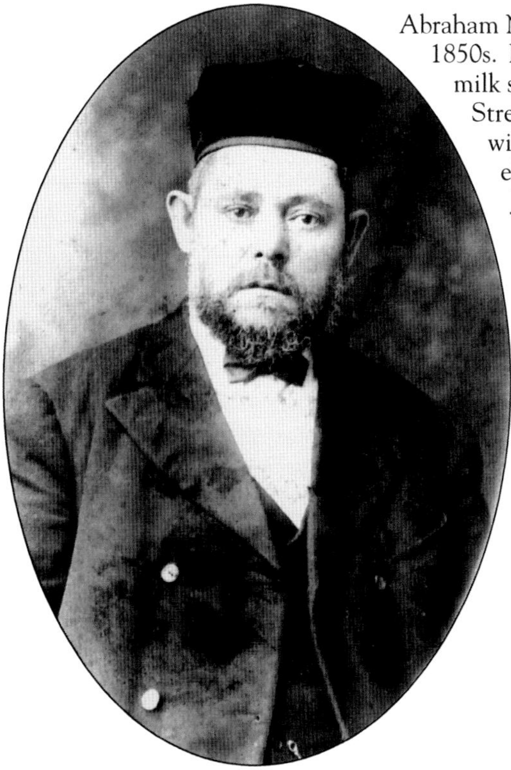

Abraham Nathans was born in Lithuania during the late 1850s. He came to Jewtown in 1888 and opened a milk store in the back of his home, at 2260 Williams Street. His store supplied the whole community with fresh goat milk. The tradition of caring for elders took place in this family according to Jewish custom, and Abraham Nathans, great-grandfather of Carl Nathans, lived with his son Morris at 3549 Frankford Avenue, where he died peacefully in 1923. (Courtesy of Carl Nathans.)

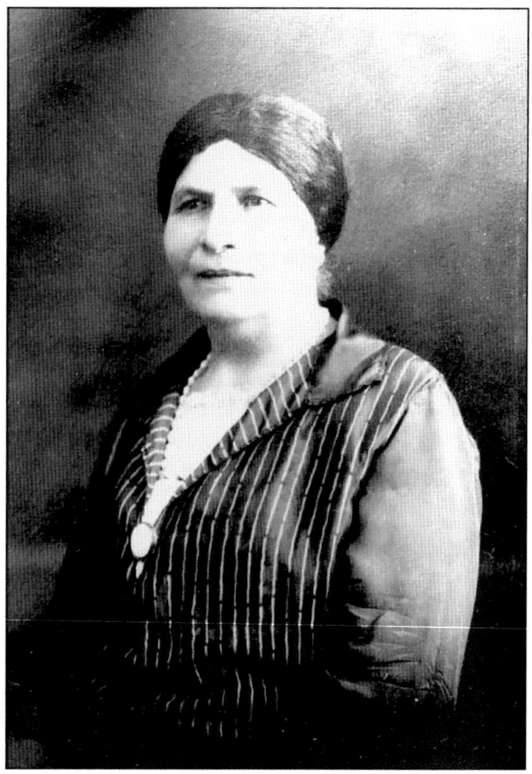

Sorah Nathans, the wife of Abraham Nathans, raised a family of five children that included Morris, Barney, Dora, Jack, and Harry. A very observant Jew, she ensured that the goats were bedded down with plenty of feed before the start of the Sabbath. (Courtesy of Carl Nathans.)

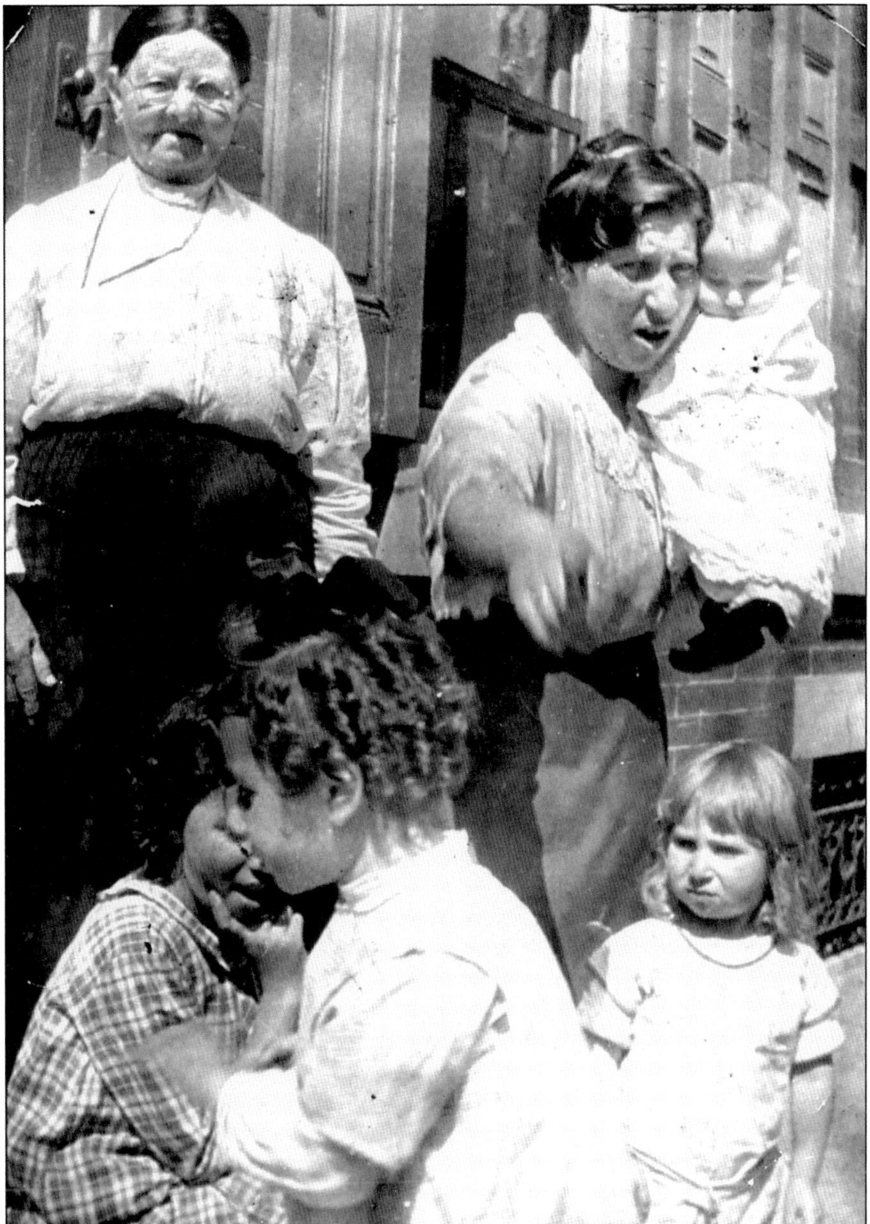

The great-great-grandmother of Carl Nathans, Mumma Temma Rosenblum, married William Berman and arrived in Jewtown during the early settlement of the colony in 1875. The couple, both born in the late 1830s, had six children: Aaron, Esther, Raechel, Harry, Jennie, and Al. This picture portrays a true sense of ethnic pride, with three generations and visiting cousins present on the sidewalk of the grandmother's home. Temma Berman, a true leader in the community, often collected funds for the rabbi in her apron and weekly rented a room for an itinerant traveler to rest during the Sabbath. Ann Medoff's mother stocked the room with fresh bedsheets and pillows. Living the life of a Jew according to Jewish custom transplanted itself very strongly through Temma Berman and her ability to rally the community to various causes. (Courtesy of Carl Nathans.)

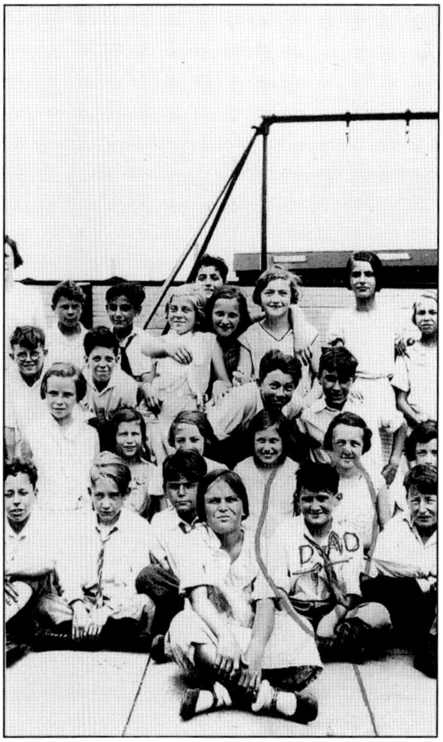

Sidney Nathans grew up at 3549 Frankford Avenue, along with sisters Esther and Adel. The children of Morris and Ida Nathans all attended the Webster School, at Frankford and Somerset Streets, and later attended the Horn School, at Frankford and Ontario Streets, for grades five through eight. (Courtesy of Carl Nathans.)

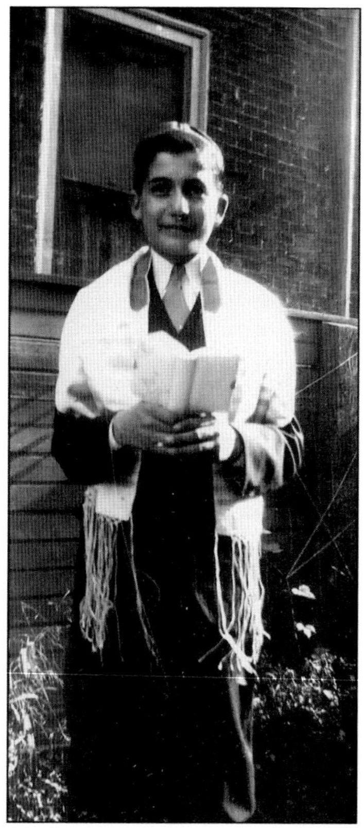

Sidney Nathans gave his parents much *nachus* (joy) when he properly prepared for his Bar Mitzvah and speech at the Kensington Jewish Community Center on Allegheny Avenue during the height of the Depression in 1933. He remained loyal to his faith and served as a president of the synagogue Temple Israel in Upper Darby, Pennsylvania. (Courtesy of Morris Nathans.)

Sidney Nathans, age 12, holds his cousin Rhoda Mae Eisenberg. Standing in front of the local men's clothing store, he proudly displays the attire of the times: knickers. After his Bar Mitzvah, a boy was considered a man and allowed—by custom in America—to wear pants rather than knickers. (Courtesy of Adel Graboyes.)

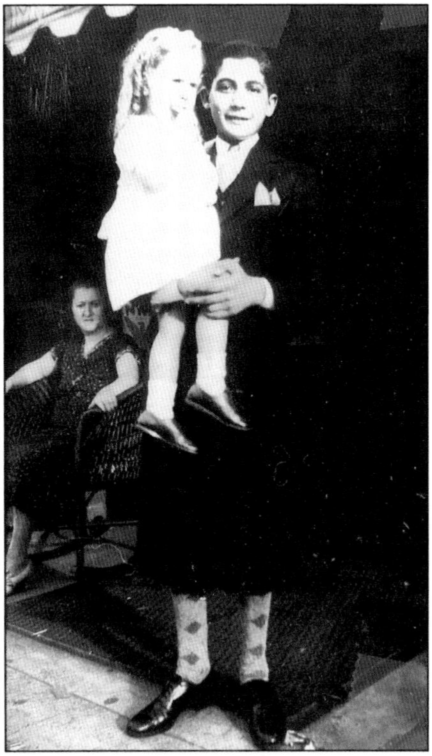

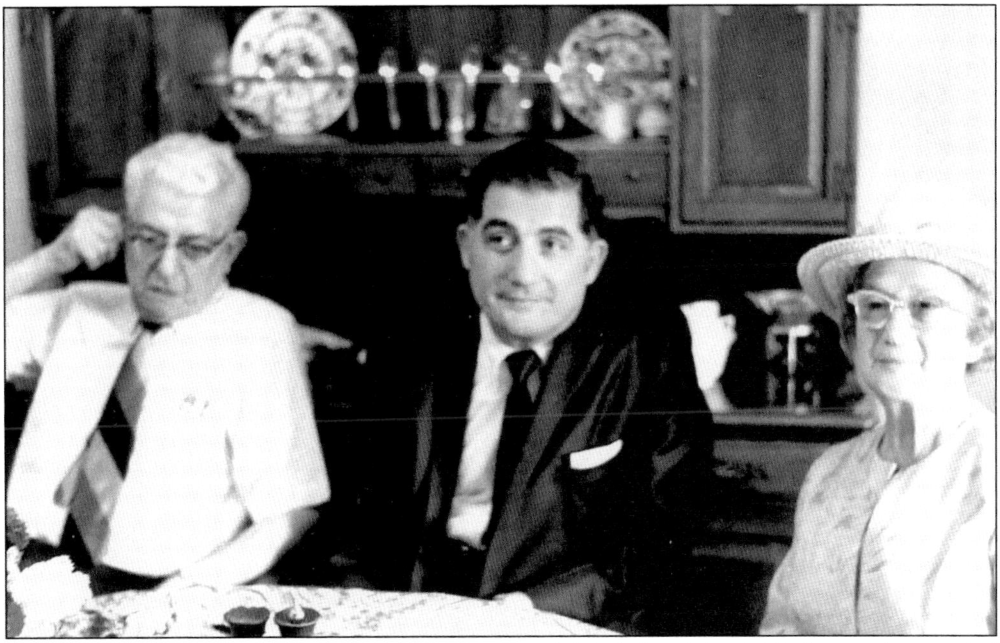

Sidney Nathans (center), the father of Carl, sits with his father, Morris Nathans, who married Ida Rebolsky. Morris and Ida Nathans both belonged to Congregation B'nai Israel in Jewtown and followed Rabbi Nahum Brenner. Morris Nathans eventually retired and moved to several localities, including the peaceful town of Mount Royal, New Jersey, along with his brother Barney Nathans. (Courtesy of Esther Zabludoff.)

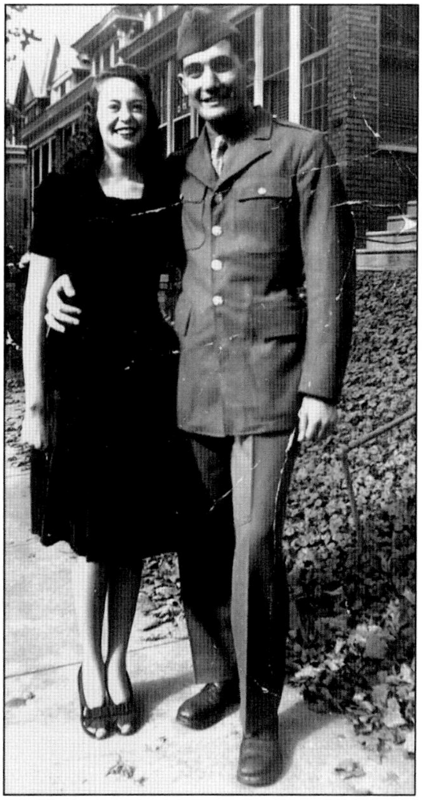

Both descendants of longtime Jewtown families, Sidney Nathans and his bride, Florence Padlasky, pose for the photographer. Shortly after this picture was taken, Nathans was shipped overseas during World War II. He spent his first two wedding anniversaries alone. (Courtesy of Carl Nathans.)

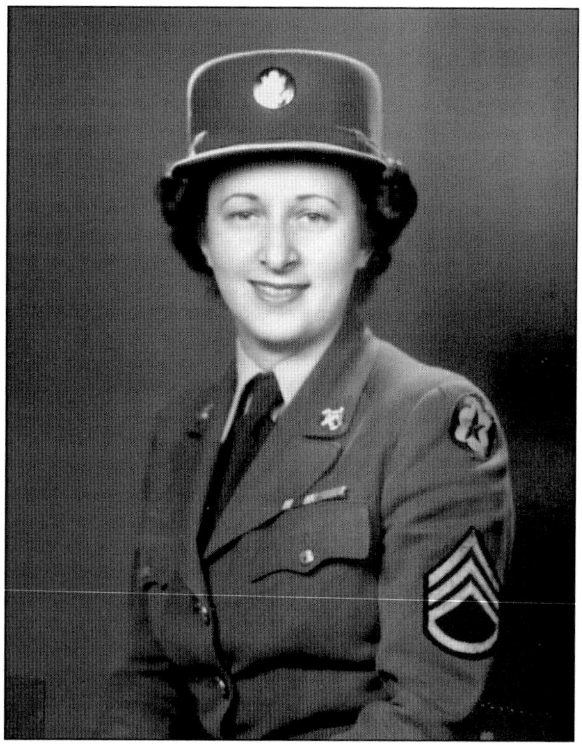

Sylvia Nathans, daughter of Jack and Lena Nathans, married Arthur Gordon. She served as a master sergeant in the U.S. Army during World War II. Afterward, she and her husband moved to Chester, Pennsylvania. Their children are Nadine, Alan, and Laurie. (Courtesy of Alan Gordon.)

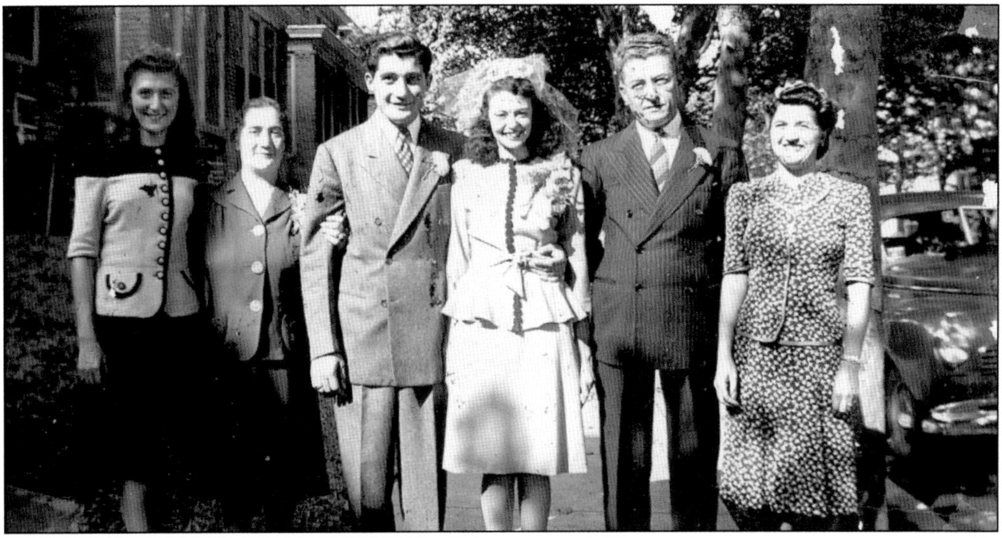

The descendants of two old Jewtown families united and never knew that their grandparents were founding members of the Jewtown community in Richmond until Carl Nathans began his research in the late 1970s. From left to right are Adel Graboyes, Ida Nathans, groom Sidney Nathans and his bride, Florence Padlasky Nathans, and Morris and Esther Nathans. They were gathered for the wedding in the 1940s. (Courtesy of Eileen Waldman.)

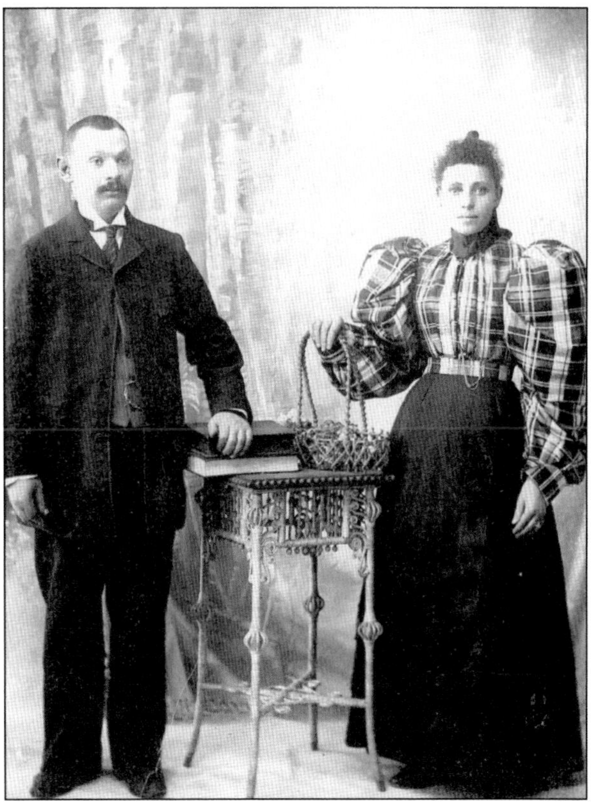

Esther Berman was from Jewtown, and her family belonged to Congregation Chevra Tehillim and followed Rabbi Benjamin Block. She and Herman Wolf were married in 1889 and moved to Passyunk Avenue, in South Philadelphia, to start a shoe business. Their daughter Rae married Harry Padlasky and had two children, Florence and William, and then moved to southwest Philadelphia. Florence's child, Carl Nathans, is named for his great-grandfather Herman. (Courtesy of William Padlasky.)

Bulletin
of the
Philadelphia College
of **Pharmacy *and* Science**

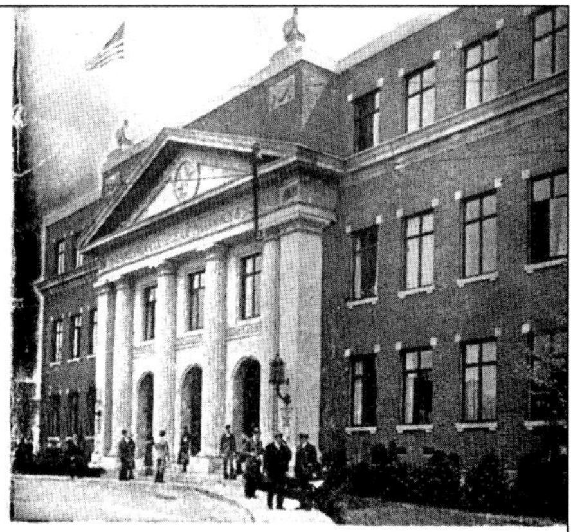

Vol. XXXVIII — APRIL, 1945 — No. 1

GRADUATES IN MILITARY SERVICE

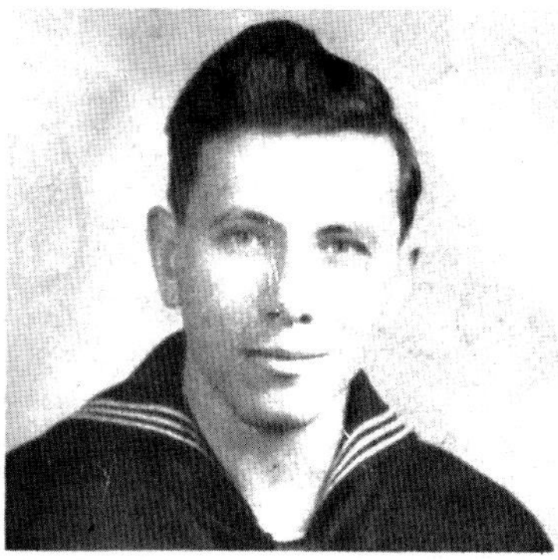

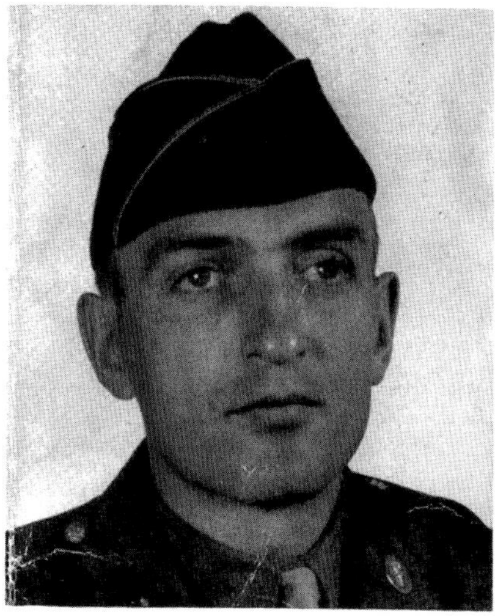

Another Gold Star has been added to the Service Flag of this College and the family, classmates and other friends are saddened by the death in action of *William M. Friedman*, 1942, on Iwo Jima. He was serving with the Fourth Marine Division as a Pharmacist's Mate, First Class, of the U. S. Navy.

Previously he had participated in the invasions of the Marshall Islands and Saipan, where he was wounded. He received the Purple Heart and the Presidential Unit Citation.

He entered P. C. P. & S. on an Alumni Scholarship and then was awarded the Breyer Scholarship. He received the degree of Bachelor of Science in Pharmacy and graduated second in his class.

Shortly before he transferred to the Marines he became engaged to Selma L. Miller, 1944.

Yet another Gold Star represents *Richard E. Farrow*, 1937, who was killed in action in Germany, February 7, where he was serving our country as Technical Sergeant in the Army. He was with a medical detachment of an infantry division. Before going into service he was the proprietor of a drug store in Haddonfield, N. J., originally established there by his father, the late Charles T. Farrow, 1896.

* * * *

John C. Decker, Jr., N. 1943, served as a stretcher bearer for the U. S. Marine Corps at Iwo Jima.

Gorgonio P. Quimba, 1937, who is a technical sergeant in the U. S. Army, was wounded in the first invasion of Leyte in the Philippine Islands. He has been awarded the Purple Heart.

Stephen Derkach, 1932, who also graduated in medicine from Hahnemann Medical College and is a Lieutenant in the Medical Corps of the U. S. Navy, has received the Bronze Star for outstanding performance of duty while attached to a Beach Battalion during the Normandy invasion.

Published monthly by the Philadelphia College of Pharmacy and Science, 43d St., Woodland and Kingsessing Aves., Philadelphia 4, Pa. Entered as Second-Class Matter, February 14, 1911, at the Post Office at Phila., Pa., under Act of July 16, 1894. "Acceptance for mailing at the special rate of postage provided in Section 1103, Act of Oct. 3, 1917, authorized on July 19, 1918."

Billy Friedman, a cousin on Florence Padlasky's side of the family, graduated second in his class at the Philadelphia Pharmacy School in West Philadelphia. The gold star proudly displayed in his home signified the ultimate sacrifice of this sailor on Iwo Jima in 1942. (Courtesy of Florence Nathans.)

Rae and Harry Padlasky always stood together as one unit. The family moved to Ridgewood Street, in southwest Philadelphia, and Padlasky served his debit (territory) in the 1940s as a Metropolitan Life Insurance agent in the Island Road Jewish community down by the new Philadelphia airport. (Courtesy of Florence Nathans.)

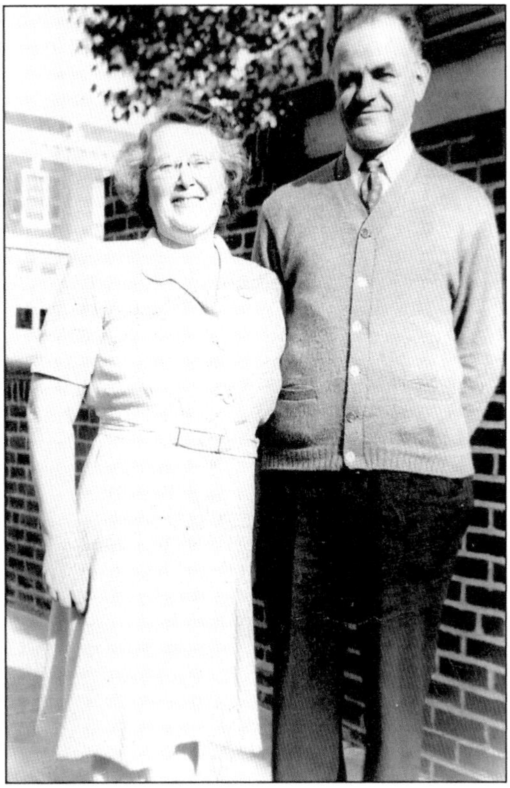

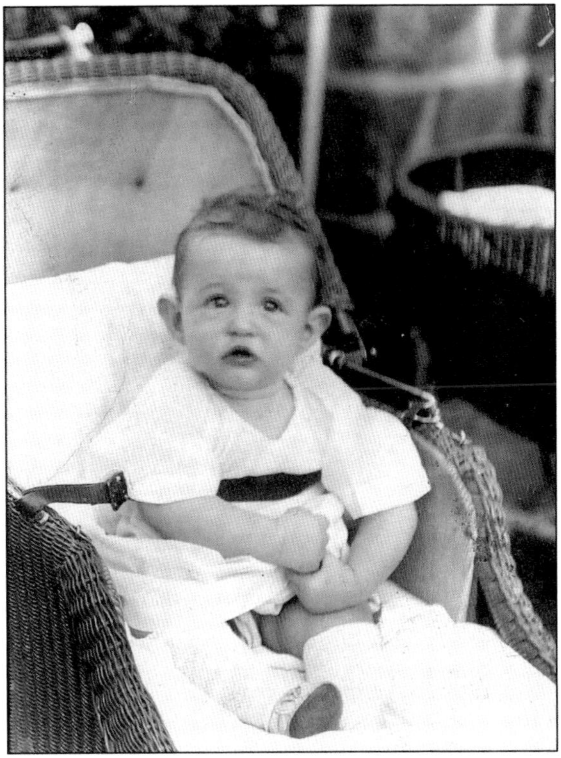

Florence Padlasky, a child prodigy at age two, was destined to adopt a life of fame through ballet and recordings. The family commented that she was stunning on stage and could have been a movie star. However, she never got over the fact that she could not hide or conceal her " big ears." (Courtesy of Carl Nathans.)

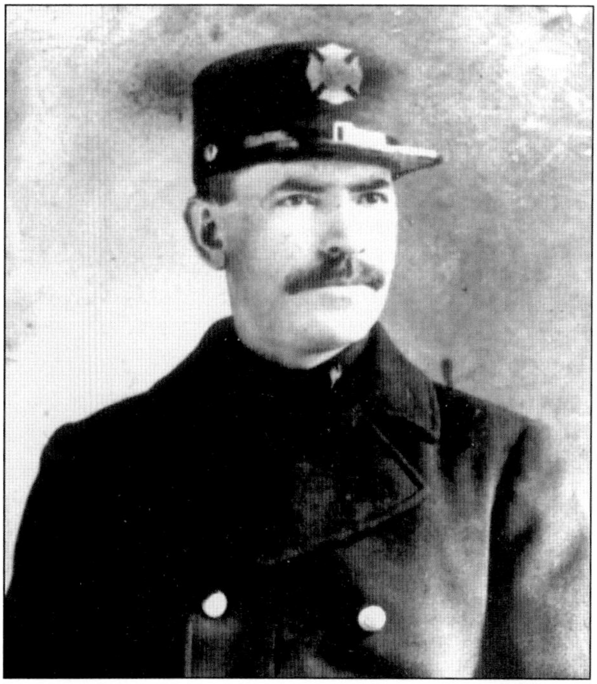

Samuel Sisenwine, a pillar in the community, served as a fireman attached to fire truck No. 10 at Frankford Avenue and Clearfield Street. He died at age 45 due to smoke inhalation while battling a neighborhood fire. He left behind eight children, who were raised by aunts and uncles. (Courtesy of Mary Sisenwine.)

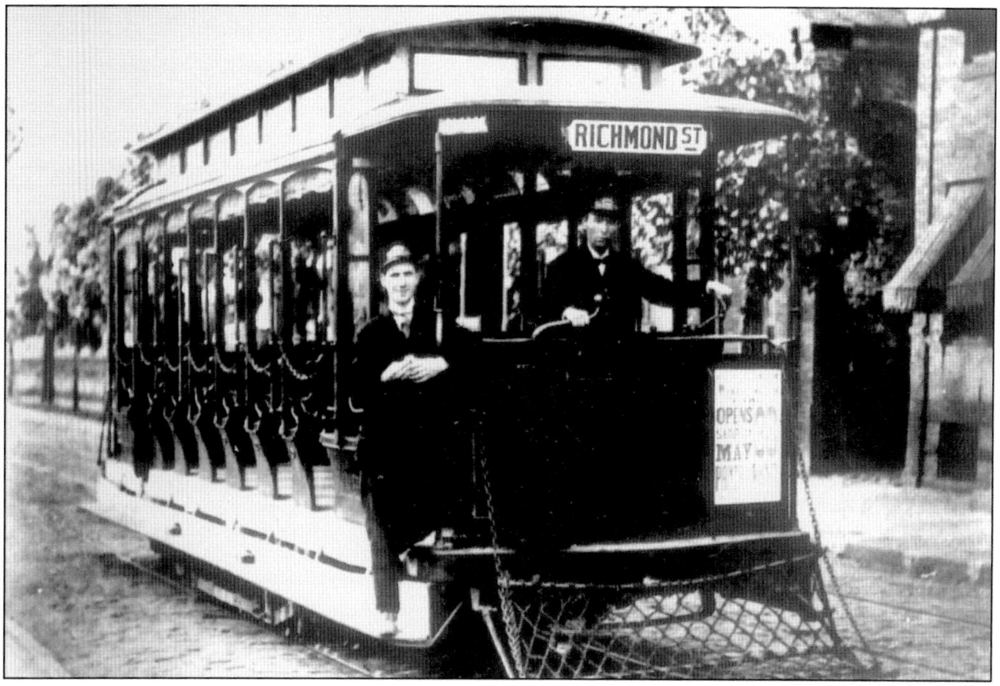

Most of the motormen for the Philadelphia Rapid Transportation Company were Irishmen who spoke English quite well. The Eastern European Jews, who knew very little English, rode these trolleys and maneuvered around the city with the help of a landsman named Joseph Berger, who spoke both English and Yiddish. Berger's family lived at 2129 East Auburn. After making several runs on the open-air Richmond trolley car, he would often have lunch with his family, who included his sons, Al and Morton Berger. (Courtesy of Al Berger.)

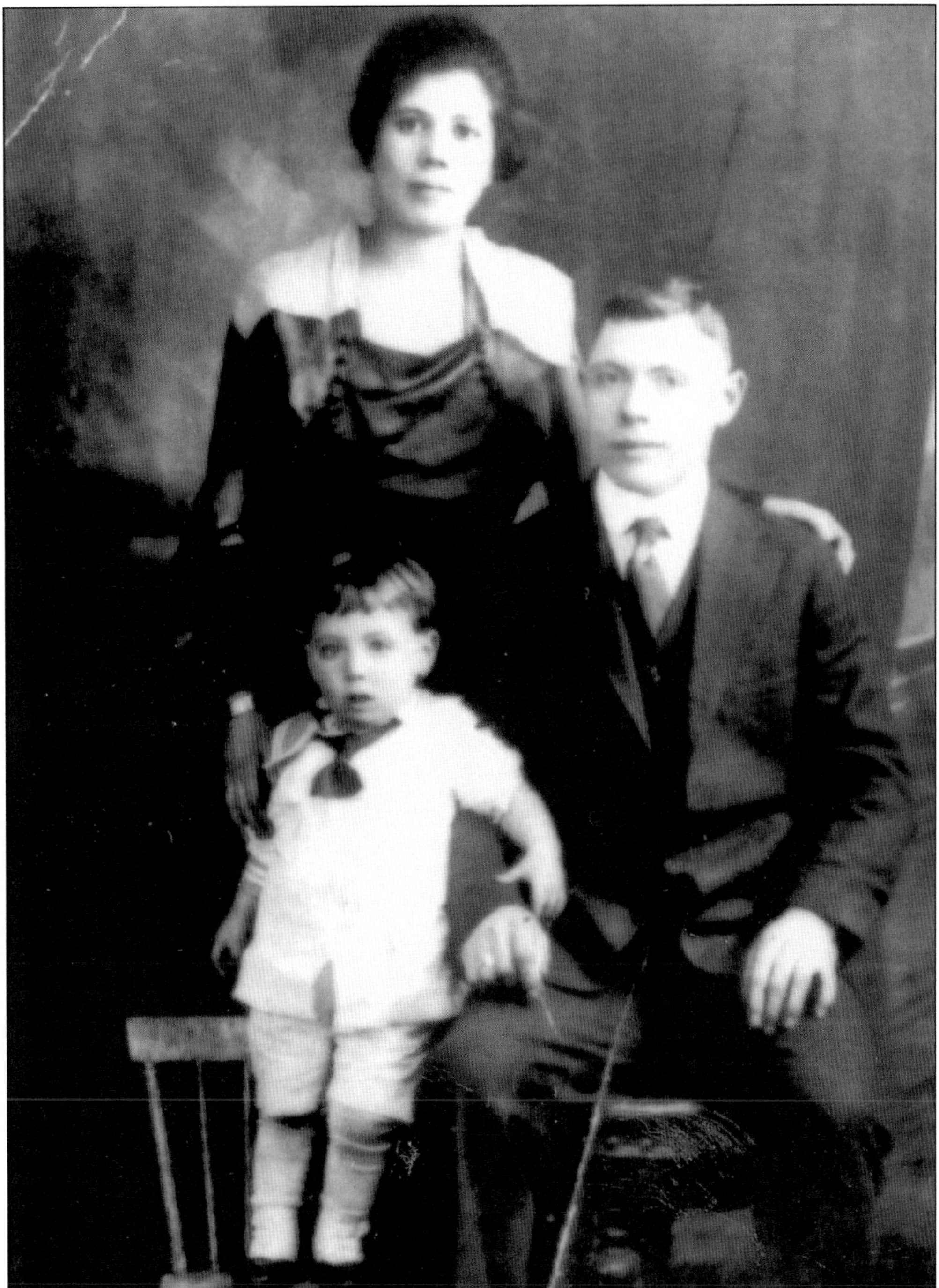

Ida and Albert Sokolof raised their son Paul at 2205 East Williams Street while they maintained a shoe repair shop during the years following 1910. The Sokolofs later moved to West Philadelphia at the other end of the route of the No. 15 trolley car, which ran out Girard Avenue. The family had to leave, however, because of a low ceiling that trapped shoe dust in the cramped quarters, making Sokolof sick. (Courtesy of Paul Sokolof.)

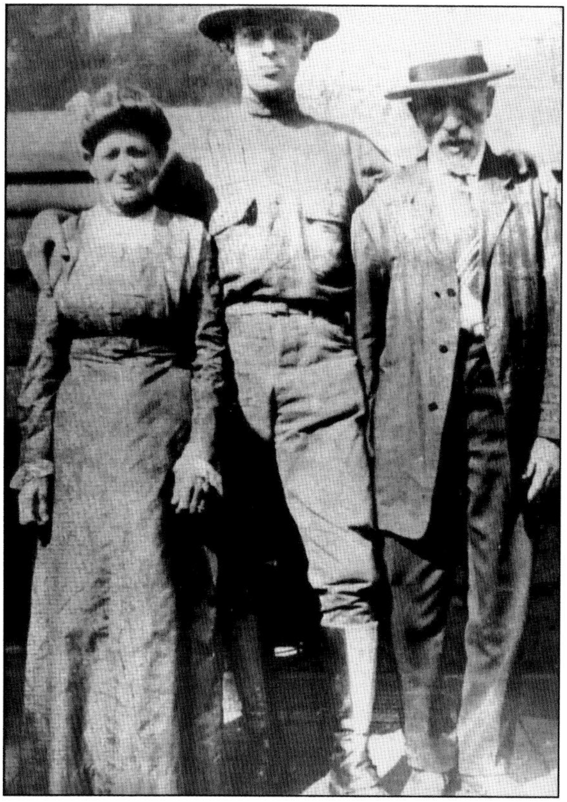

Soldier Harry Feinsinger is shown with parents, Temma and Louis Feinsinger, during World War I. The Feinsingers came to Jewtown with a great deal of zeal for their Judaism, so much so that Temma sat outside on the stoops with several other women reading from the Hebrew scriptures. The women discussed points of great interest, as did the men on late Saturday afternoons. (Courtesy of Anita Berman.)

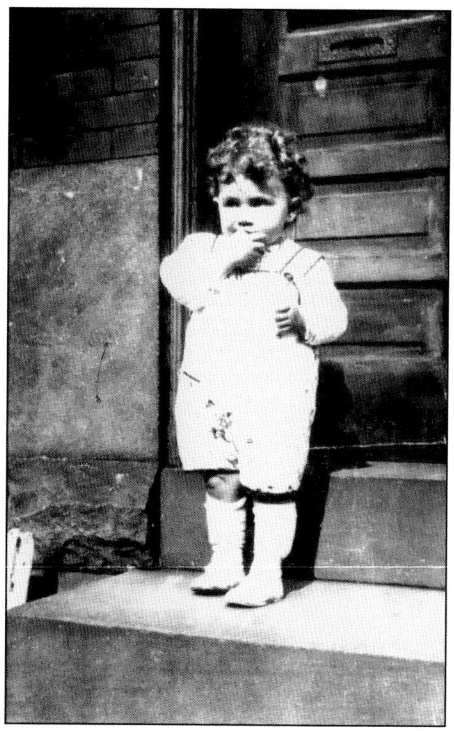

Temma Medoff, the granddaughter of Louis and Temma Feinsinger, pauses for a moment on the solid granite steps. Steps like these were found throughout Philadelphia from the late 1870s on. (Courtesy of Anita Berman.)

Harry Rottenberg bought the chicken slaughterhouse at 2222 East Auburn Street from the late Reverend Dantovitz. The religious requirements for a *shochet* (ritual slaughterer) went hand in hand with those for the person selected to offer prayers from the *beama* (pulpit) for the entire congregation. The community accepted Rottenberg, who lived at 2304 East Cambria Street with his wife, Bertha, who immigrated from Budapest, Hungary, in 1921. (Courtesy of Bertha Rottenberg.)

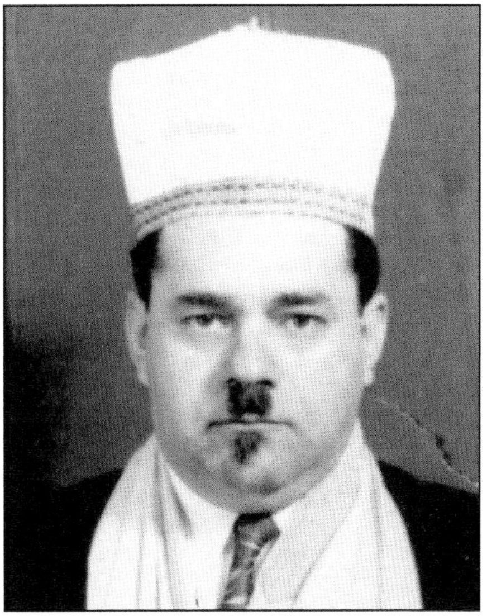

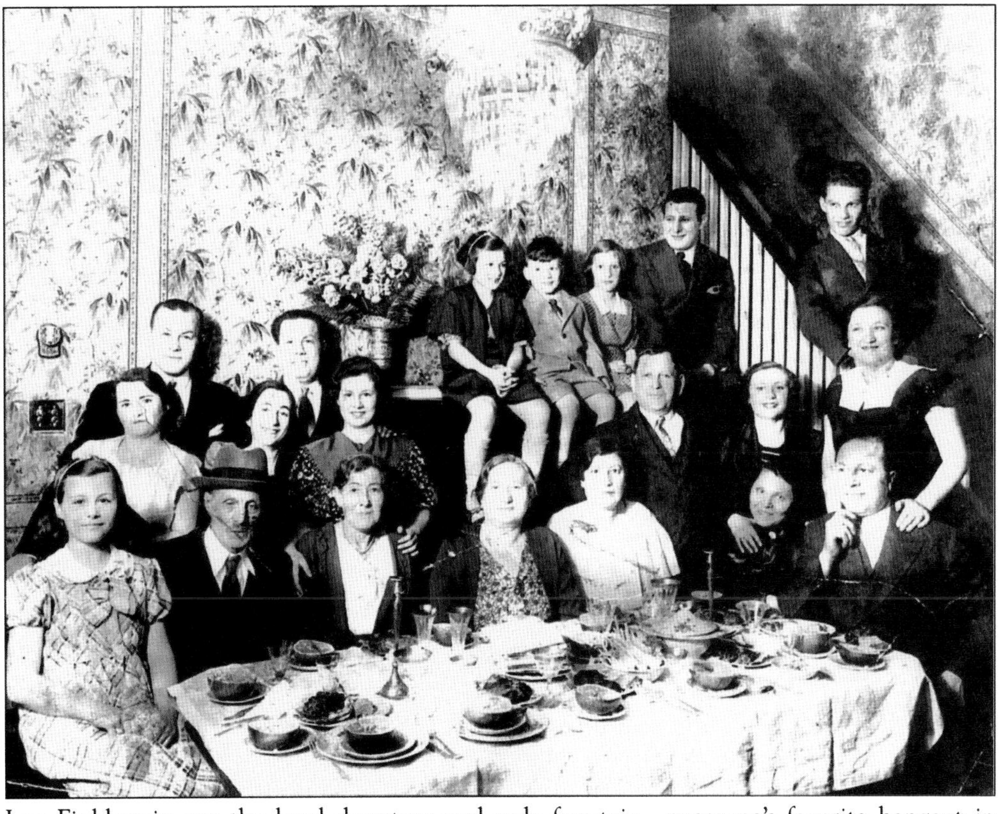

Len Finklestein ran the local drugstore and soda fountain—everyone's favorite hangout in Jewtown. Family affairs were often held above the store in the large dining room with its old-fashioned chandelier, which brightened the entire environment. With so many people crowded into one room, these family gatherings were a real treat. Finklestein cooked for all the children, Elaine, Jerry, Herbert, and other relatives. Seated are Edith and Harry Bookman, and on the steps is their son Alan. (Courtesy of Alan Bookman.)

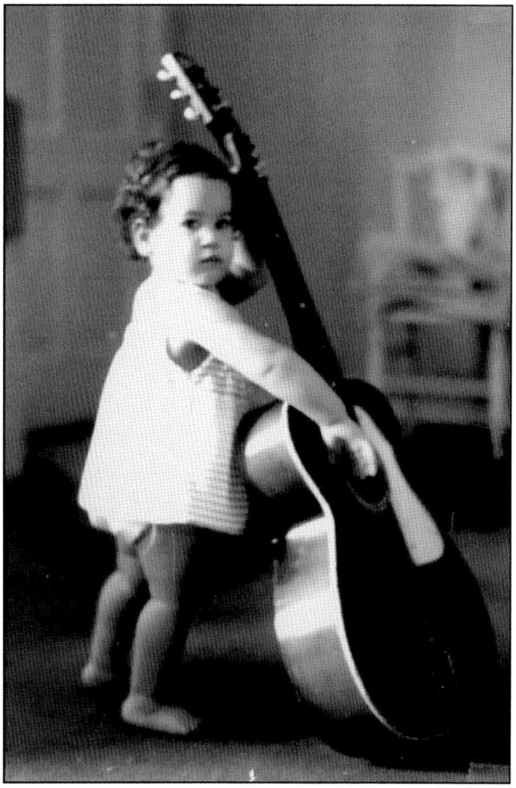

Heather Dawn Waldman, daughter of Eileen and Bruce Waldman, begins the generation of music lovers. Grandmother Rae Padlasky took her daughter Florence to ballet and vocal training lessons, and in turn, the talent lives on from generation to generation, with her daughter Eileen doing the same for Heather. (Courtesy of David Waldman.)

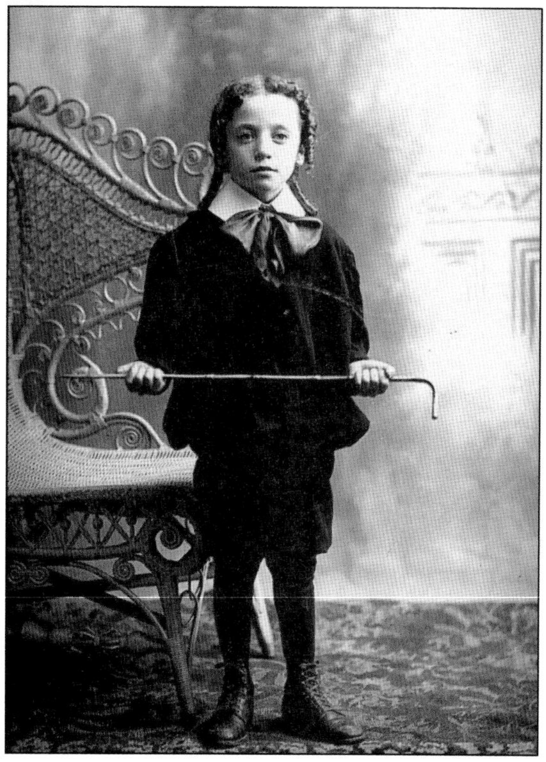

Izzy Wolf, the brother of Rae Padlasky, is pictured here in a studio sporting a handsome haircut and walking stick, which speaks of the times: the years just after 1910. He became the proud parent of Alvin, Temma, and Herman Wolf. (Courtesy of Selma and Ruth Bender.)

Many early synagogues in Philadelphia stood two stories high for the inclusion of a balcony where, according to the Jewish rituals of the day, women sat separated from the men during prayer services. Isadore Yanos recalled that his mother and Aunt Bess sat upstairs and maintained a good view of him as a child. After intermission of services, he knew that he had to appear in his seat in a timely fashion and cut short his socialization with his buddies outside. (Courtesy of Isadore Yanos.)

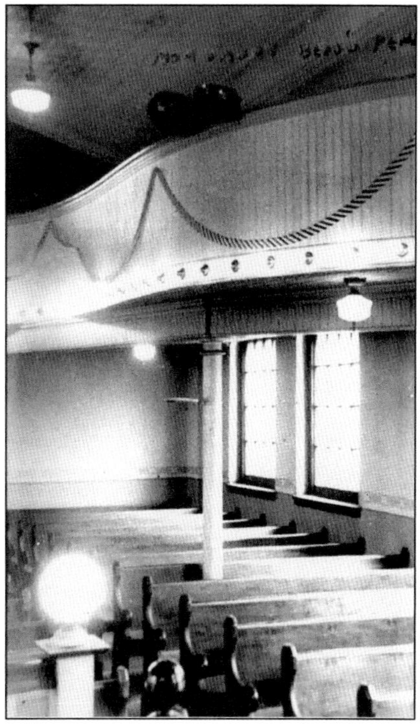

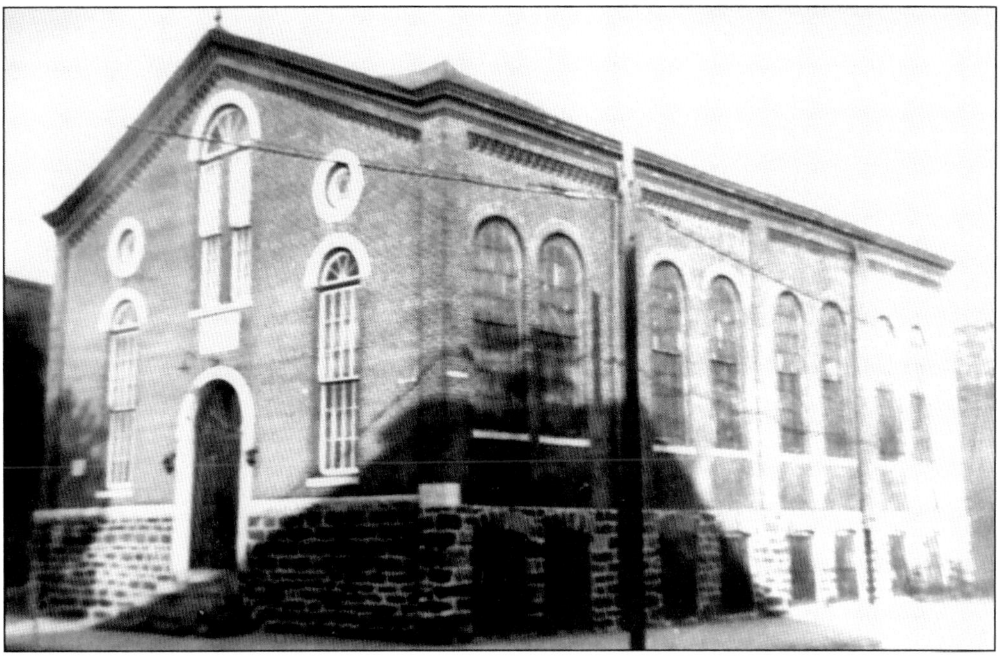

A second synagogue served the early Jewtowners: Chevra Tehillim, founded by Rabbi Benjamin Block, who slaughtered chickens according to Jewish ritual. The two-story synagogue was the gathering place for Jews who arrived in Jewtown after fleeing from Russia in the late 1880s. An entrance to a small courtyard led to the basement and the social hall, which had a small chapel, heated by a potbelly stove, where the men prayed in the winter. (Courtesy of Carl Nathans.)

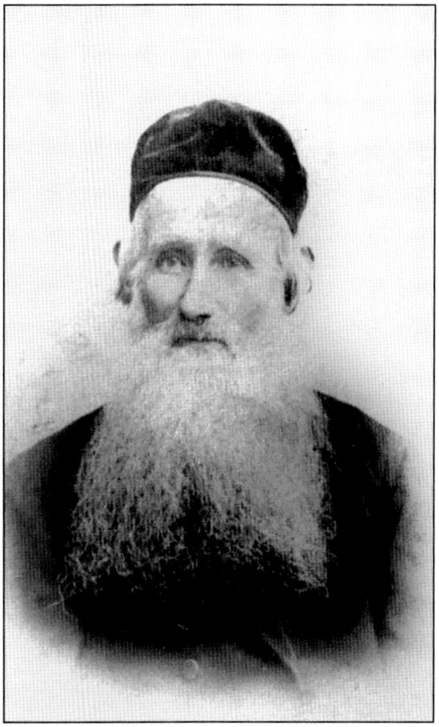

Joseph Yanos ran the Chevra Tehillim Shul as a *shames* (caretaker). A man with a quiet demeanor, he collected money for various worthy Jewish charities and loved the Sabbath, a love that he passed along to his child Isadore Yanos. Isadore recalled opening the door to the his home at 2219 East Williams Street and observing the table set for the Sabbath with a large challah (loaf of bread) and a smaller challah baked especially for him and placed at his setting on a spotless white tablecloth. (Courtesy of Isadore Yanos.)

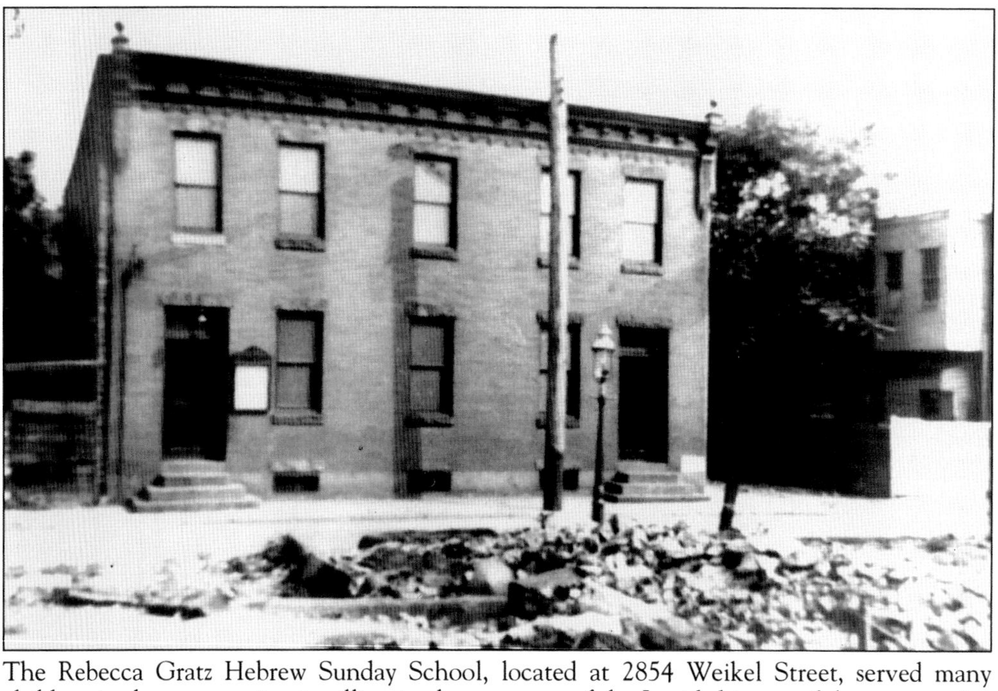

The Rebecca Gratz Hebrew Sunday School, located at 2854 Weikel Street, served many children in the community, instilling in them a sense of the Jewish history of the community, which began in the late 1880s. Classes were conducted in Yiddish and English for all to learn. Teachers included Dr. Gersonkrantz and Rev. Morris Elkin. In the evening, classes were held for new immigrants wishing to learn English. (Courtesy of Isadore Yanos.)

Three

THE SYNAGOGUES

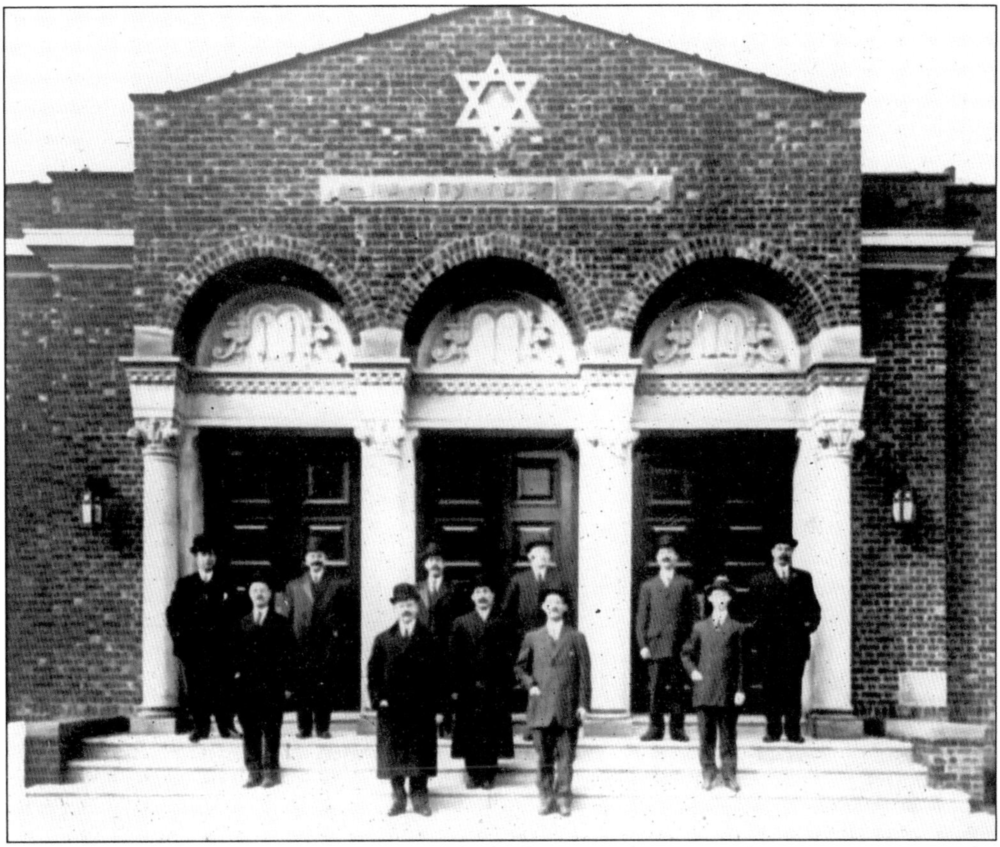

The Jewish community under the Frankford El centered on its religious institutions, the synagogues. Inside, the buildings housed the heritage of the Jewish people, with many old prayer books, as well as scholarly works brought from the old country. The Polish, Hungarian, and Russian Jews who settled along the Delaware River in the northeast section of Philadelphia during the late 19th century built their merchant community around the synagogue. Due to real estate considerations and the desire to blend into their neighborhoods, the Jews built their religious edifices one or two blocks from the main shopping districts. Finally, in 1909, after 20 years of renting quarters, Congregation Adath Zion of Frankford opened its synagogue at 4300 Paul Street, one street over from the Frankford Avenue shopping district. (Courtesy of the Adath Zion Archives.)

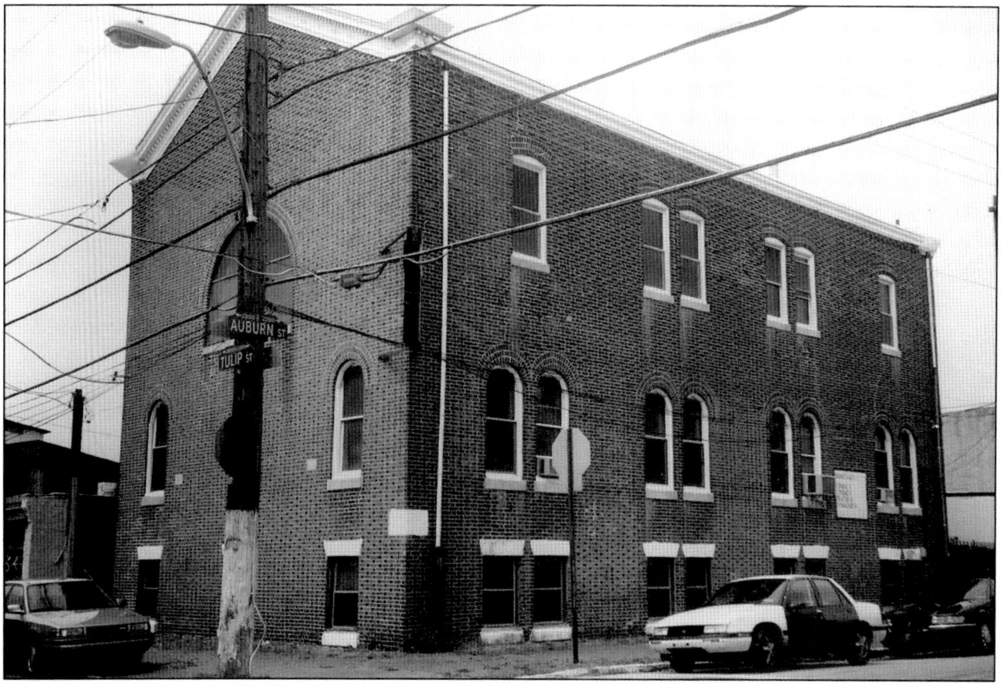

Very few communities had competing synagogues diagonally across the street from one another; Jewtown was an exception. Congregation B'nai Israel was founded and organized only a few years after the founding of the settlement in 1877. The synagogue built its home in the early 1900s, after renting rooms for religious ceremonies for more than 20 years. Located on the southwest corner of Tulip and Auburn Streets, the synagogue looked like some of the higher educational institutions found in Europe. (Courtesy of Allen Meyers.)

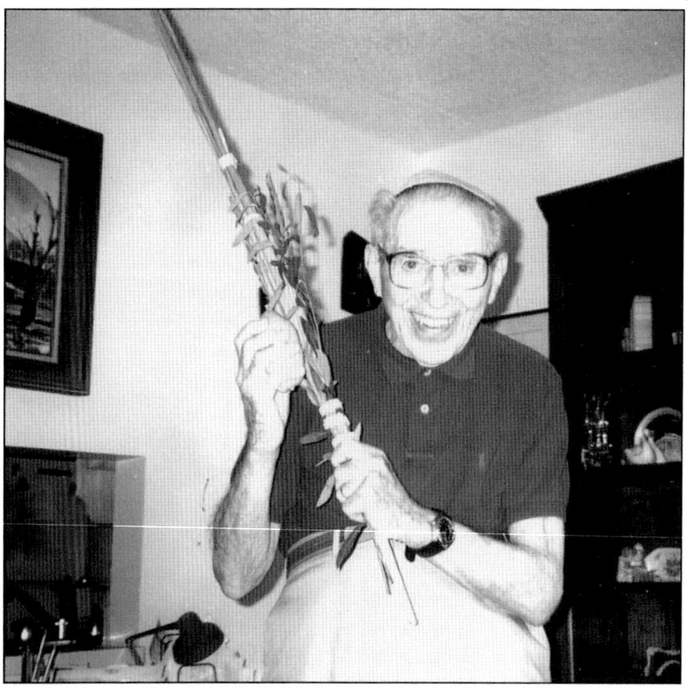

Herb Baker, the nephew of Rabbi Jacob Baker, was born on September 13, 1912, the second day of the new year. He always said to people, "you know me," since many people came to Yom Kippur services eight days later to participate in his *bris* (rite of circumcision). Now a widower, Baker clings to his upbringing as a devout religious Jew, with the *luvav* and *estrog* (palm and citrus fruit) to celebrate the fall harvest in his Martin Run retirement apartment in Broomall, Pennsylvania. (Courtesy of Herb Baker.)

Chevra Tehillim (reciting of Psalms) was founded in July 1887. Originally, the congregation met at 2244 Williams Street and served a Jewish community of more than 65 families. The first synagogue had a second-floor balcony for the women. The new synagogue, located on the northeast corner of Tulip and Auburn Streets, served the congregation under Rabbi Benjamin Block. The round, stained-glass windows were crafted by Isaac Silverman. (Courtesy of Allen Meyers.)

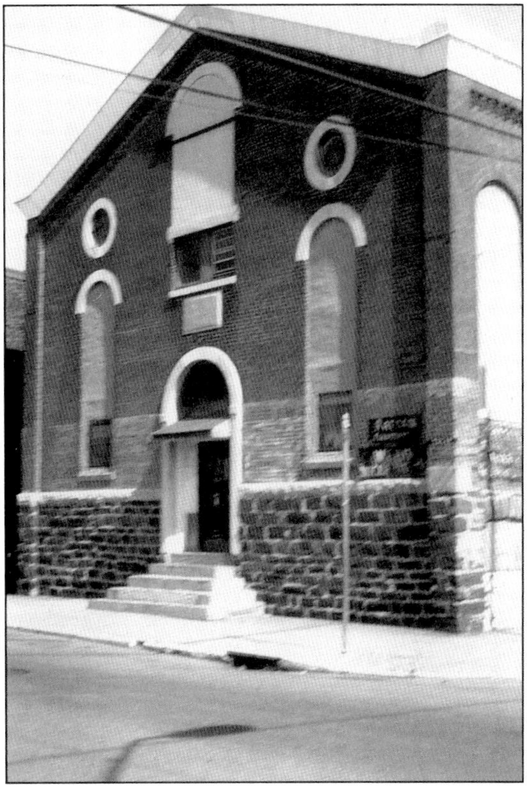

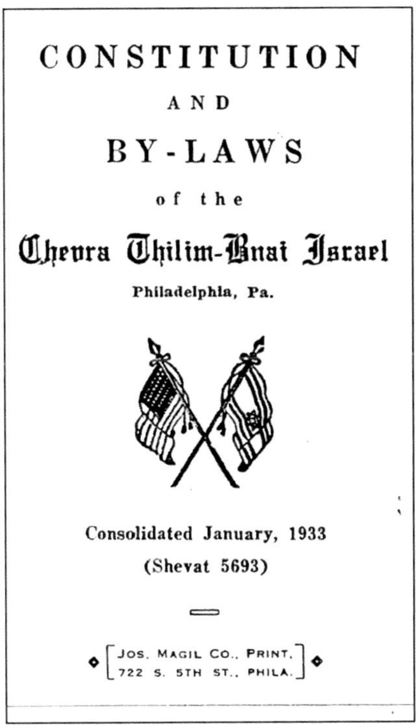

CONSTITUTION

AND

BY-LAWS

of the

Chevra Thilim-Bnai Israel

Philadelphia, Pa.

Consolidated January, 1933

(Shevat 5693)

[JOS. MAGIL CO., PRINT. 722 S. 5TH ST., PHILA.]

More than 50 years had passed since the founding of the settlement known as Jewtown when the Great Depression forced the marriage of both competing synagogues into one congregation in the early 1930s. The rules were amended in this official document to make this union unoffending to all parties. The unification, explained Herb Baker, could be found in the fact that the people two generations later were completely comfortable in identifying themselves as Jewtowners and expressed it with an element of pride. (Courtesy of Carl Nathans.)

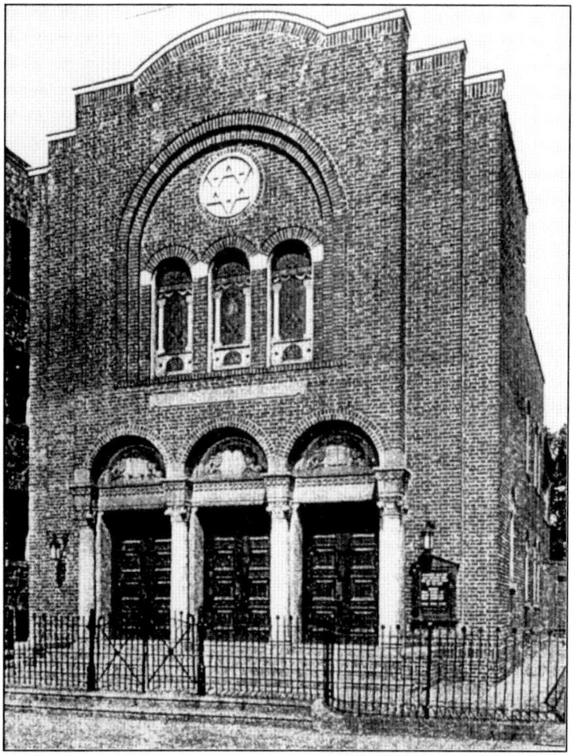

Congregation Adath Zion was composed of many merchants, predominantly German and Austro-Hungarians, in the community along Frankford Avenue. Founded in 1895, it built the first edifice shortly after 1910. One generation later, with the end of the Great Depression, the congregation in 1937 began a building campaign to enlarge the synagogue under the leadership of Rabbi Max L. Forman. The new second-story of the synagogue served as a meeting place for the Young People's League, B'nai Brith Lodge No. 1212, and as the local chapter of the Deborah Lung Hospital.

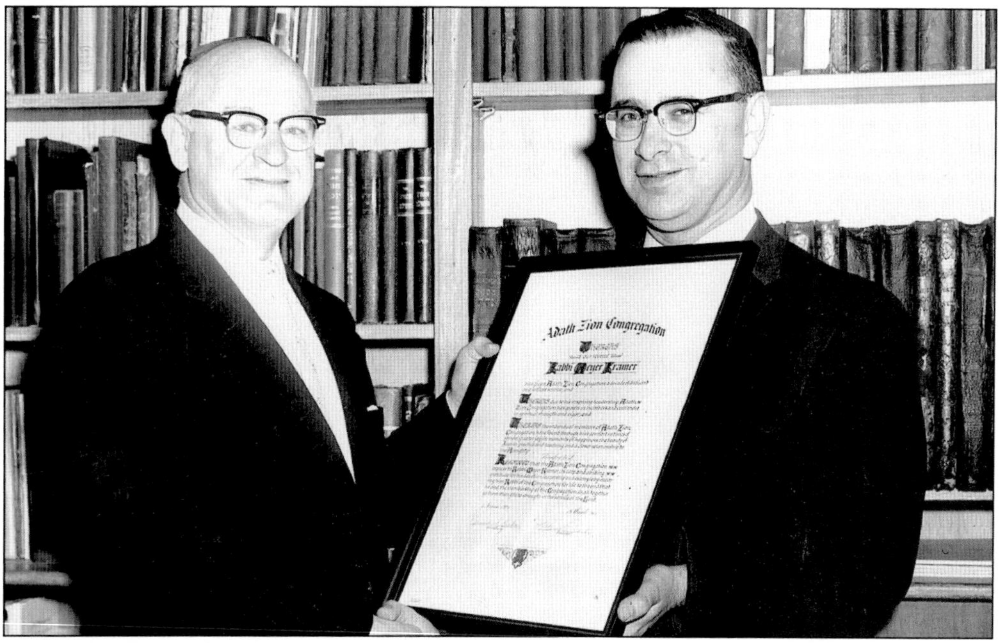

The leadership at Congregation Adath Zion, which served the Jewish merchants of Frankford Avenue, became stronger with each passing generation. Rabbi Meyer Kramer (right), a graduate of Yeshiva University in New York, along with longtime lay leader Dr. Maurice Beck, guided the community through a period of urban change that witnessed the migration of the congregation to the farmlands in the great northeast section of Philadelphia in 1956.

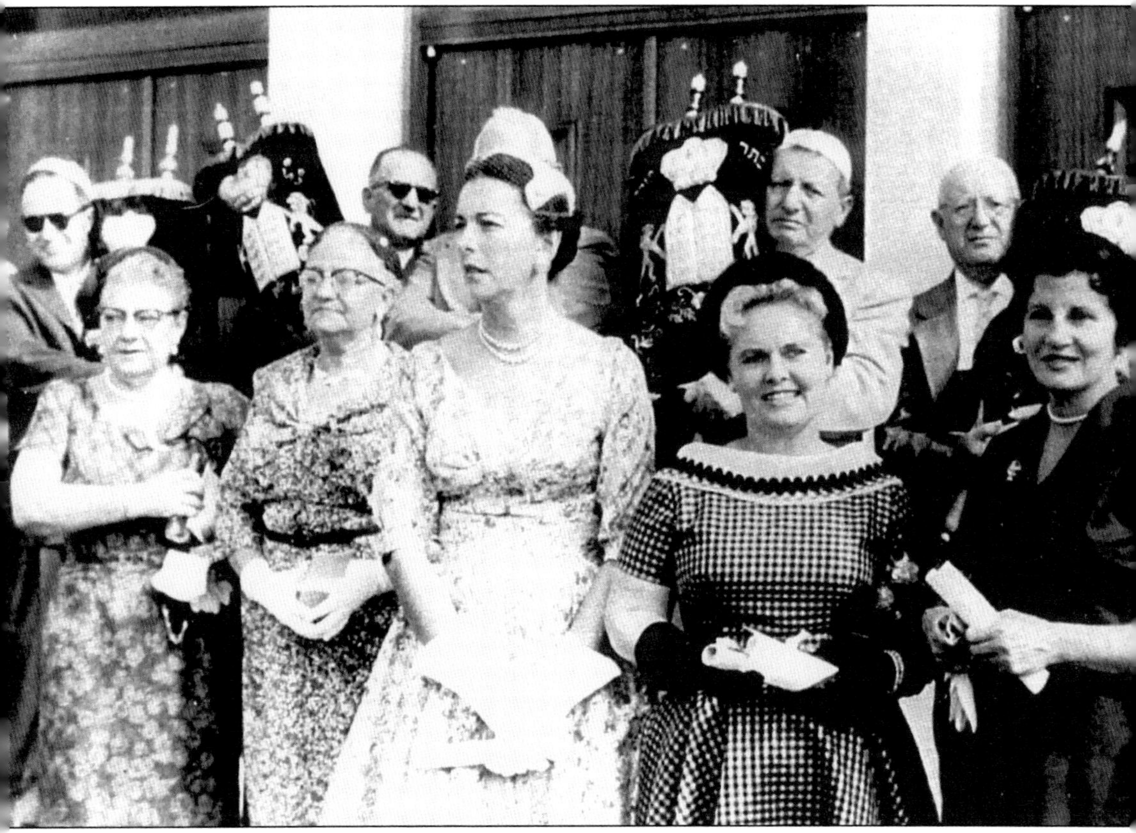

The driving force for change in Congregation Adath Zion of Frankford could be found in the women who served as one arm of the synagogue. In 1956, the leadership of Fay Zeaman and her husband, Bernard Stern, witnessed the march of the holy scriptures from Paul Street to Adath Zion's new home on Pennway Street in the Castor Gardens section of Oxford Circle. (Courtesy of Fay Stern.)

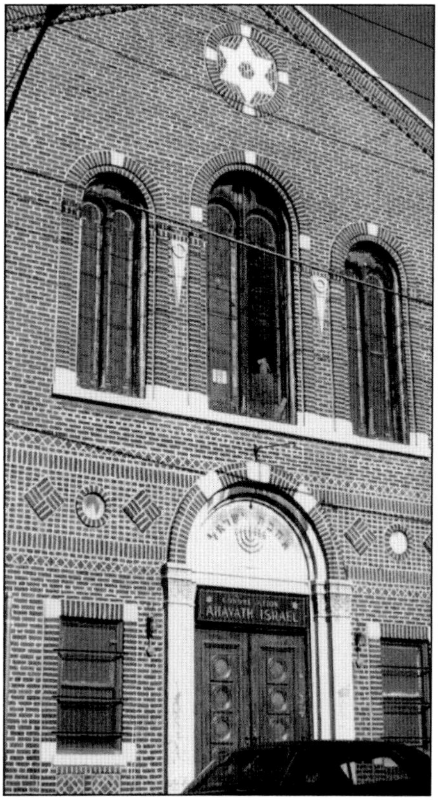

Emanuel Wirtshafter, a Hungarian Jew, settled with his son, Henry, in the Fishtown section of Philadelphia along the Delaware River during the 1890s. Wirthshafter's department store, situated in the 2000 block of Frankford Avenue, attracted other immigrants who settled in the community. Ahavath Israel-Anshei Kensington found permanent quarters in two cottages at 2302—2304 Mascher Street in 1905.

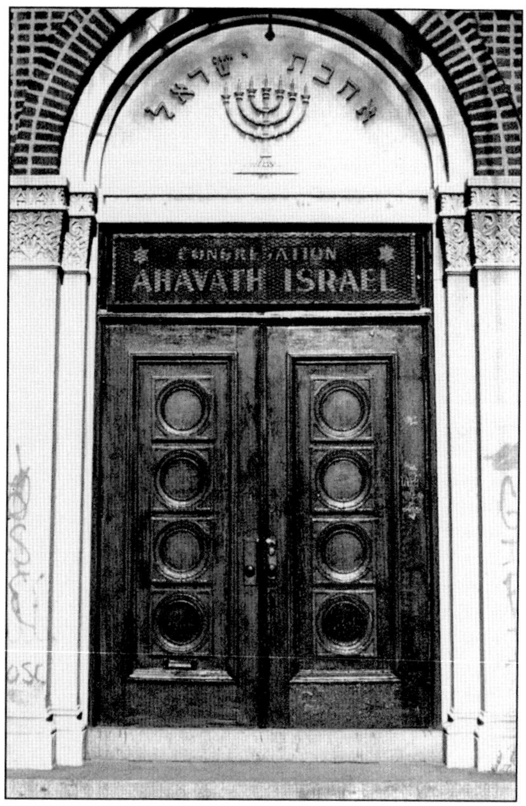

The Jews of Fishtown and Kensington included Ben Zion Jessar, Manny Wirthshafter, Sam Erickson, David Rabinowitz, and Sol Block, who signed the charter of Ahavath Israel in the city deed book, number 28, page 392, in 1903. After renting quarters in various halls and holding service above storefronts, the Hungarian congregation hired the famous city architect Louis Magaziner and paid $10,500 to have the building company Sokoloff and Glicksman create a religious edifice in 1912.

The *beama* (the center of activities where the scriptures were read) served the Jewish merchants of the community for more than 75 years. Jewish *simhas* (happy occasions) and sorrows were commemorated on this stage throughout two world wars, the Great Depression, and the creation of the modern state of Israel. Children who received their Jewish education only blocks from their homes atop the storefronts on Front Street and Kensington Avenue loved their shul.

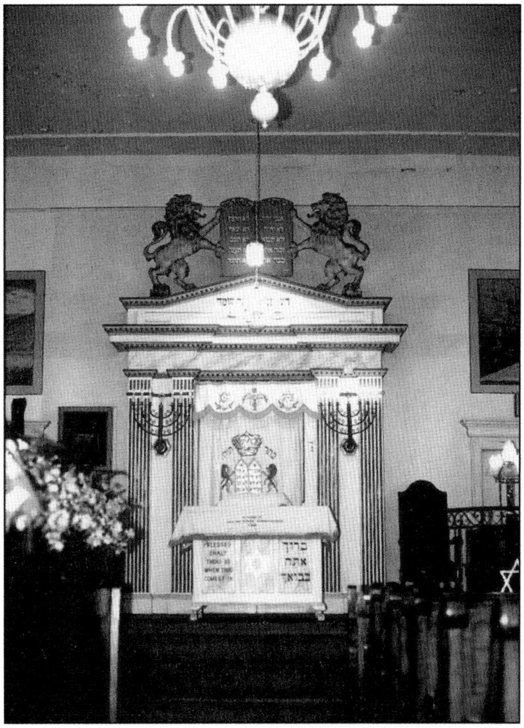

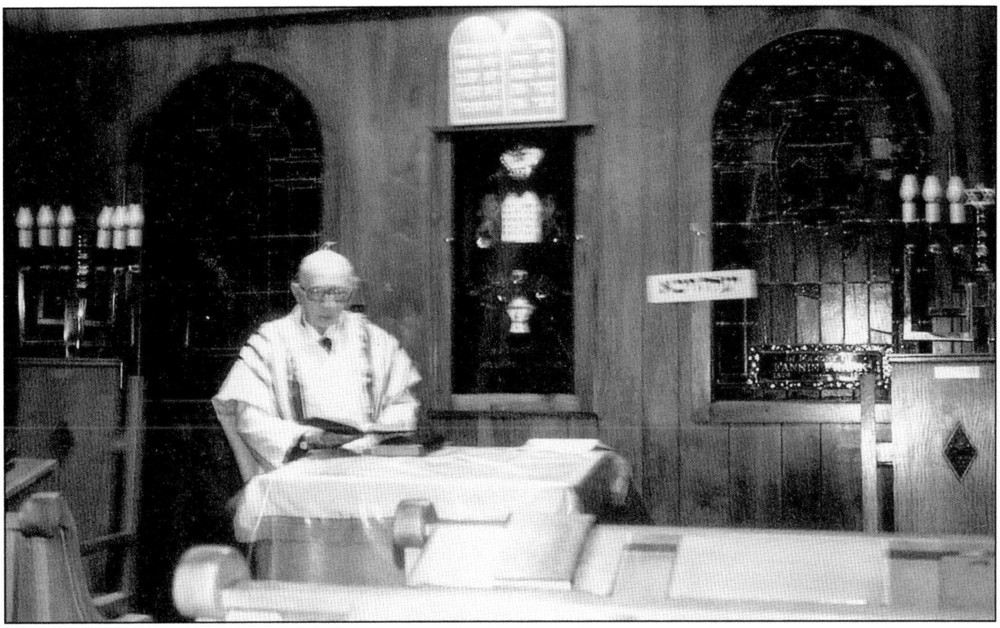

Rabbinical leadership in the Philadelphia Jewish community is a longstanding tradition that sometimes endured several generations. Rabbi Isidor Solomon, born in Palestine, came to Ahavath Israel in 1940 and immediately bonded with the community. Allen Meyers, the author, met with Rabbi Solomon in the early 1980s and assisted him in his daily activities by driving him around the city to perform his chaplaincy duties of visiting the sick. The synagogue closed after the High holidays in 1981. (Courtesy of Allen Meyers.)

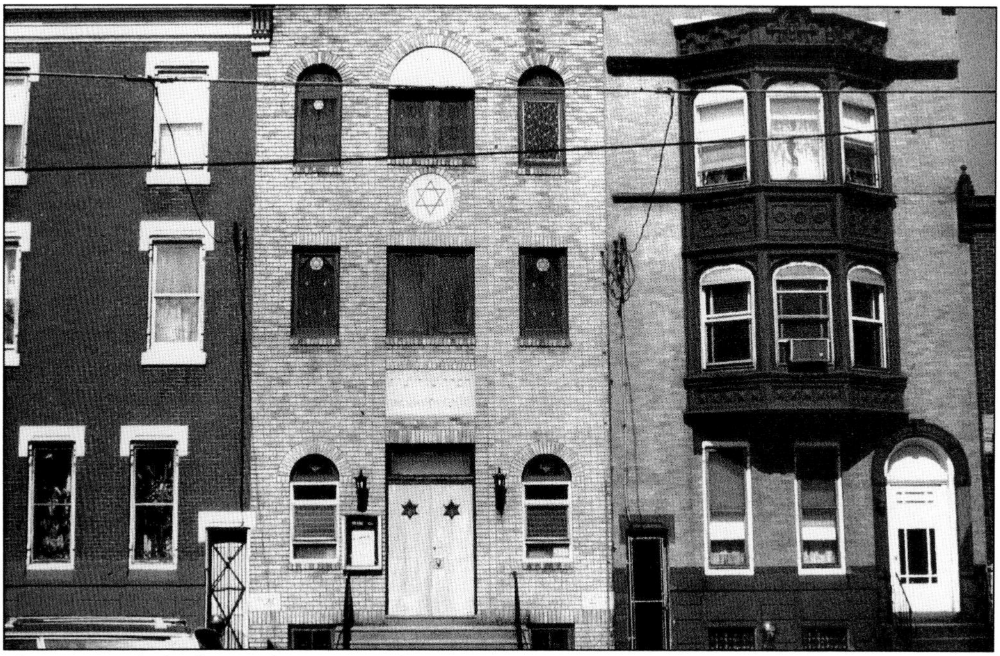

Shaare Yitzchok, better known as the Kensington Jewish Community Center, came into existence as the sixth and last congregation to form as the result of a concentrated business district with its pulse at Kensington and Allegheny Avenues in the early 1920s. The merchants, led by Max Packer and Jacob Stosh, opened their businesses as quarters for the new congregation until a suitable building at 2033 East Allegheny opened its doors in 1926. (Courtesy of Allen Meyers.)

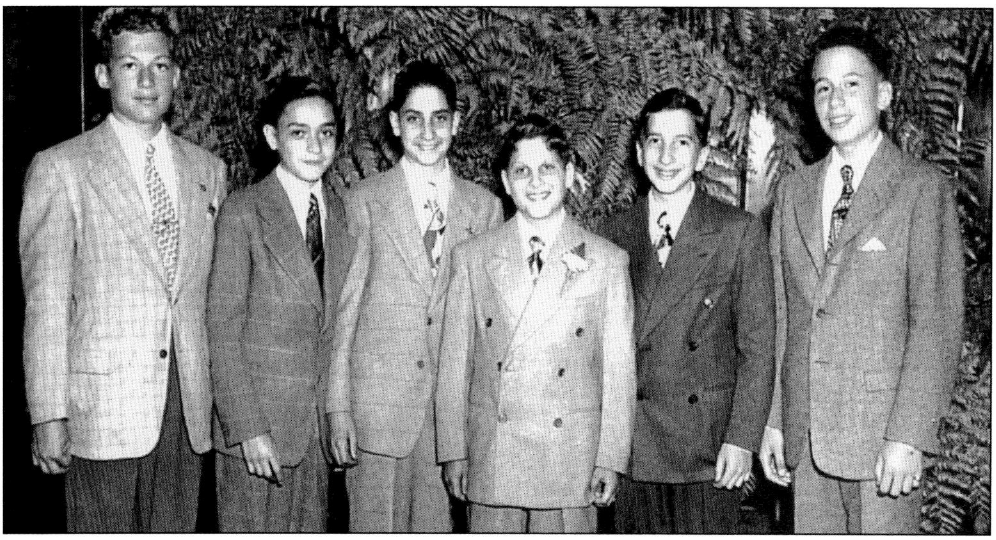

The activities in early years at Shaare Yitzchok centered on the education of the young people whose parents had stores from 2800–3500 Kensington Avenue, under the Frankford El. The Hebrew school, which met at the synagogue, gave rise to lifelong friendships. Herb Bobman celebrated his Bar Mitzvah with his friends Peter Fischer, brothers Norm and Art Loev, Ray Obod, and Stewart Brown. The boys even formed a baseball team from the synagogue, named the Kensington Rockets. (Courtesy of Herb Bobman.)

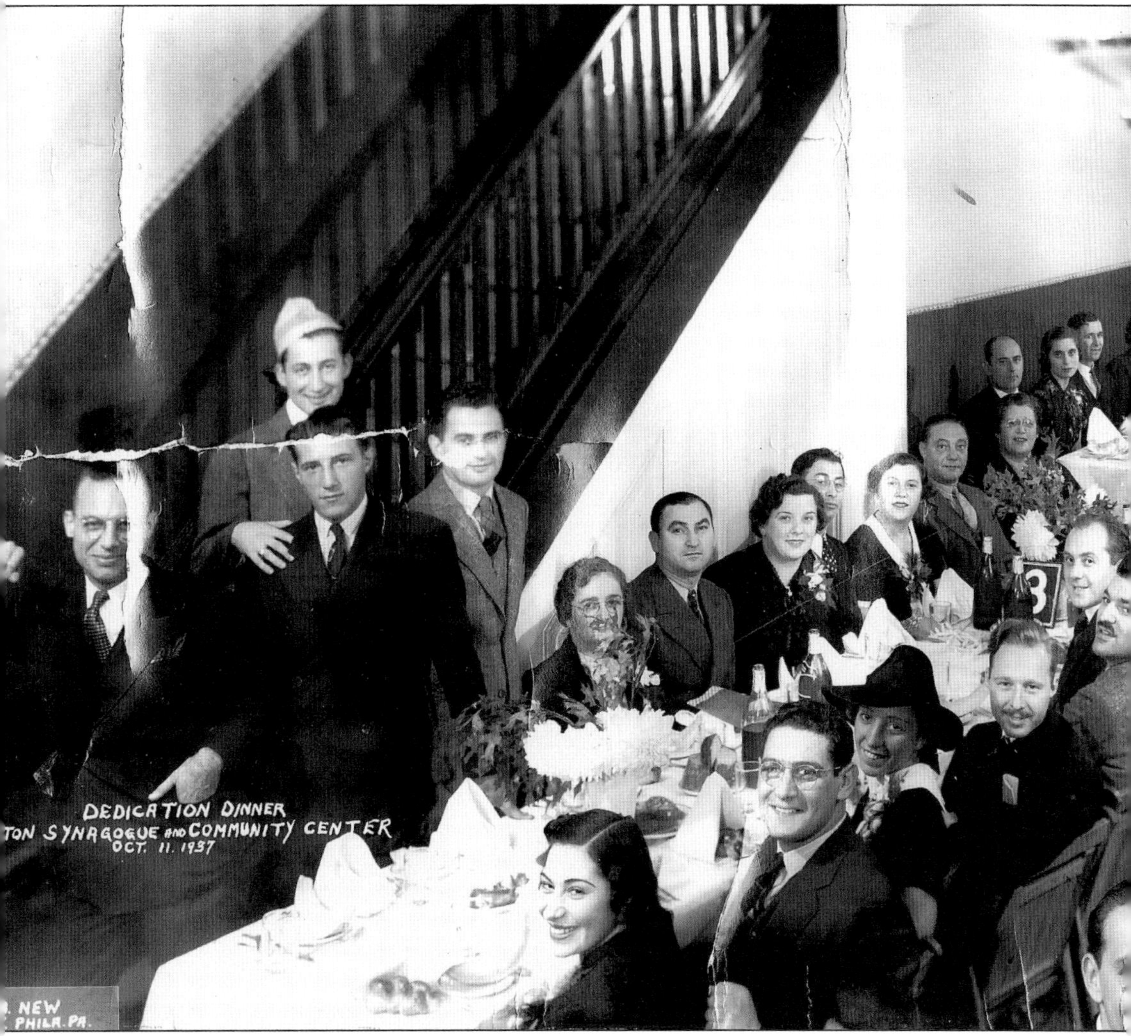

As the membership of Shaare Yitzchok expanded in the 1930s, the Jews of Kensington who had formed the congregation realized that their children's needs were a priority . A fund-raiser to acquire a building two doors away from the synagogue was launched in 1937. The congregation held a dinner on October 11, 1937, in the social hall downstairs to announce new plans and a new name: the Kensington Synagogue and Community Center. (Courtesy of Charles Shuben.)

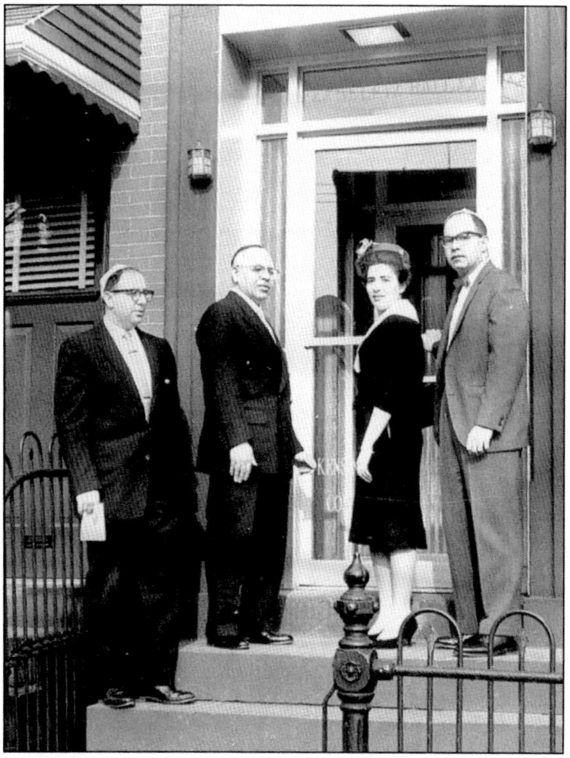

In 1963, the leaders of the Kensington Synagogue and Community Center decided to reinvest in the future of their beloved center of activities, at 2027 East Allegheny Avenue. The children who had grown up and now ran their parents' businesses remodeled the building for their adult activities. From left to right are Rabbi Zeri Greenwald; Charles Shuben, president of the men's club; Florence Gold, president of the sisterhood; and Dr. Sidney Snyder, president of the synagogue. (Courtesy of Charles Shuben.)

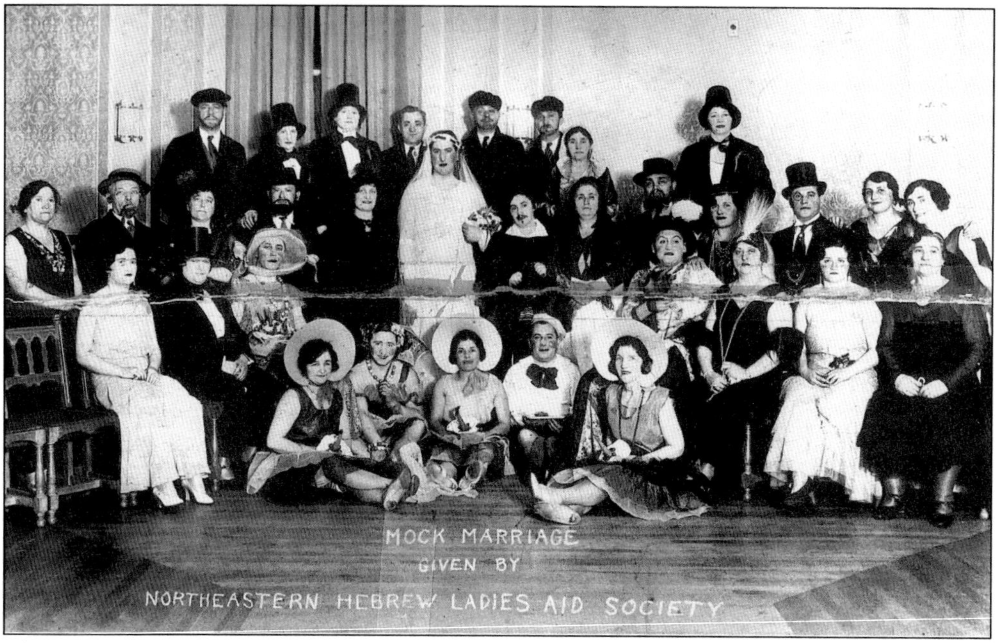

The Kensington Synagogue had a great reputation for duplicating the activities that worked in other Jewish organizations. The year-end social event and major fund-raiser for this predominantly Russian-Jewish congregation was *Mock Marriage*, a skit about a large family marrying off its only daughter. The Northeastern Hebrew Aid Society put on the show, which everyone— Jews and non-Jews could come and see for a fee. (Courtesy of Marvin Levin.)

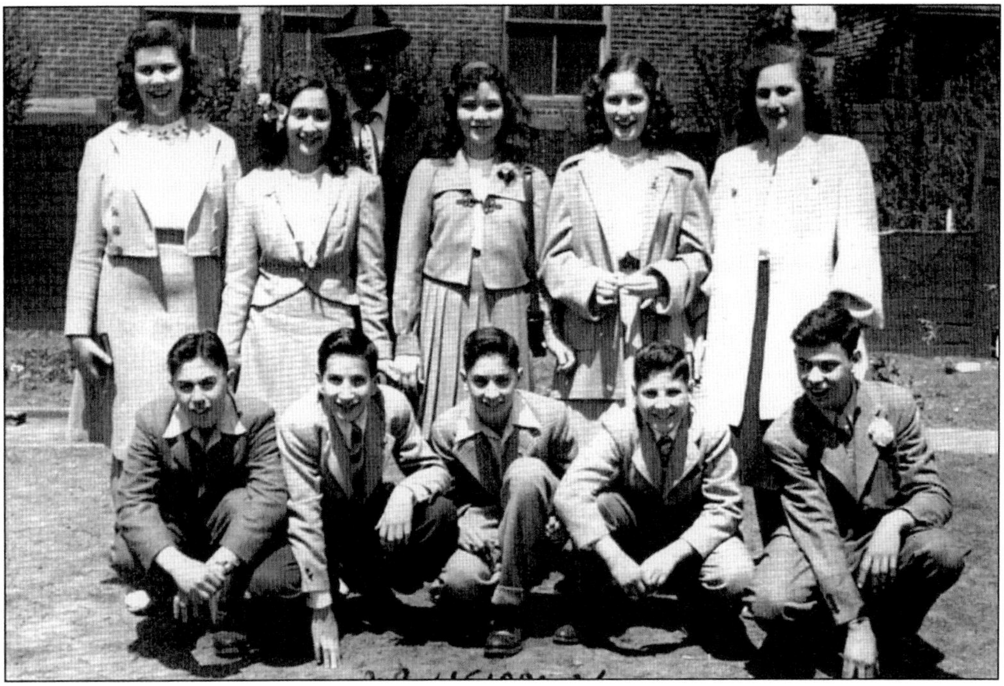

Joining in pictures for the fun of it became a socially accepted pastime for many. Philadelphian Jews participated in the ritual with a flair of their own by signing their Sunday school graduation photograph. The names spelled out around the photograph create a historical record: Elaine Salden, Elaine Goldberg, Sandra Zwickel, Bea Ruttenberg, Blanche Shapiro, A. Grobman, Norman Love, Herb Bobman, and the teacher, Mr. Weissman. (Courtesy of Ray Obod.)

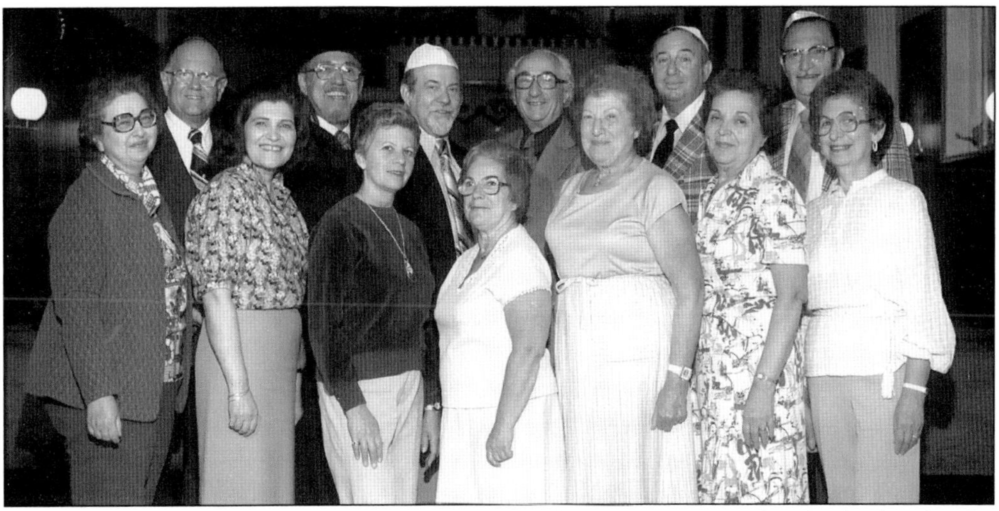

The women of Kensington Synagogue had many things in common besides husbands who collectively ran the men's association. They organized numerous events that bonded the community into one unit similar to a small town where only one synagogue serves an entire community. The desire to put on dinners, shows, fund-raisers, and the best play ever, *Fiddler on the Roof*, served as the fabric which kept the synagogue in existence for more than 60 years. (Courtesy of Charles Shuben.)

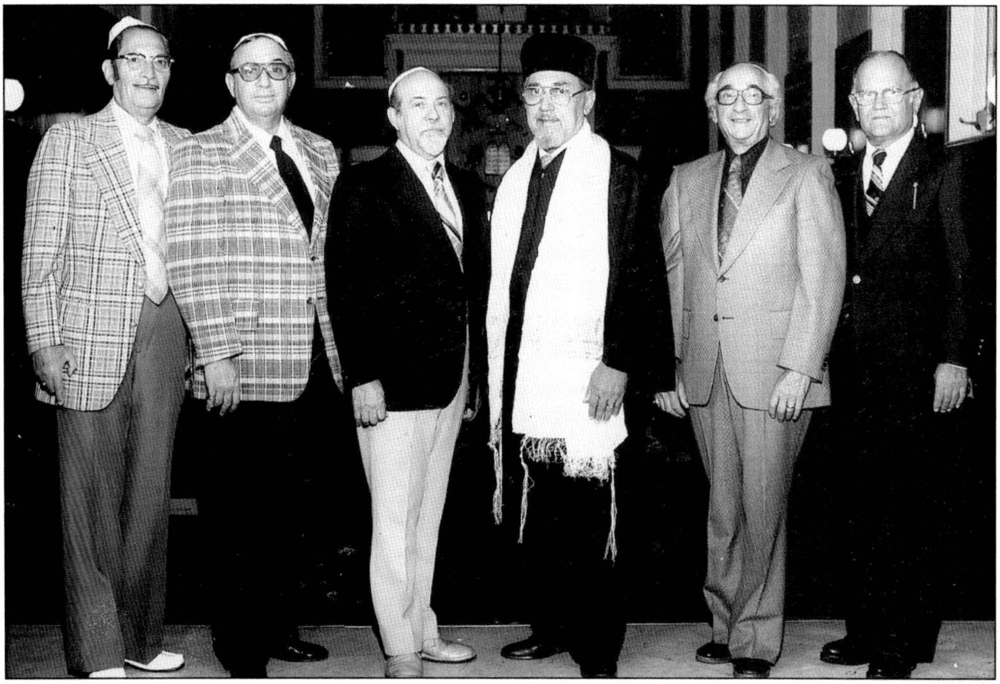

The men of Shaare Yitzchok worked within their circle of friendship to give thanks to a long and lasting congregation that united under Judaism to give something back to the community for its long years of dedication. Longtime friends Joe Bogdanoff, Charles Shuben, Len Gold, Rabbi Harry Cole, Al Frost, and Izzy Seidman decided in 1986 to honor the synagogue on its 60th birthday with—you guessed it—a show and dinner. (Courtesy of Edith Seidman.)

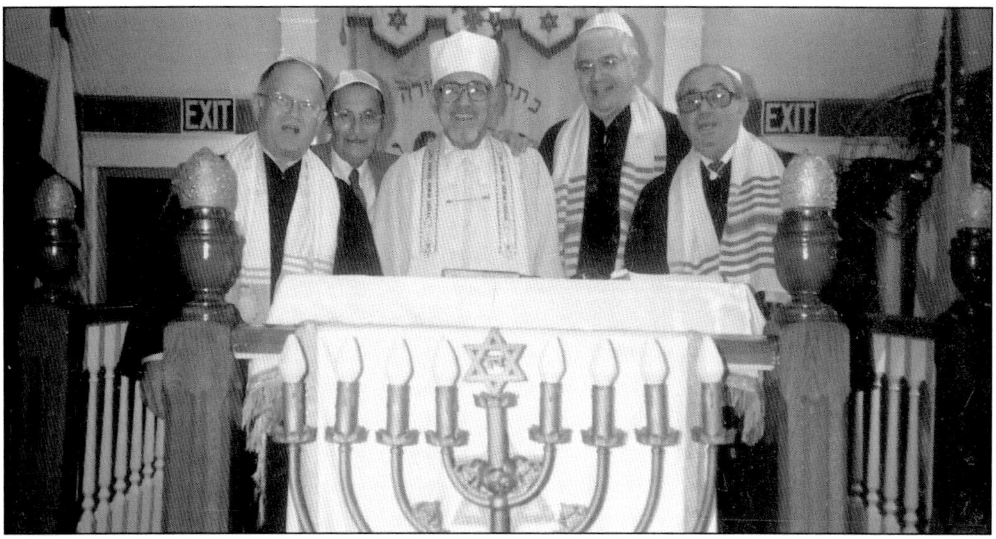

It was a good time to say good-bye and be thankful for all the wonderful years that the men and women shared in their beloved row house shul on Allegheny Avenue. Rabbi Harry Cole (center) united the remaining guardians of the synagogue for a last pose on the *beama*, where for more than 65 years the call for community prayer sounded every Saturday morning. The synagogue closed and merged with Shaare Shamayim in the far northeast section of Philadelphia. (Courtesy of Edith Seidman.)

Four

My Means of Travel

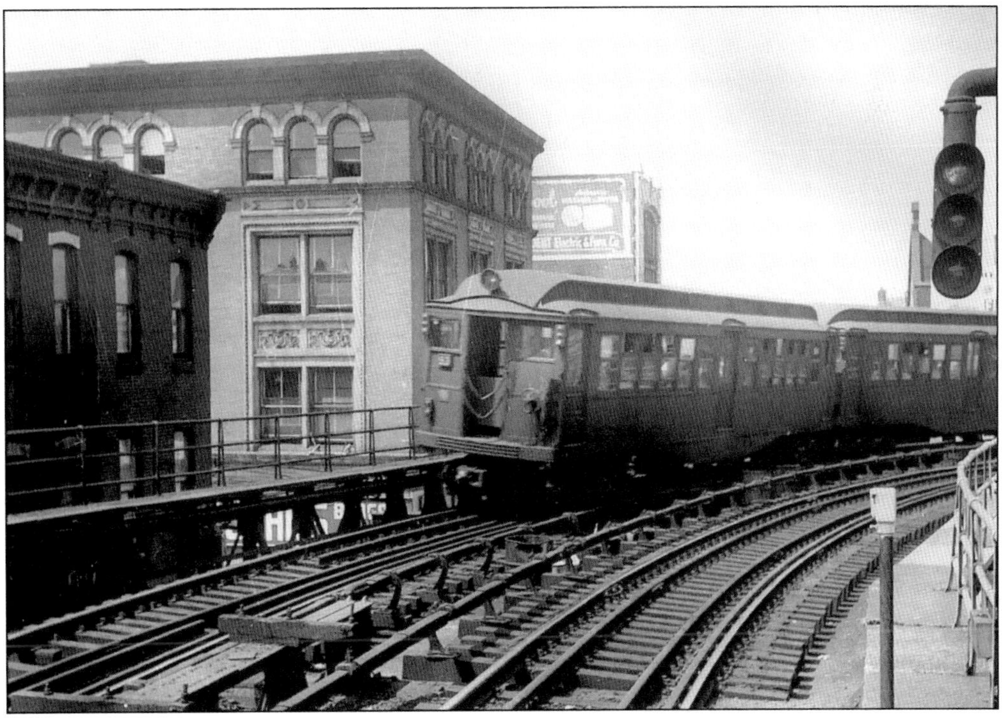

The early development of public transportation took place in the River Wards corridor, which connected the outlying districts to the downtown sections of Philadelphia. A railroad with a right-of-way through a densely populated area seemed almost impossible as the city developed in the early 20th century, but plans for just that system were in place by the late 1890s. The opening of the Market–Frankford line in 1922 started a whole new era in real estate, business, and residential living patterns. Visits to relatives around the city could be easily made by hopping on the El to downtown or to West Philadelphia. The trip going into town included a ride by the Kent movie theater, near Kensington Avenue and Front Street, where the tracks curved at a very sharp turn. Rounding that turn, the passing train would made a loud, shrill sound, which could be heard throughout the neighborhood. (Courtesy of Dick Short.)

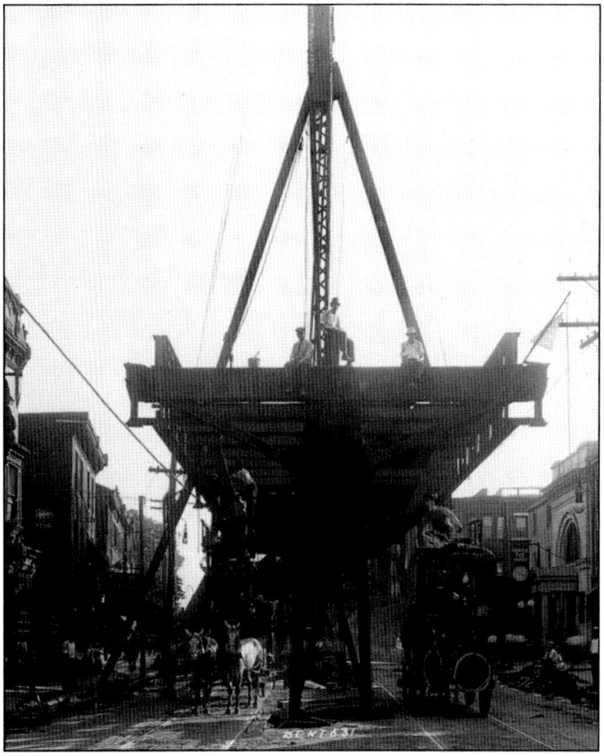

The construction process of the Market–Frankford line, which included lifting heavy timber more than 40 feet in the air, took more than eight long years to complete. The laborers relied on horses and wagons to do the bolstering of the ironwork that would carry the elevated train from Frankford to its downtown destination. Less than a mile from the location of this photograph, a concrete water trough for horses remained for more than 60 years after the El was completed. (Courtesy of the Philadelphia City Archives.)

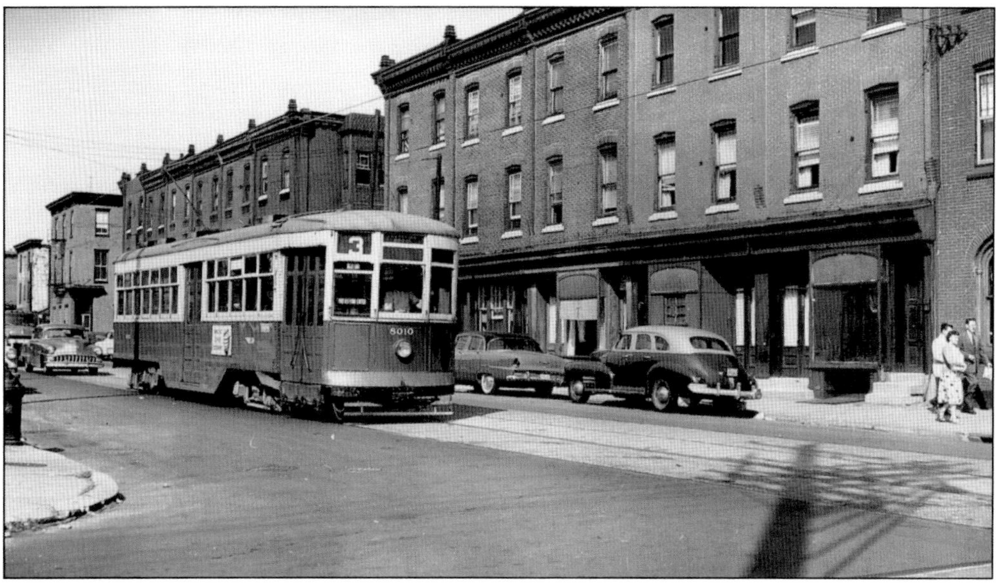

Trolley cars were part of everyday life in Philadelphia. The Route No. 3 car traveled from its terminal in Frankford, at the Bridge-Pratt Street carbarn, to another predominantly Jewish neighborhood in North Philadelphia: Strawberry Mansion. The No. 3 ran under the Frankford El for most of its journey until it turned west on Berks Street on its way over to Columbia Avenue before looping around in Fairmount Park off Thirty-third Street. (Courtesy of Dick Short.)

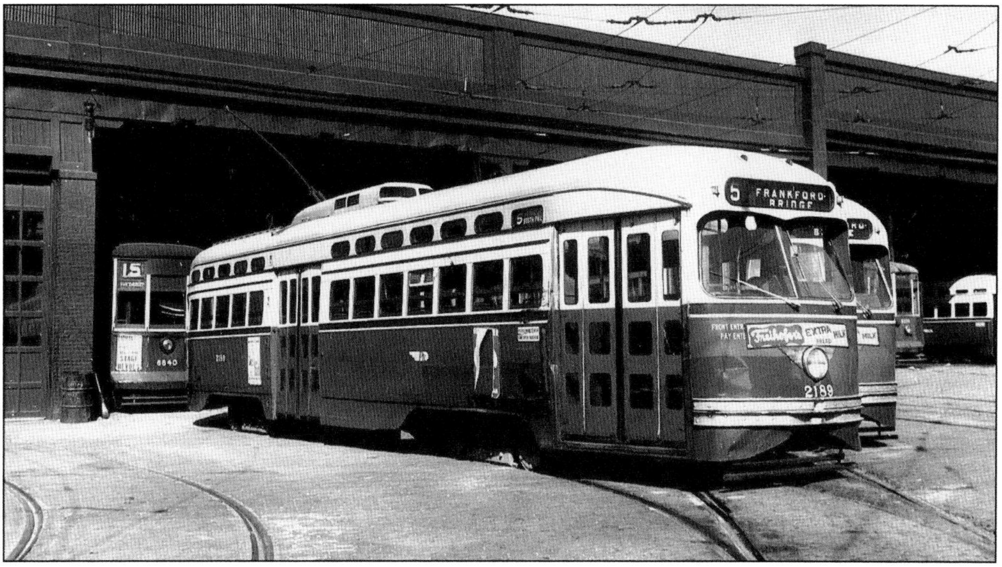

Whole family outings were conducted on trolley cars. Each trolley car connected people not only to relatives but also to various services and shopping venues. The Route No. 5 car ran from South Philadelphia to Frankford along Third Street and over Frankford Avenue past many hospitals and community parks. The long ride via No. 5 was a favorite of Esther Meyers, the mother of Allen Meyers, who usually did not have the energy after shopping to climb the steep steps of the Frankford El. (Courtesy of Dick Short.)

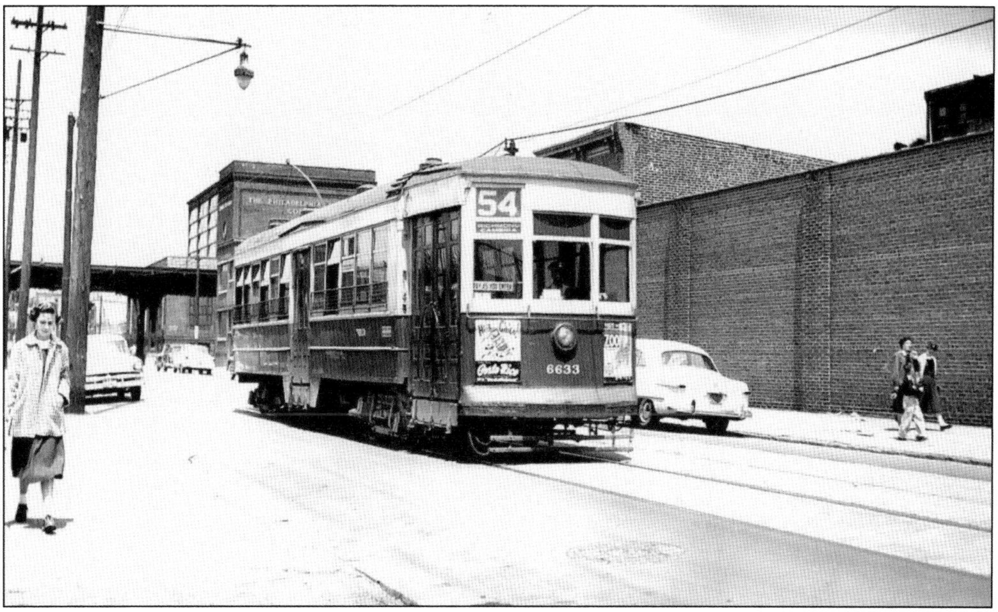

The Route No. 54 car traveled from the Schuylkill River to the Delaware River along Lehigh Avenue from Thirty-third Street eastbound past Dobbins Vocational High School (at Twenty-second Street) and the old Northeast High School (at Eighth Street) on its way to Richmond and Somerset Streets. Students were outnumbered only on days when the Phillies baseball team played its home games at Connie Mack Stadium, across the street from Dobbins. (Courtesy of Dick Short.)

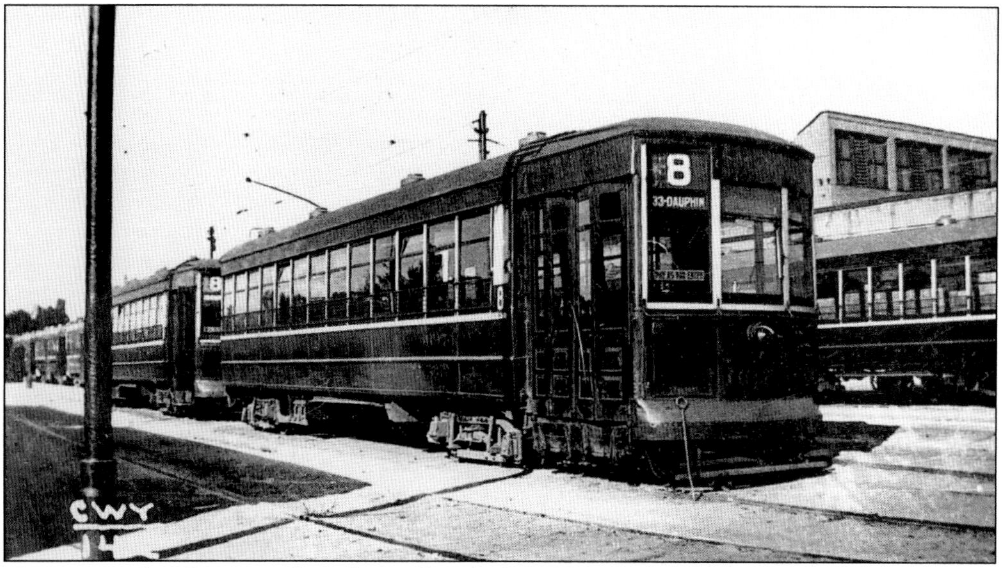

The routes of trolley cars often changed with the addition of new neighborhoods or national events. With the onset of World War I, Route No. 8 ran along Susquehanna Street, terminating at Richmond and Norris Streets, in order to transport thousands of skilled laborers to the shipbuilding lines along the Delaware River. Packed with men and women daily, the trolleys literally delivered people from their doorsteps to the factories. (Courtesy of Dick Short.)

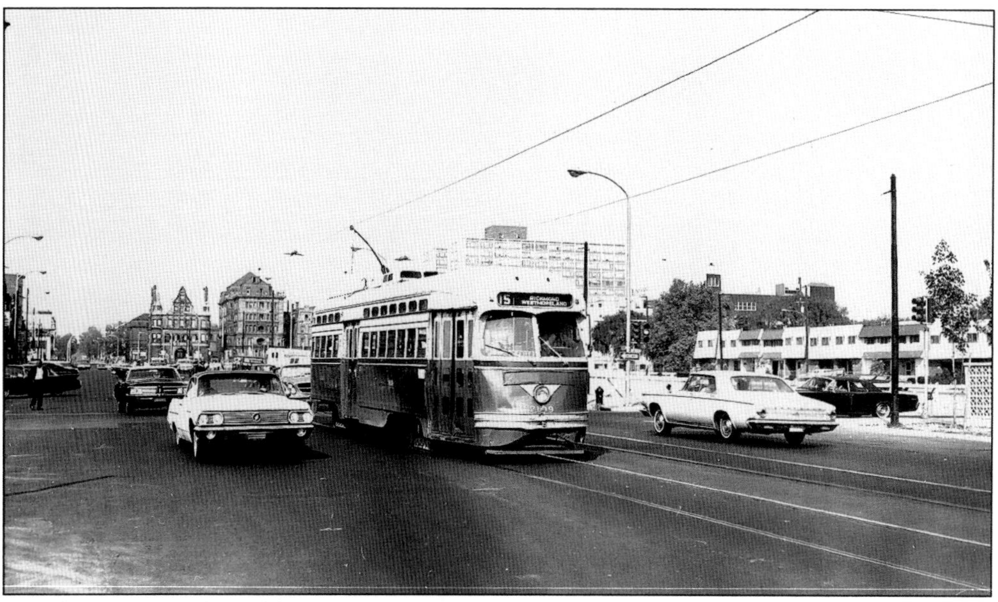

Another east–west bound line connected Kensington, North Philadelphia, the zoo, and points west of the Schuylkill River all for the price of one ticket. The Jews of Richmond relied on the No. 15 line to go shopping at the famous Marshall Street marketplace off Girard Avenue. On return trips, the whole trolley car filled up with the smells of fresh rye bread, corn beef, and Jewish pickles. (Courtesy of Dick Short.)

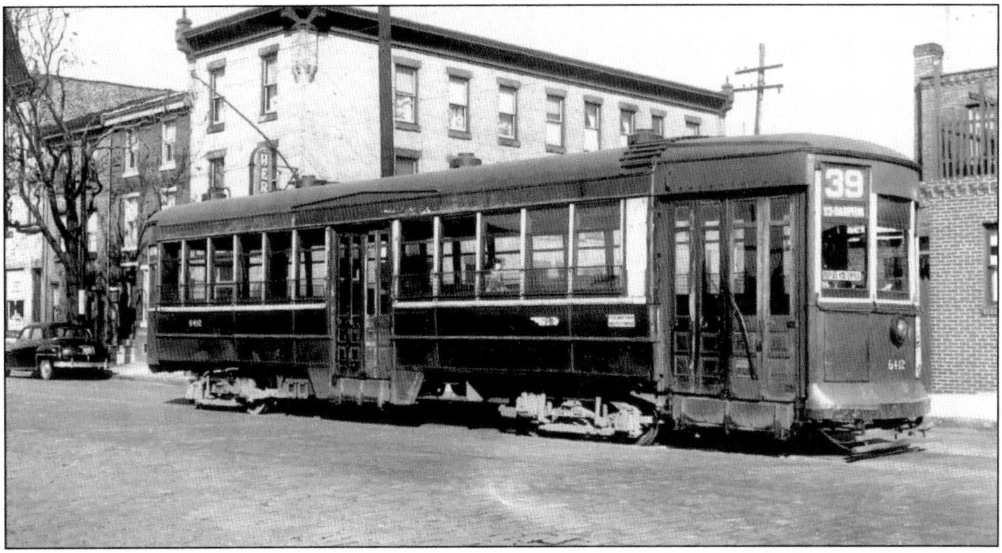

Sometimes trolley cars had twins, or look-alikes, which caused a great deal of confusion since they ran on similar streets and the same tracks. When unsuspecting riders in a hurry did not pay attention, they usually boarded the first trolley that came along. For example, the Route No. 39 followed another trolley's route plan. Often the riders did not have any idea of the mix-up, usually because the motorman forgot to change the sign and trolley car route number during a layover. (Courtesy of Dick Short.)

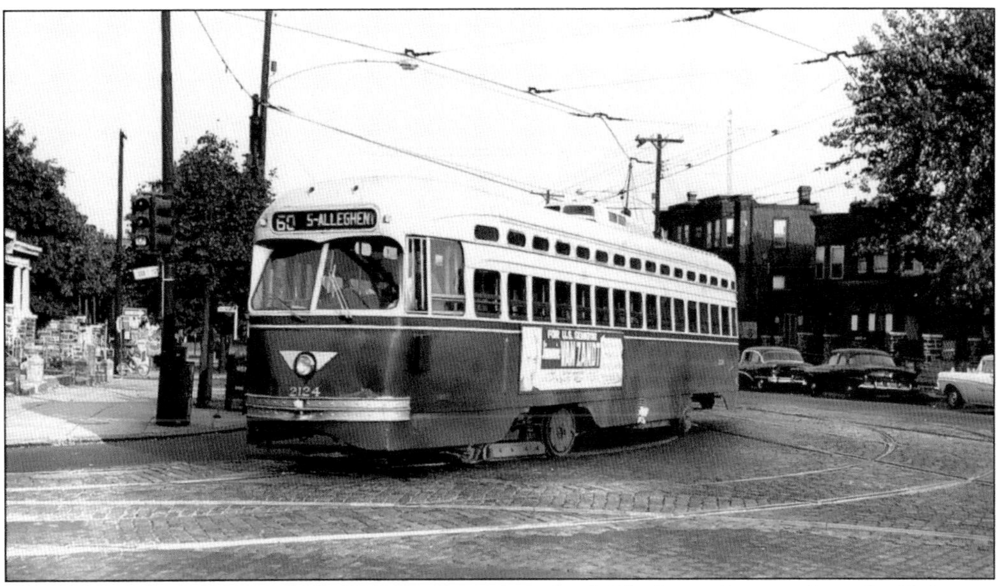

The Route No. 60 car traveled along the entire length of Allegheny Avenue from the Delaware River to the Schuylkill River, connecting many Jewish business districts. The grid set up by William Penn, with all streets intersecting in a boxed design, aided early Jewish immigrants who lived one or two neighborhoods away from each other and wanted to visit very easily. The major connections took place farther east at Front Street, Kensington Avenue, and Richmond Street, where other Jewish businesses depended on foot traffic, as well as trolley riders connecting to more lines. (Courtesy of Dick Short.)

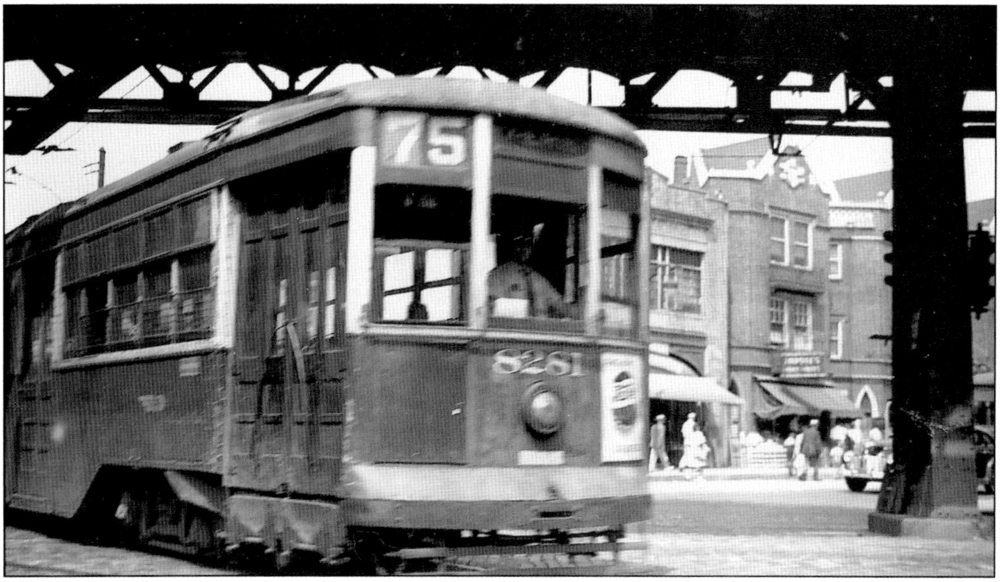

Trolley car No. 75 crosses under the El at Margaret Street. A ride in the country became a treat for those who rode on Route No. 75 from Bridesburg westward through Frankford to Wyoming Avenue. The No. 75 connected several Jewish communities, including Logan (near Broad Street) and Feltonville (at D Street), to the Frankford Business district. (Courtesy of Gus Spector.)

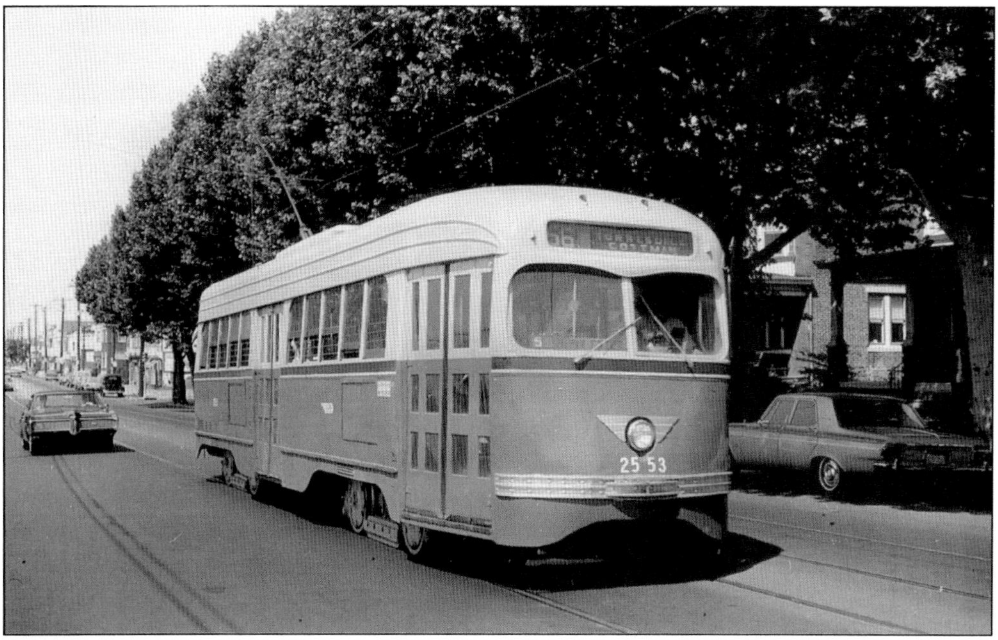

Trolley cars served the general public in a variety of ways: getting to work, going to school, taking in a ball game, and visiting other Jewish families who ran businesses throughout the city. The Route No. 56 car ran from Erie and Hunting Park Avenues to Torresdale and Cottman Avenues. The trolley went up to the Disston Saw Company, off Longshore Avenue, where Jews established storefront businesses in the 1920s and formed the Northeast Jewish Community Center. (Courtesy of Allen Meyers.)

Five

SCHOOLS

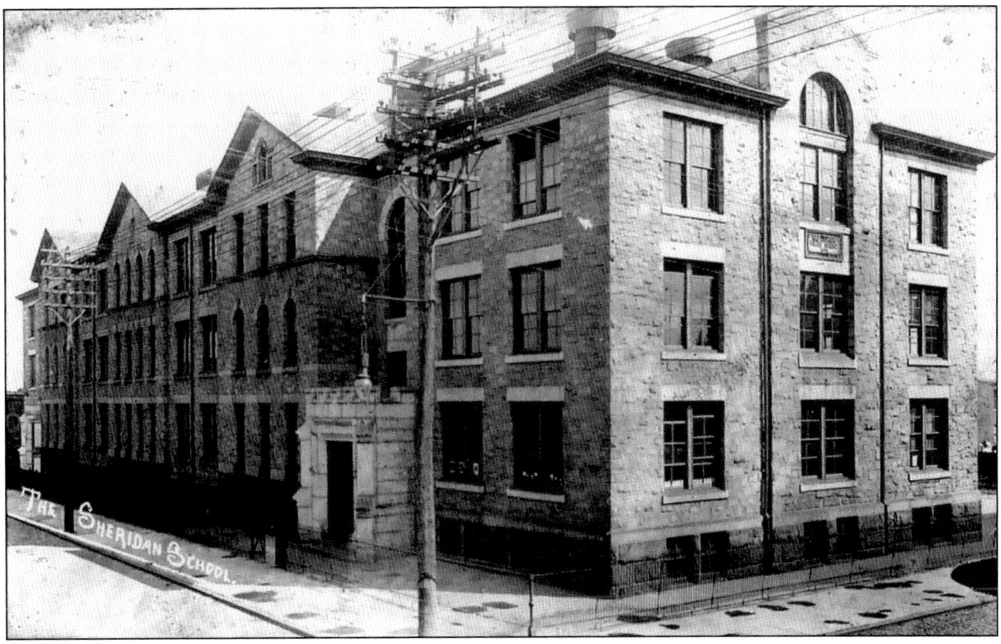

For the most part, there were two types of schools available to children in Philadelphia: public schools and parochial schools run by the Catholic Church. The Jewish immigrants sent their children off to school to better themselves and to prepare for adult life. The bonds and alliances made by children growing up in the most industrial section of Philadelphia led to lifelong friendships regardless of ethnic or social class. Once at school, the children learned their lessons in modern surroundings, since most of the schools, such as the Phillip Sheridan Elementary School, at G and Ontario Streets north of Allegheny Avenue, were built in the late 19th and early 20th centuries to meet the needs of a growing immigrant population. Cecilia Matless, the daughter of a shoemaker, graduated in June 1928, which was a victory all by itself since many female students did not complete the elementary curriculum and instead helped in the home. (Courtesy of Betsy Gherson and Hope Matless.)

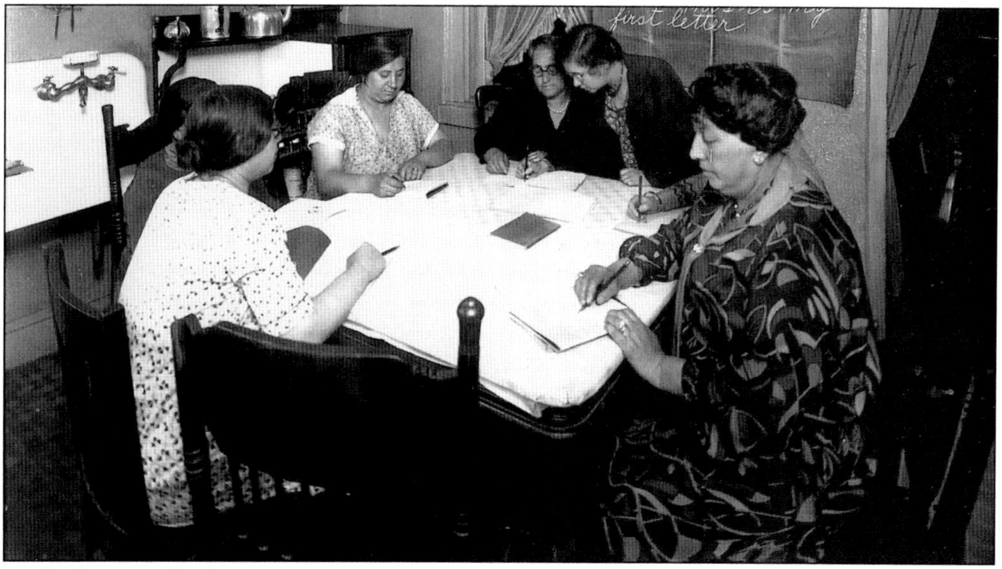

With the arrival of so many immigrants during the early 1900s, learning English became a central theme in the Philadelphia public schools. At schools throughout Philadelphia, small classes were held in the evening for women who wished to learn to read, write, and speak English. Evening classes made it possible for many immigrants to maintain a day job. (Courtesy of Walter Spector.)

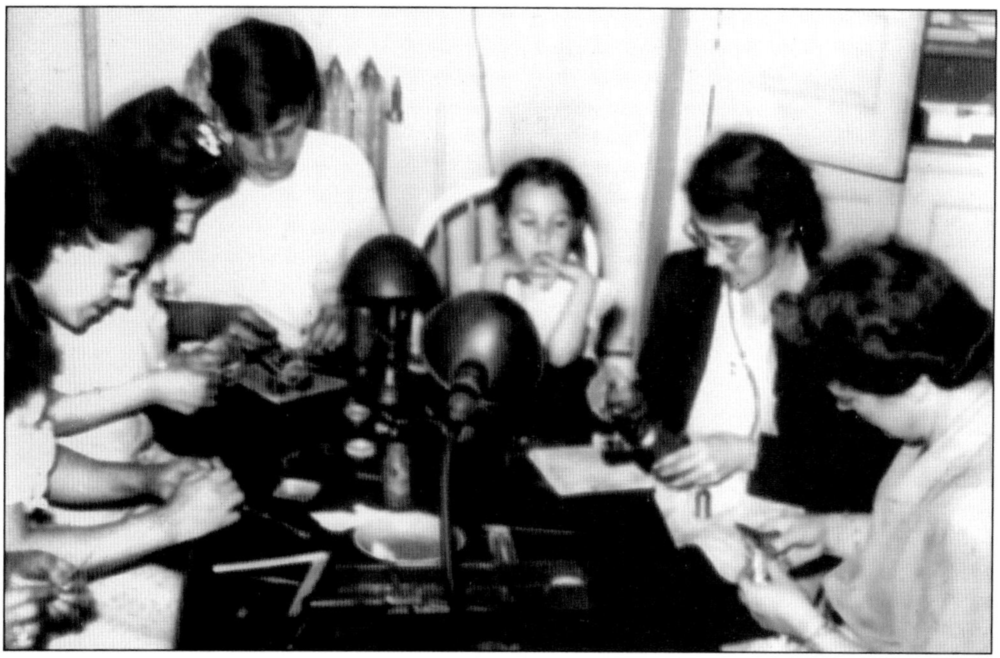

Schools opened up for all portions of the population, especially in the Kensington section. Trade schools and learning organizations, such as the prominent Light House community institution that ran two programs near Second and Lehigh Avenues, abounded in this community. (Most people know only of the athletic program Light House provided to the youth of the neighborhood.) Women studied trades such as jewelry making, as shown in this photograph, taken a few blocks north of Lehigh Avenue. (Courtesy of Frank Bender.)

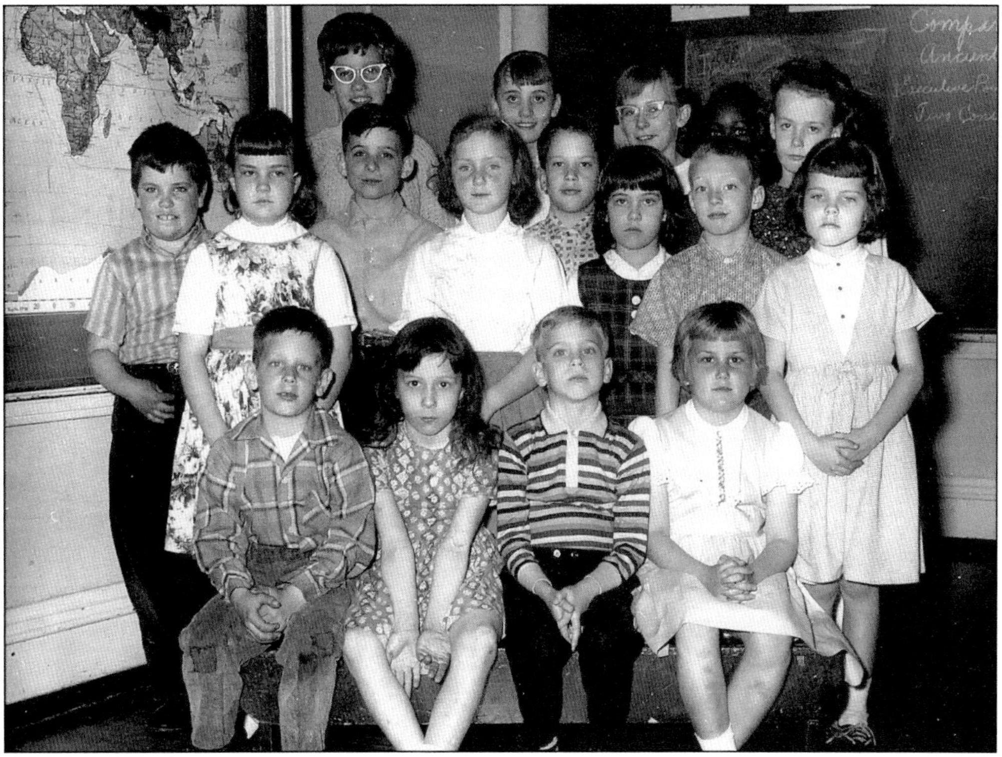

For the Jewish children of Kensington, the public schools were the place to make new friends and pals. This 1965 photograph portrays happy children of working parents enjoying their childhood not far from their homes. Elliot Seidman, the son of Edith and Izzy Seidman of the Seidman appliance business, attended the John Webster Elementary School, at Frankford and Ontario Streets. (Courtesy of Edith Seidman.)

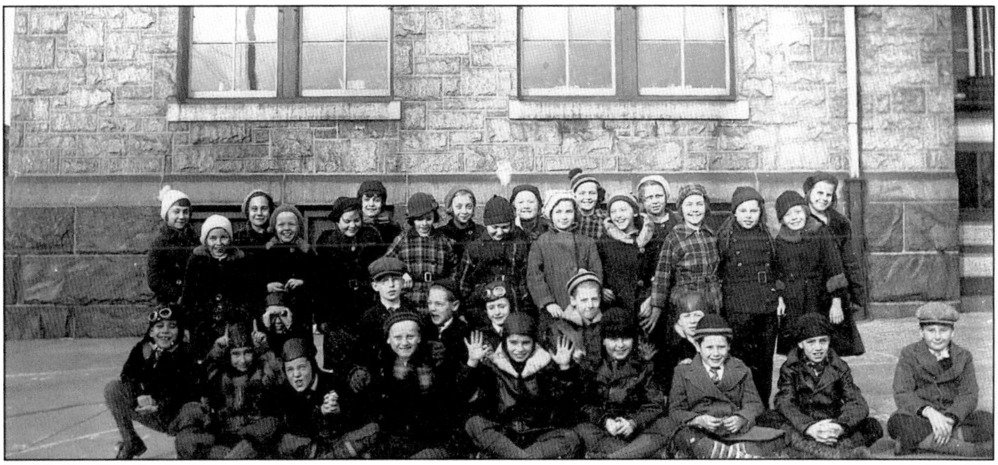

School is out, and it is recess time in the play yard. Lawrence Levan, whose parents ran the well-known chocolate and candy store on Kensington Avenue, is pictured with his class at the Phillip Sheridan Elementary School. Making friends is easy for someone who can invite classmates over to the chocolate-dipping room in the basement of the family store. (Courtesy of Lawrence Levan.)

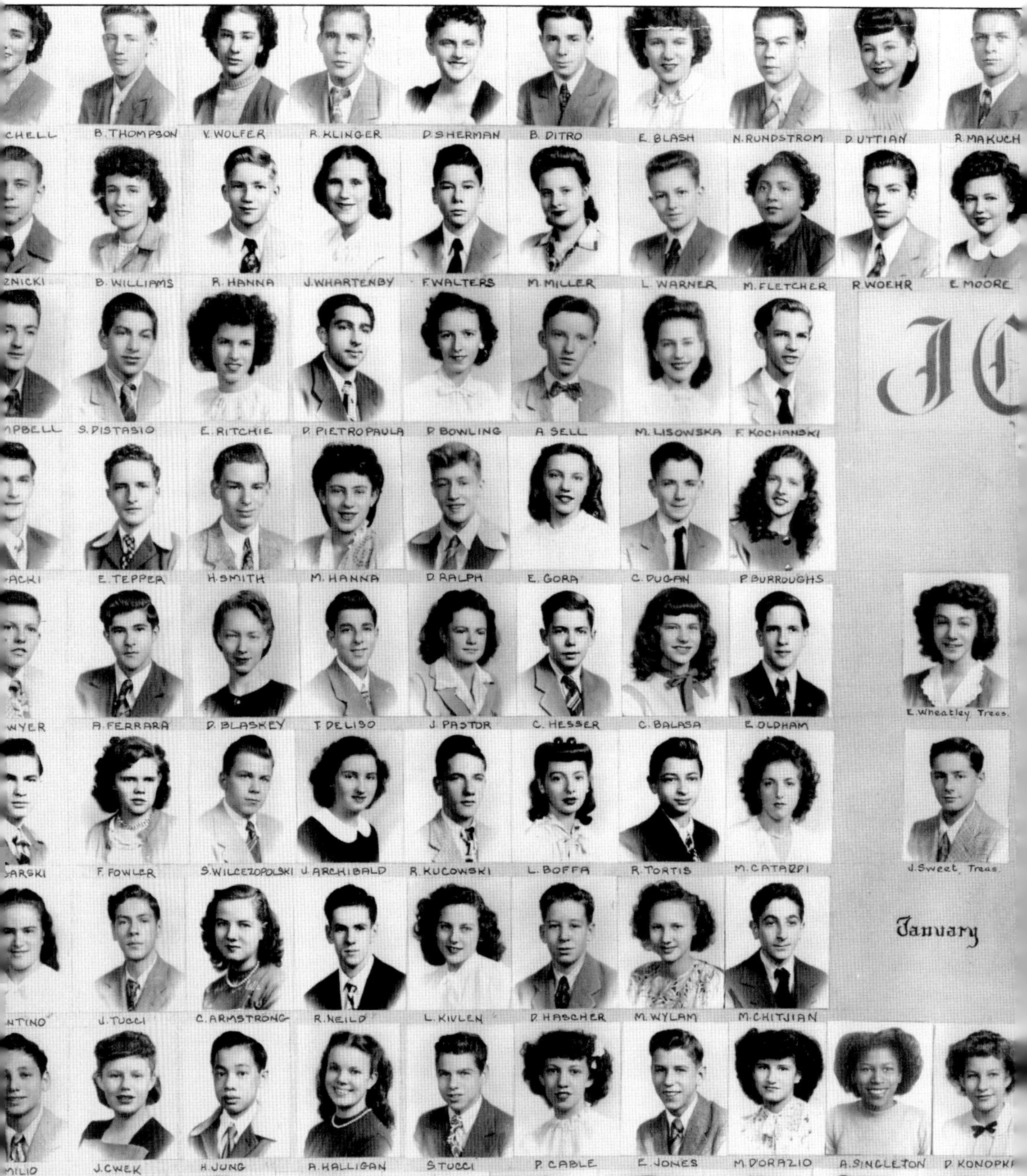

One of the greatest joys of attending the Philadelphia public schools during the 20th century was the opportunity to attend a brand new junior high school, a kind of rite of passage for 12-year-olds. The John Paul Jones Junior High School, located at Ann and Memphis Streets, had a number of feeder schools from the high industrial and business neighborhoods of Kensington and Richmond. Morris Baren, the son of Unity and Frankford grocery owner, lived at 2314 East

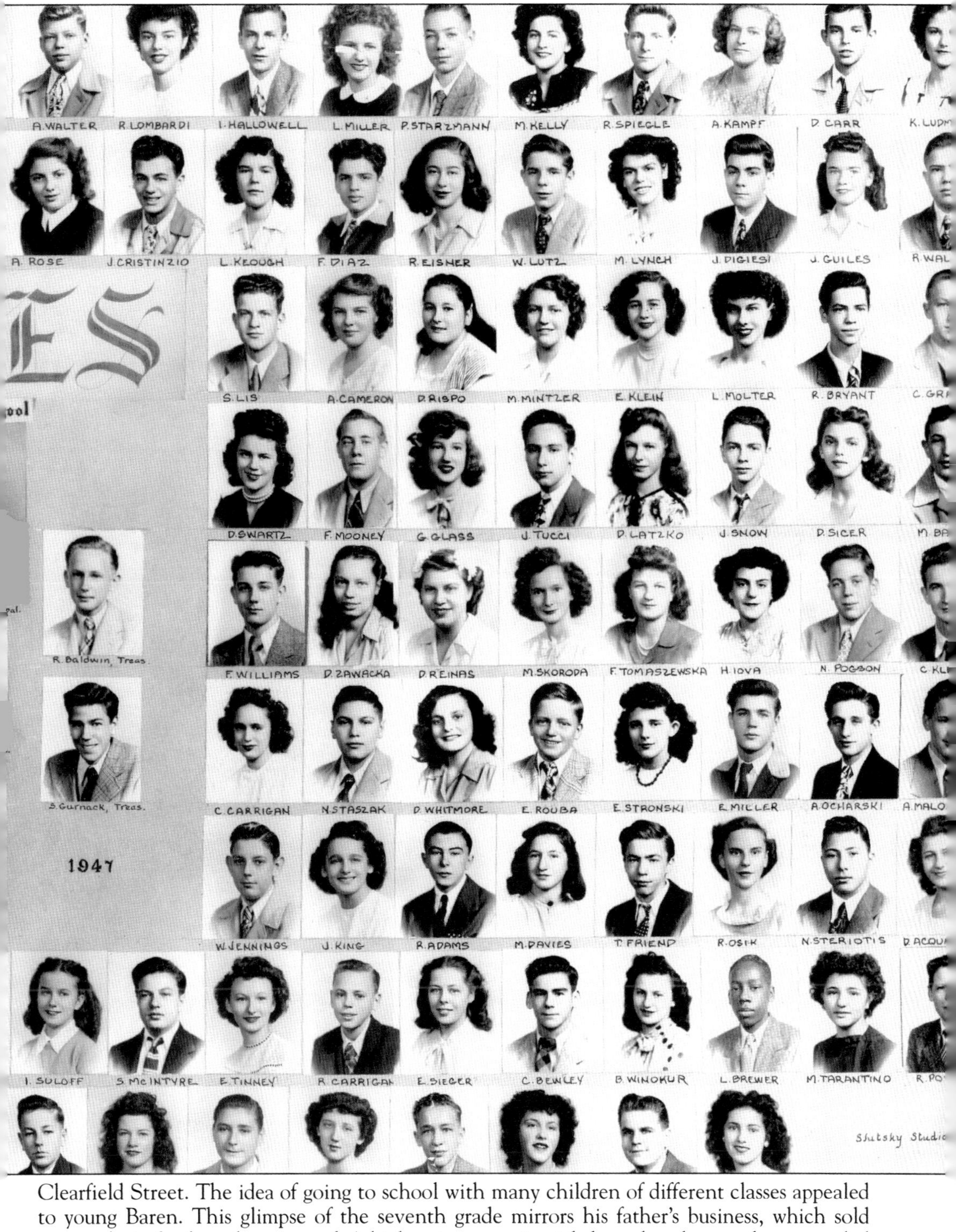

Clearfield Street. The idea of going to school with many children of different classes appealed to young Baren. This glimpse of the seventh grade mirrors his father's business, which sold many ethnic foods under one roof. A high point came in eighth grade, when students traveled downtown by themselves to have their graduation picture taken at the famous Slutsky Studio. (Courtesy of Morris Baren.)

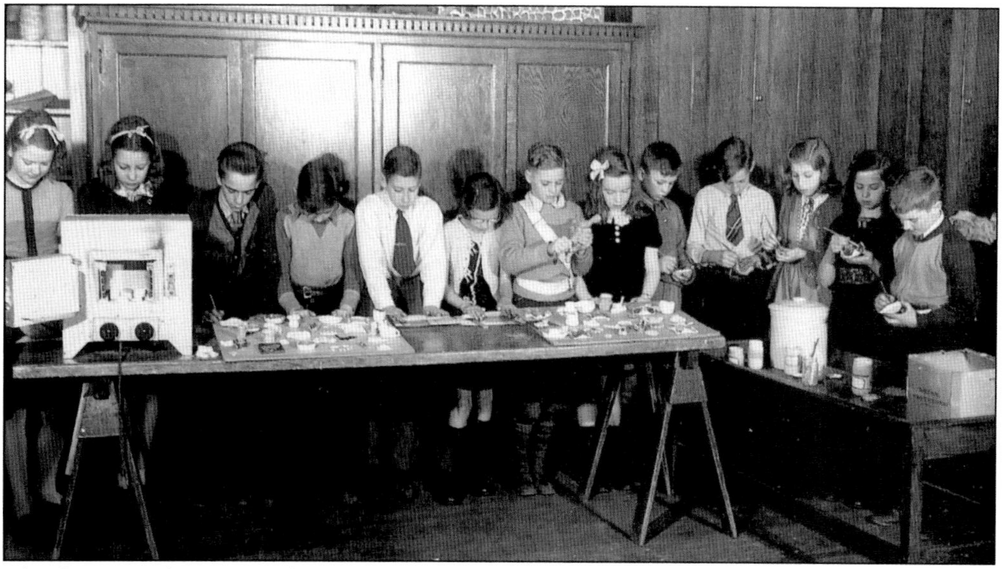

The focus on doing something with your hands was a valid passport to the future for the children of Fishtown and lower Kensington. The Isaac Sheppard Elementary School, at Howard and Cambria Streets, took note of teaching the children a vocation in the latter grades. Edie Brody, Pauline Abramson, Helen Gordon Feldscher, Irma Rothman Alexander, and Francine Sherman all took the ceramics class. (Courtesy of Edie Brody.)

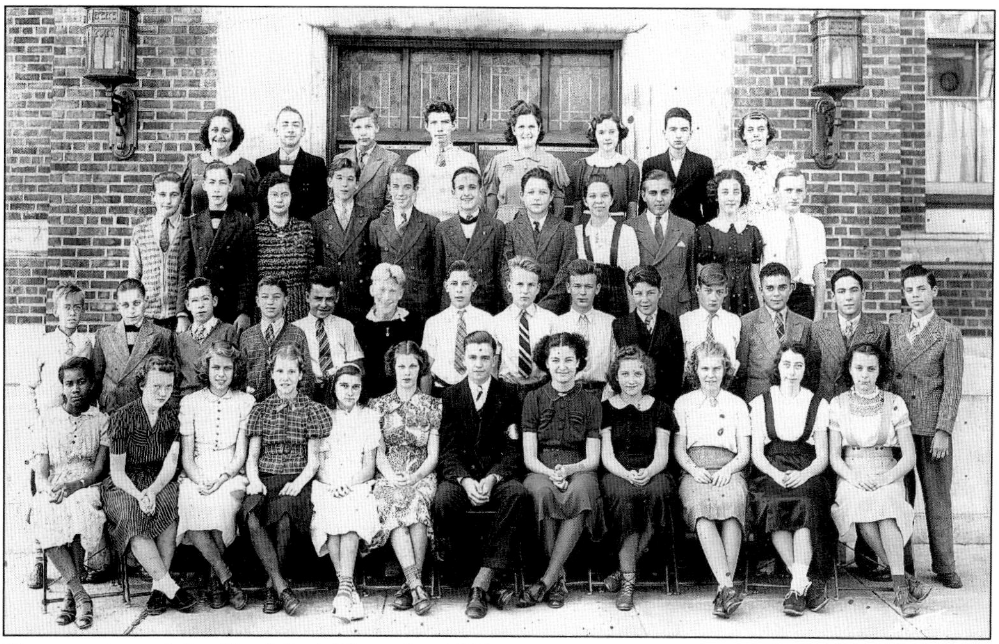

The opening of the Frankford El in the 1920s gave new meaning to "the other side of the tracks." The John B. Stetson Junior High School, located at B Street and Allegheny Avenue, served the Kensington Jewish children whose parents owned businesses under the El and on the west side of Kensington Avenue. Jerry Schaff of the Fifth and Cambria business district attended Stetson in 1938 with friends Allen Pever and Stewart Abraham. (Courtesy of Jerry Schaff.)

The location of the original Northeast High School, at Eighth and Lehigh Avenues, made it convenient to many students in a variety of neighborhoods that radiated out from the secondary school. The all-boys school, which opened as the manual training school, gave way to a more academic curriculum in the 1920s and attracted boys from Strawberry Mansion and Swamp Poodle (Twenty-second and Lehigh), as well as from Kensington, Fishtown, and Richmond. A popular way to arrive at school included hitchhiking along Lehigh Avenue or hopping the Route No. 54 trolley car.

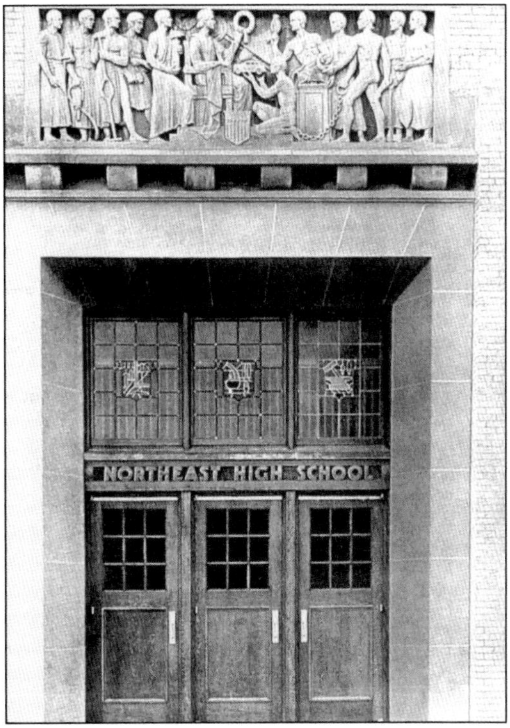

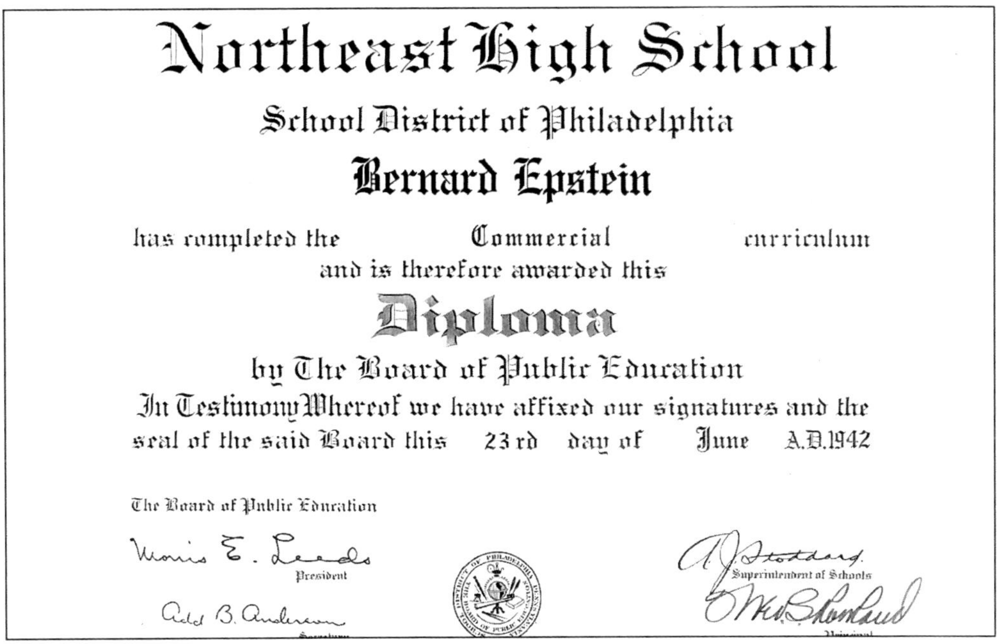

Northeast High School

School District of Philadelphia

Bernard Epstein

has completed the Commercial curriculum
and is therefore awarded this

Diploma

by The Board of Public Education

In Testimony Whereof we have affixed our signatures and the seal of the said Board this 23rd day of June A.D.1942

The Board of Public Education

President

Superintendent of Schools

This diploma was found tucked into a 1942 Northeast High School yearbook by author Allen Meyers. In the winter of 2001, Meyers was invited to a rural farm auction in Harleyville, Pennsylvania, by Walter Spector. He noticed the yearbook among some left-behind material, considered to be of no use to anyone. Not so in this case, however, for perhaps because of this picture, the diploma may someday be reunited with its rightful owner, Bernard Epstein, or his family. (Courtesy of Allen Meyers.)

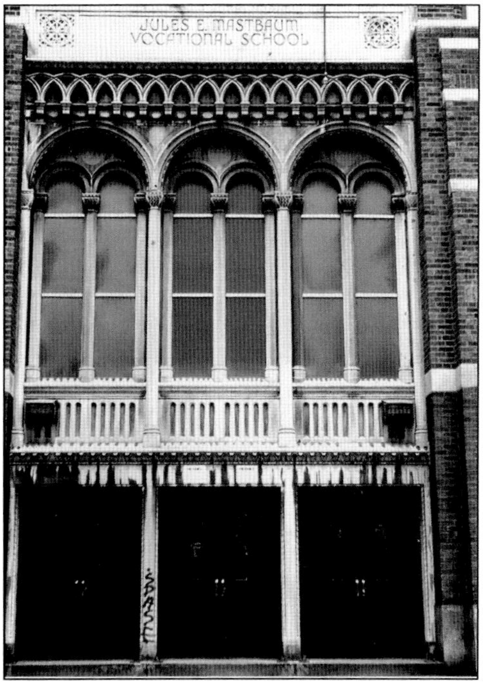

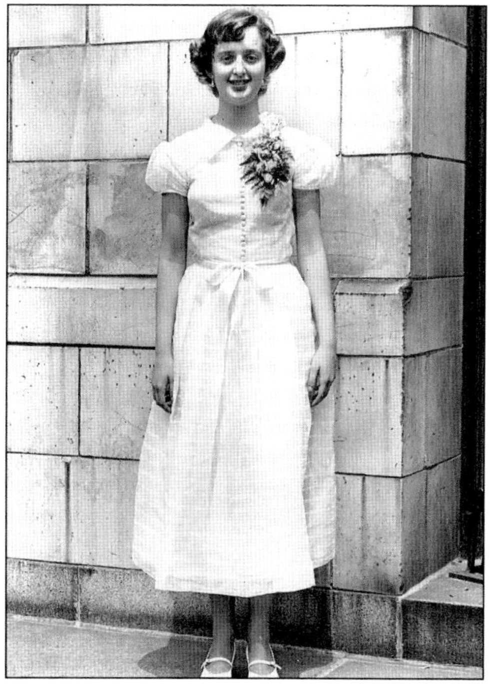

The emphasis on providing a trade for every student took precedence in Philadelphia during the early 20th century. The Jules E. Mastbaum School (left), a multistory institution with both commercial and trade courses opened in Kensington, off Frankford and Allegheny Avenues, in the 1920s. Janice Kleinman Spivack (right), the daughter of a Richmond business owner, dreamed of her prom day at Jones Junior High School. Upon graduation, she earned her Sunday school teacher certificate from the Minnie Mayer Hebrew School.

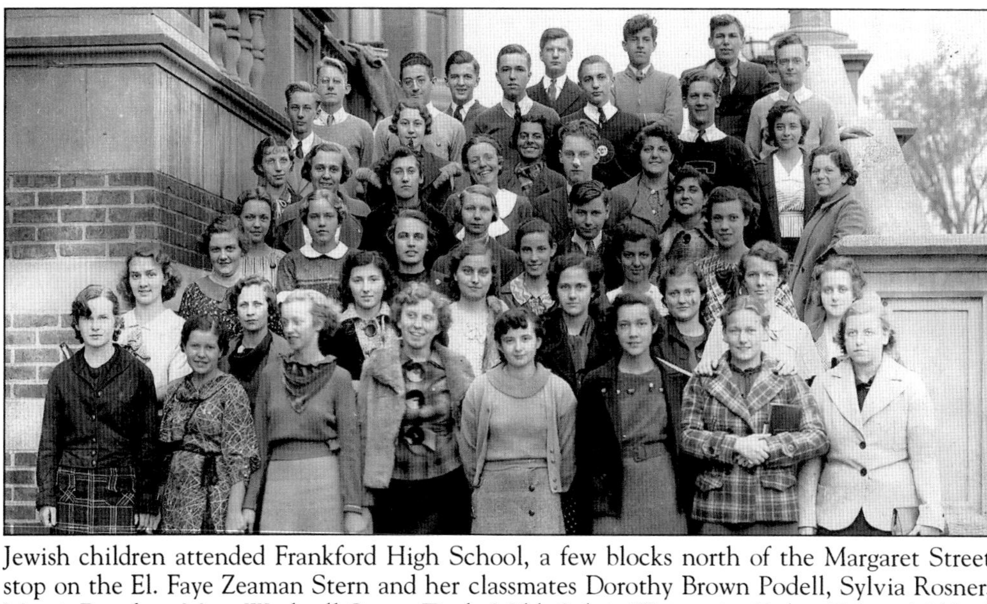

Jewish children attended Frankford High School, a few blocks north of the Margaret Street stop on the El. Faye Zeaman Stern and her classmates Dorothy Brown Podell, Sylvia Rosner, Morris Dreyfuss, Myra Wachtell Stern, Trudy Mild, Sylvia Weinstein, Esther Tobin, Mildred August, Norman Lauer, and Sylvan Schwartzman took French together and graduated in 1936. (Courtesy of Faye Stern.)

Six

Family and Friends

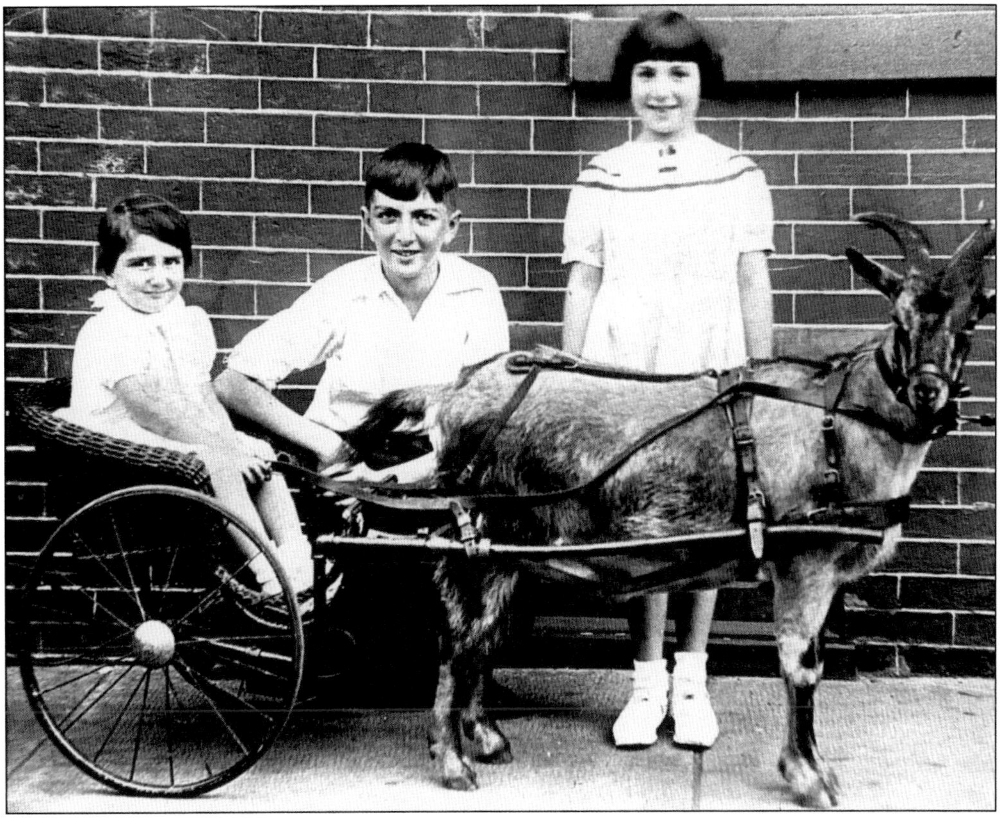

The memories of the past can be stored away in one's conscious being for a lifetime. They will never diminish in size, shape, or importance if they are treated with reverence, for they are part of one's being. The Jewish people of the Kensington area grew up in times that included the Great Depression, Nazi Germany, and the loss of loved ones during World War II. For many, their family and circle of friends grow less each year as they grow older and the only refuge is the picture in one's mind that makes one happy. The photograph of the Ben and Bessie Sirlin children along Richmond Street below Allegheny Avenue is a classic. Leonard, Sylvia, and Marilyn posed with the goat from the street photographer in the 1930s. (Courtesy of Marilyn Sirlin Scherwin.)

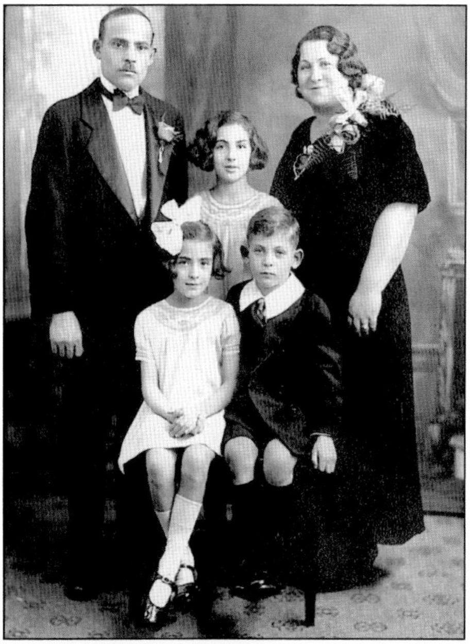

Immigrants had their family photographs taken in America to share a sense of wholeness. The status associated with studio portraits made them desirable and worth saving up for. The investment for Sam and Ida Levin meant that one day they could pass on their heritage through photographs. Levin ran an upholstery shop in the 3100 block of Kensington Avenue He and his wife proudly shows off their three children, Evelyn, Leonard, and Sylvia in this 1940 family memento. (Courtesy of Myra W. Helfand.)

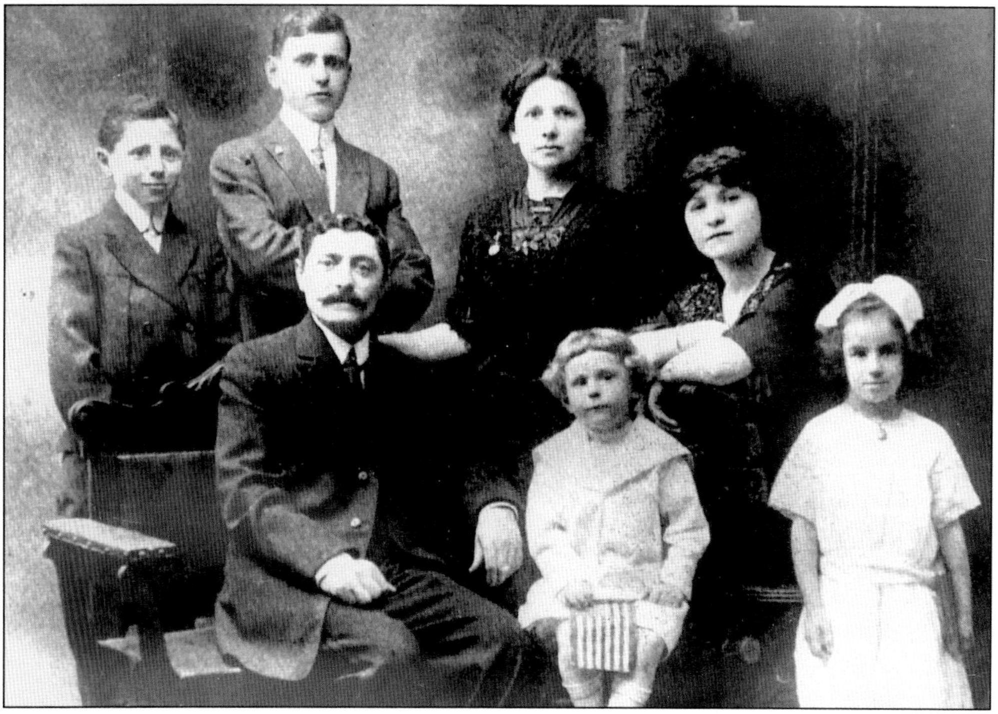

Family portraits often help tell the history of a family when a written record is not available. From left to right are sons Harry and Jake, father Louis, mother Rebecca, son David, and daughters Mary, and Dinah Levin. The family arrived from Russia and settled in West Philadelphia, while others went to the Island Road community in southwest Philadelphia—its rural nature reminding them of the old country. Harry Levin and his wife, Reba, opened Levin's Hardware store in the 3000 block of Kensington below Allegheny Avenue. (Courtesy of Harry Levin.)

The Kleinman family arrived from Russia and settled in the Richmond section adjacent to Jewtown and Kensington. David and Eva Kleinman had three children, Ethel, Beatrice, and Janice. At the end of the Route No. 60 trolley car line and the Route No. 15, Richmond Street listed many Jewish business owners in the 1920s through the 1940s. Family members and people from their small town in Russia were now new neighbors. (Courtesy of Janice Kleinman Spivack.)

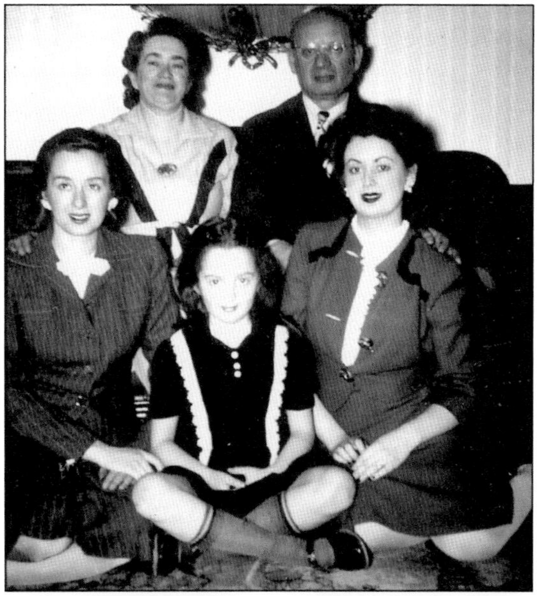

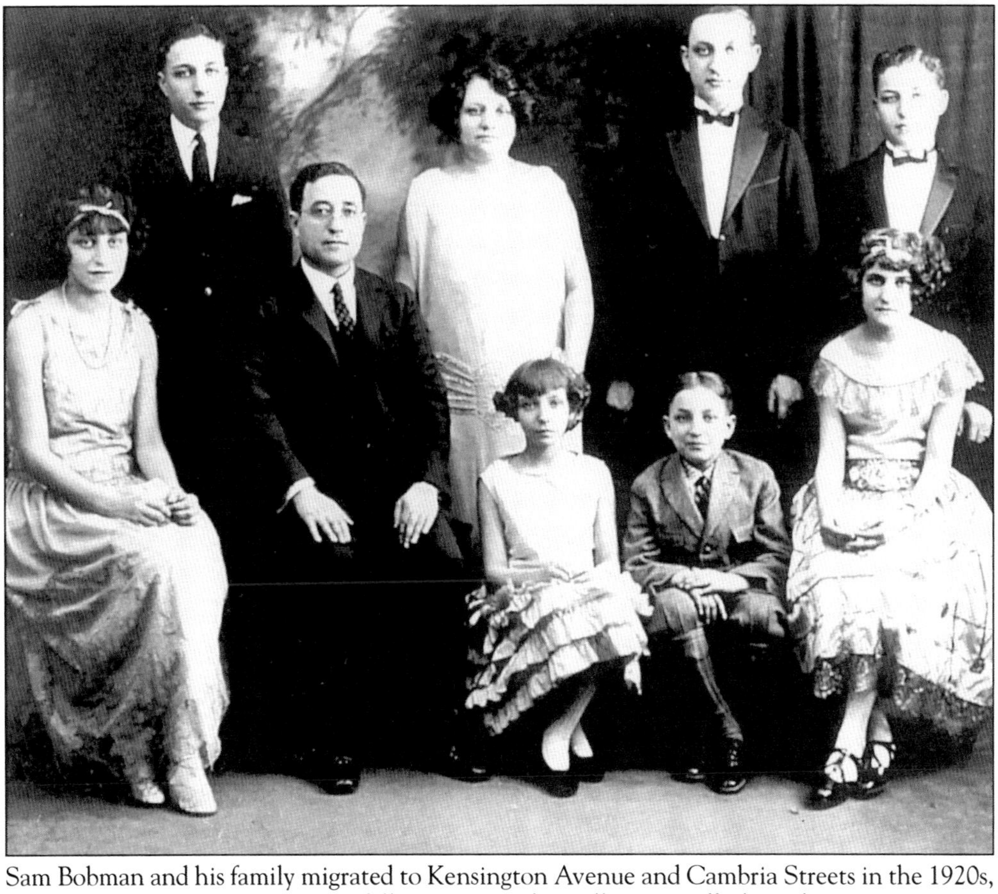

Sam Bobman and his family migrated to Kensington Avenue and Cambria Streets in the 1920s, as the new Frankford El went into full operation. The trolley car traffic brought many customers to his store. (Courtesy of Herb Bobman.)

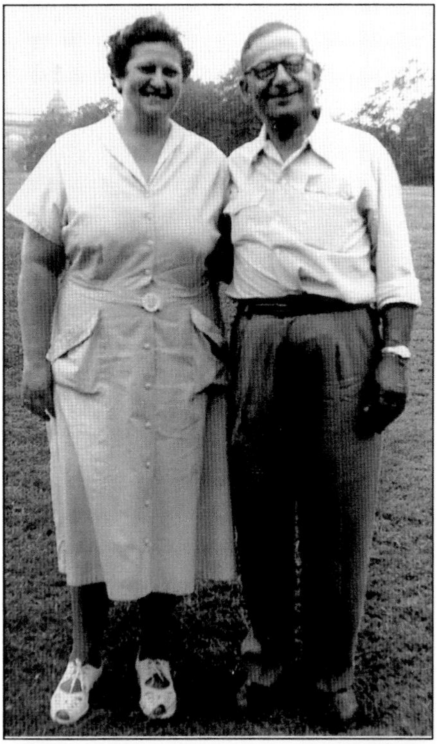

On the Fourth of July, everyone pulled out an old Brownie Six black box and snapped photographs of the family enjoying an outing in Fairmount Park. The five children of William and Reba Matless, formally from Romania, settled in Kensington. The tradition of living close to family members carried forward into the next generation with the children, who are now married couples. Sarah, Abe, Cecilia, Helen, and Rae later lived near each other, a mile north of the Frankford El terminal from the Frankford El off Bustleton. (Courtesy of Hope Matless.)

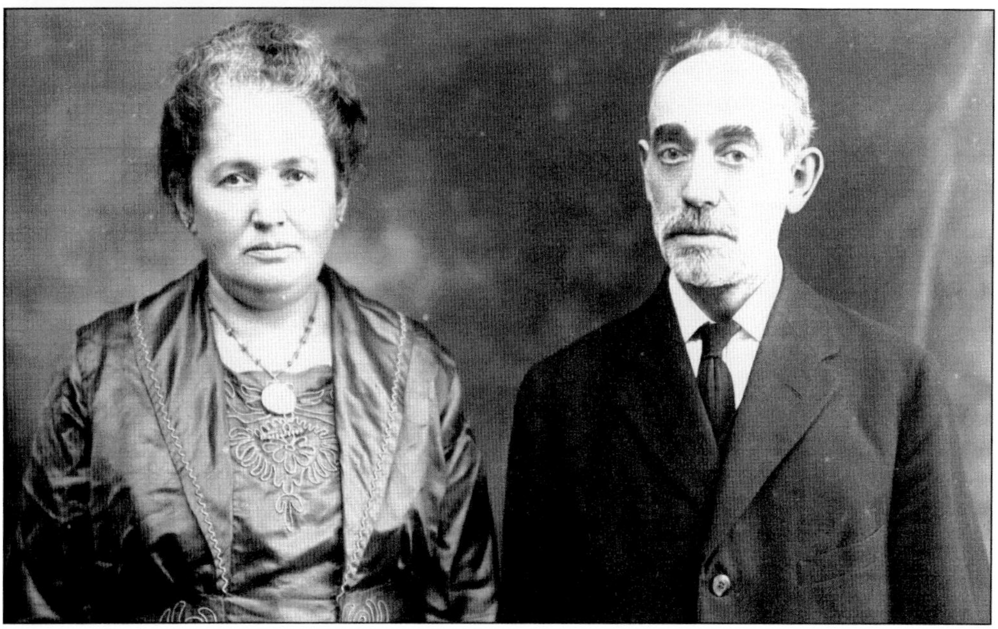

Bessie and Abraham Ettinger could name all the people and places up and down Richmond Street—Nate Friedman, Goldman candies, Gordon shoes, Penner flooring, Love's clothing, Chodosh clothing, Schatz shoes, Pecarsky furniture, Samson department store, Sid Levin the butcher, Cooper clothes, Minkosky shoes, Zilberg's fabrics, Levin's shoe repair, Nagel's Hardware, Lit appliances, Karashoff photography, Sabloksky five and dime store, Rooklin's men's wear, and Jacob's Kiddie Shop. (Courtesy of Janice Kleinman Spivack.)

Getting ready for an affair in a Jewish household is always an exercise in who is going to get dressed first. "Did you forget anything at the cleaners, dear? That tie doesn't match, and oh, those shoes from the Boston shoe store must be worn to match your suit." Finally, when all the commotion calms down, it is time to take nice pictures downstairs in the living room. David and Eva Ettinger pose near the stairs in 1944. (Courtesy of Janice Kleinman Spivack.)

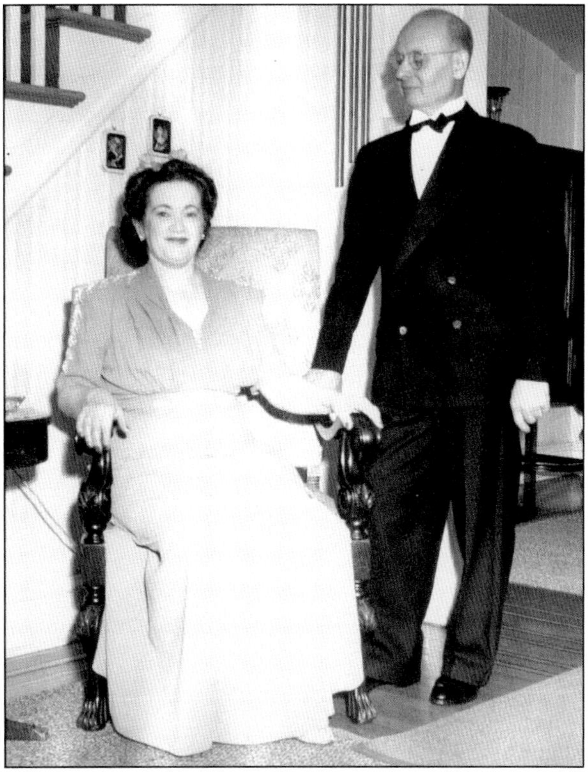

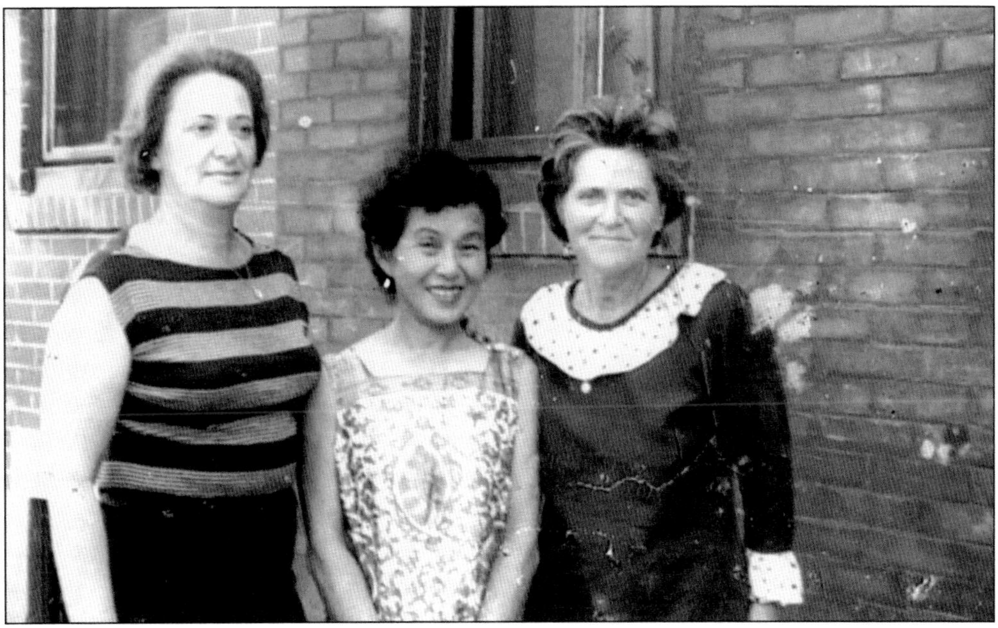

From left to right are Phoebe Potnick, her sister-in-law Fusano Jacobs, and her sister Sylvia Jacobs. The sisters' brother Douglas Jacobs served in the Korean War and returned home with his wife, Fusano, a Japanese woman who converted to Judaism. This photograph was taken on Coral Street off Frankford Avenue, where Sylvia's children, Richard and Marlene, grew up. (Courtesy of Marlene Adler.)

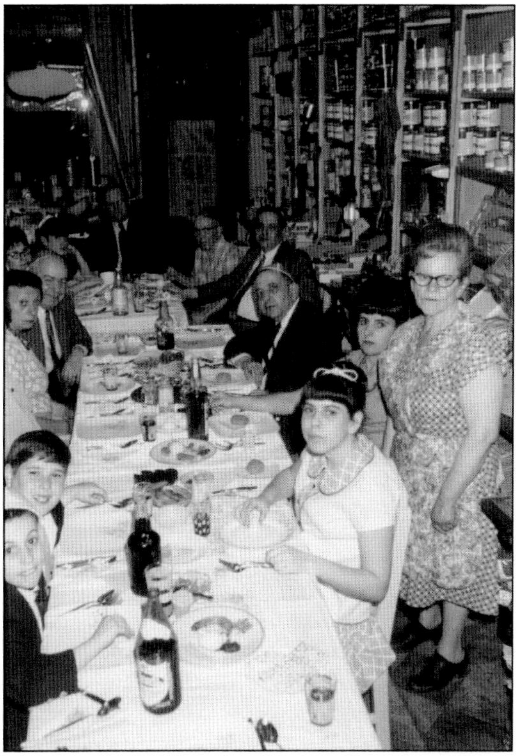

The old adage of making do with what you have is a good way to journey through life. Izzy and Edith Seidman can tell that from the bottom of their heart; they struggled to make a living in the 3300 block of Kensington Avenue selling hardware and appliances during the 1950s. The Seidmans made room for two tables butted together to make one long setting for all who came to visit and eat good Jewish cooking and share in family talk on many Jewish holidays. (Courtesy of Edith Seidman.)

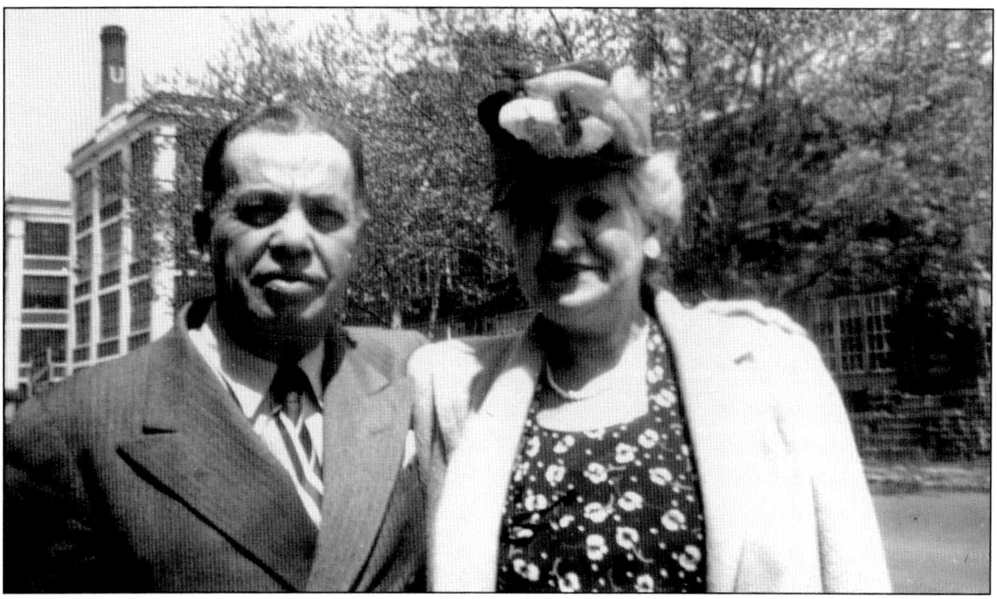

The hats of the 1940s were something else. From 1933 to 1952, David and Jenny Prince owned a pharmacy two blocks north of the Frankford El at I and Tioga Streets. Prince made up cold tablets and his own brand of cough syrup, which he labeled himself. The neighborhood had famous industries that included the Richardson Dinner Mint factory with its famous V and Goldenberg's world-famous peanut chews, at I and Westmoreland Streets. (Courtesy of Lee Prince Waters.)

Away from the neighborhood yet still at home is the way Willis and May Fleisher conducted their lives. The Fleishers owned Shelbourne Mills, a textile factory in Kensington at H and Westmoreland Streets. The factory switched over to making khakis during World War I and ran 24 hours a day. Willis relied on public transportation and refused to use company taxi coupons to arrive at his home, at 17th and Jefferson Streets. (Courtesy of Ruth Fleisher Kohn.)

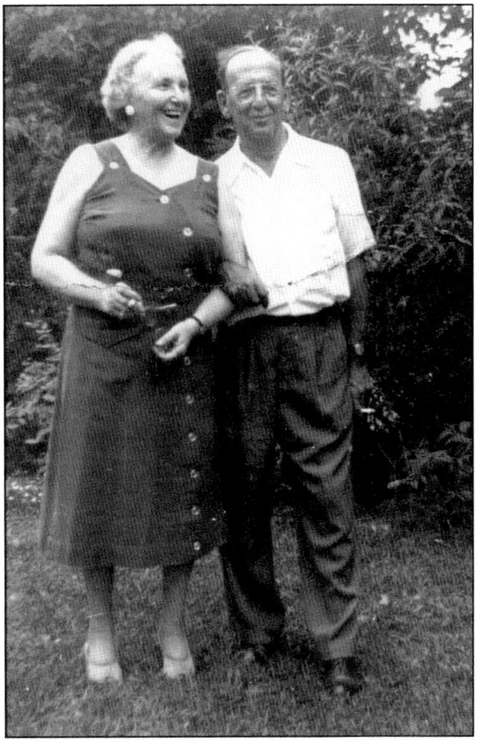

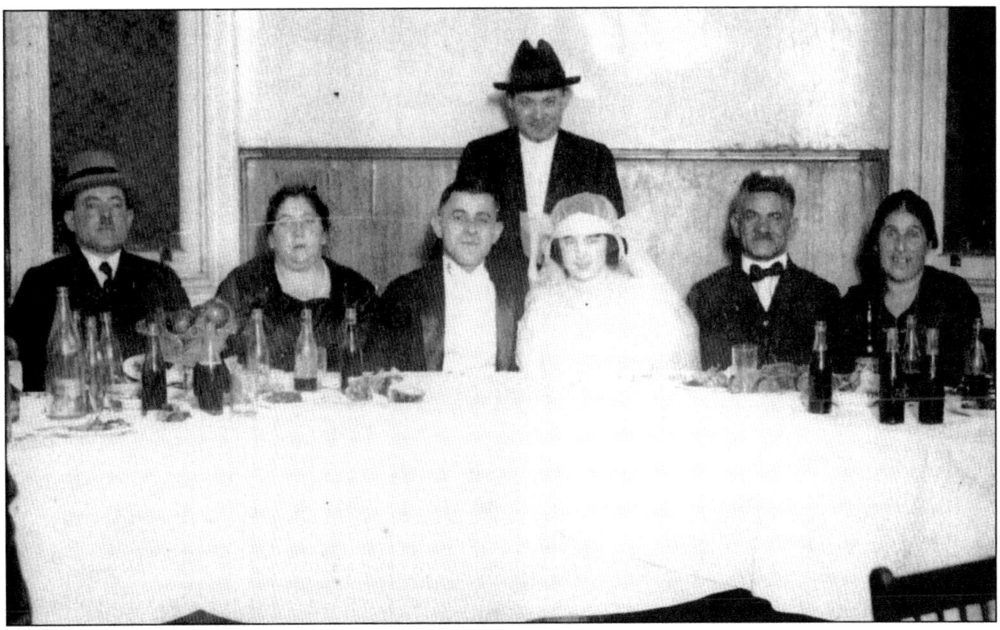

The old-fashioned wedding in a Jewish family is an age-old tradition. In America, the table is set no differently than it is in Kiev, Russia—bottles and bottles of spirits line the head table. Sam and Ada Schlutz (center), from the famous wallpaper company, celebrate their wedding with their guests at a Jewish catering hall shortly before 1920. (Courtesy of Lillian Schlutz Spiro.)

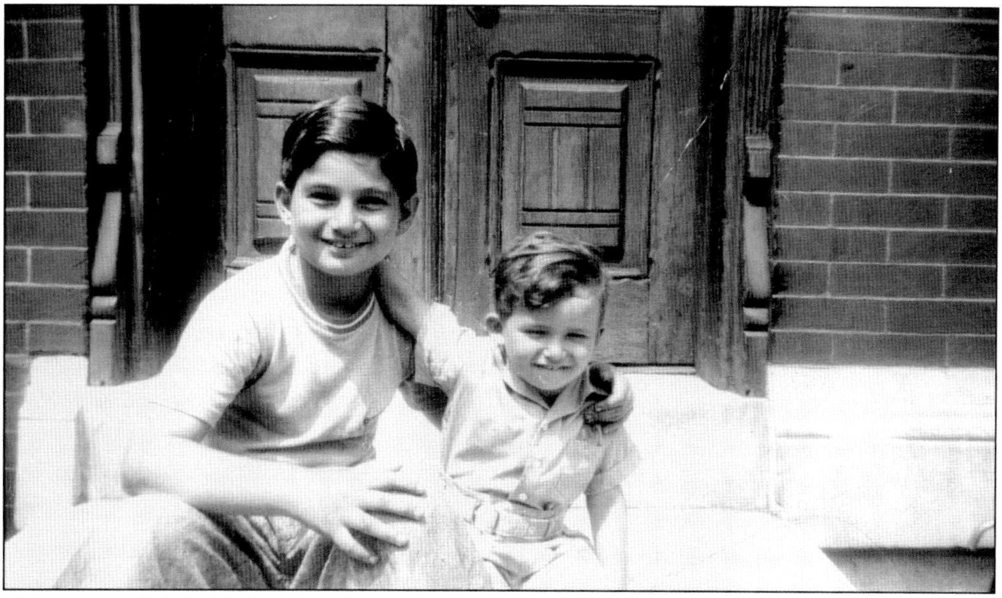

The stoops of Philadelphia's row homes are a very near and dear setting for siblings to share the tender moments of early childhood. Irwin Bennett and his brother, the children of Meyer and Yetta Bennett, watched others play the Battle of Waterloo or king of the mountain near the street named for the activity until many homes were condemned. A hot meal awaited the boys after a hardy day of playing in the neighborhood. (Courtesy of Irwin Bennett.)

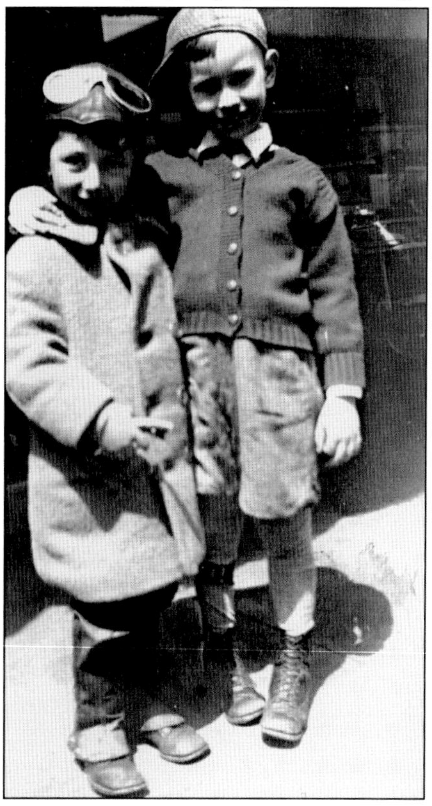

Merv Tuckman (left) sports his new fashionable Lindbergh goggles under the Frankford El. The son of Bill and Shirley Tuckman, he lived at 3210 Kensington Avenue. Lawrence Levan, from 3230 Kensington Avenue, was his best friend. Now grown men, the two met again during the writing of this book. They clearly recall their trips to the famous Iris movie house at 3100 Kensington Avenue. What a great *simha* (happy reunion) to see one's childhood friend so many years later. (Courtesy of Merv Tuckman and Lawrence Levan.)

A front yard of pavement under the Frankford El is just fine for Ray Obod—the son of Moe and Gussie, who sold linens and curtains at 3051 Kensington Avenue—to try out his new tricycle. Later in life, Obod's friends included Jerry Fristberg and Arthur Love. The children enjoyed McPherson Square, a large park good for sledding in the wintertime, and used the best boxball court behind the stores on Ruth Street. (Courtesy of Ray Obod.)

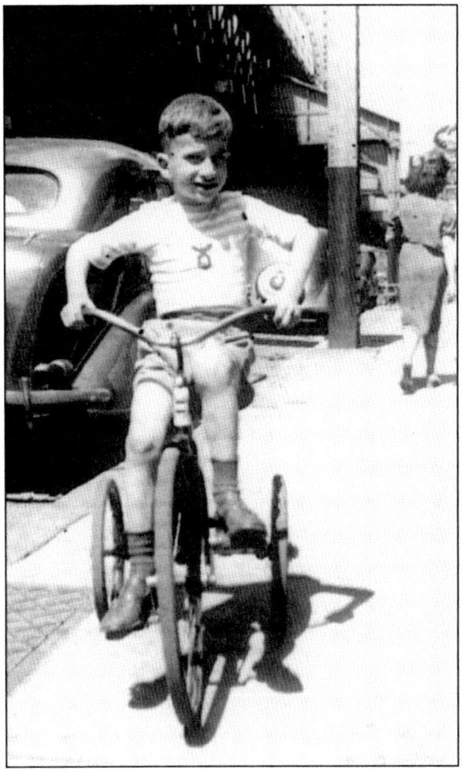

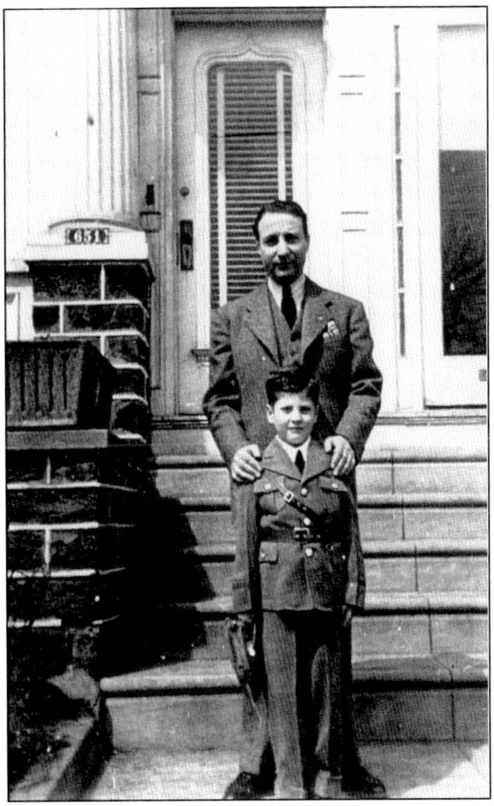

Sam Bobman and his son Herb strike a father-and-son pose. The Bobman family loved the fresh air and the sound of the Frankford El as it brought more customers from all over the city to the clothing stores in Kensington and Frankford. That pace of hustle and bustle came to a grinding halt on the High Holidays, when the family gathered at Zadye Morris Bobman's house at 651 East Allegheny Avenue.(Courtesy of Herb Bobman.)

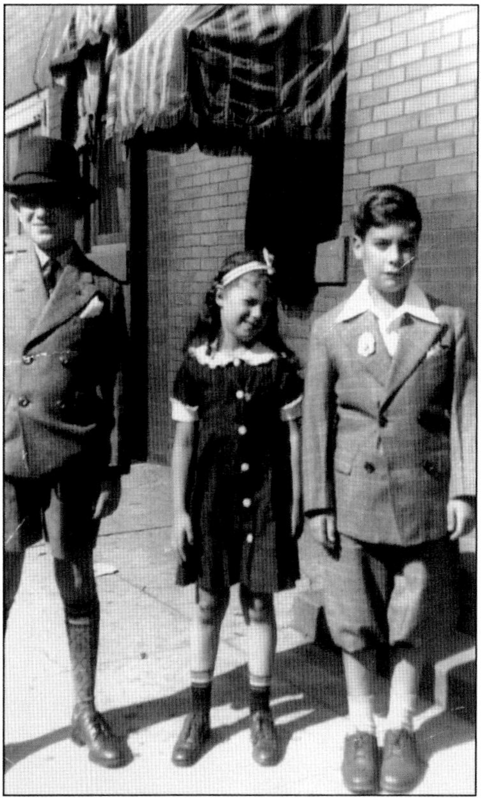

Dave and Freda Baren ran a delicatessen at this location. Their children Ida and Morris Baren (right) are pictured outside with Gilbert Grossman. A thrill for boys age 13 and older was the footrace along Allegheny Avenue with Rabbi Alexander Levine to see who got to the Kensington Jewish Community Synagogue first. This determined who had to serve on the "minyan posse." If the rabbi won the race, the boy had to honor the agreement and gather other members to make the quorum of 10 adult males to conduct the call to community prayer. (Courtesy of Morris Baren.)

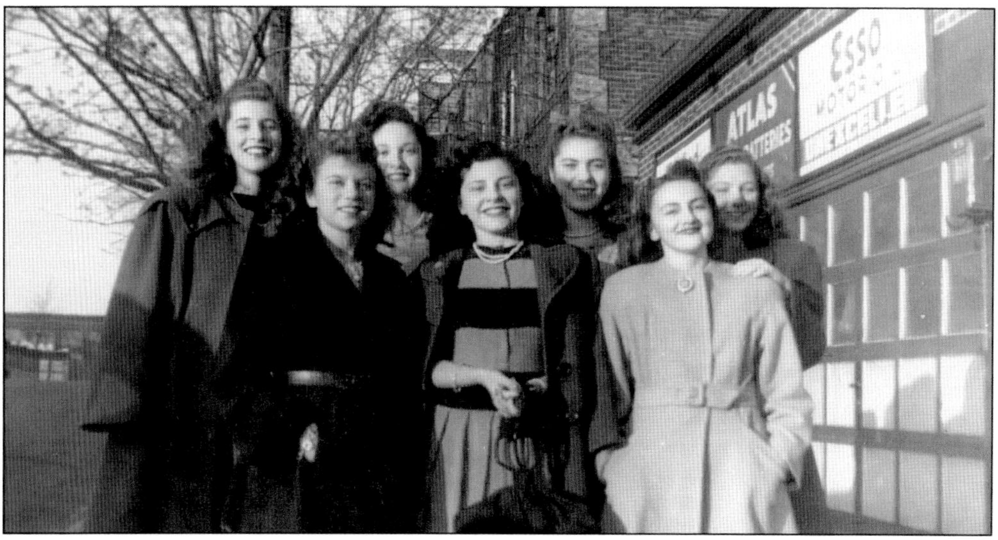

Having lots of friends became important to many girls who aspired to popularity. Acquaintances were made through the Kensington Jewish Community Center, and lifetime friendships blossomed. The Sunday School Society met above the old Horn and Hardarts restaurant, on the northeast corner of Kensington and Allegheny Avenues. From left to right are Lee Prince, celebrating her 16th birthday, and her friends Naomi Shuster, Evelyn Kauderer, Marilyn Brown, Claire Shapiro, Vicki Lubeck, and Judy Gordon. (Courtesy of Lee Prince Waters.)

Sisters helped each other weather the worries of World War II. Ruth Perl and Sophie Remstein relied on each other during the 1940s. They even picked out the clothes each other wore. The popular style for women who worked in the factories while the men were off at war included the Rosie the Riveter outfit, complete with slacks. After the war, the women returned to wearing dresses. (Courtesy of Alan Remstein.)

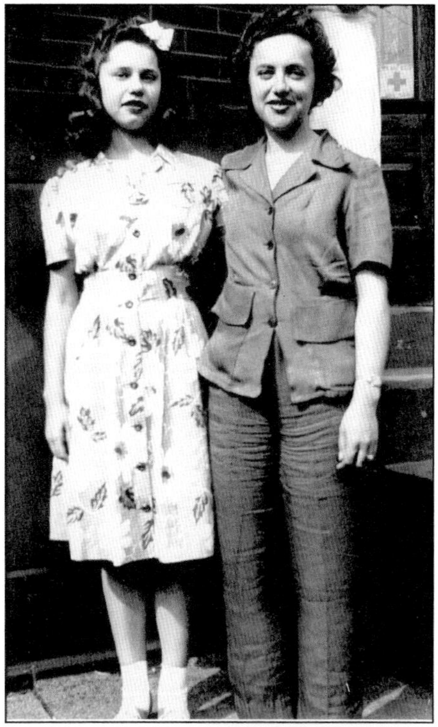

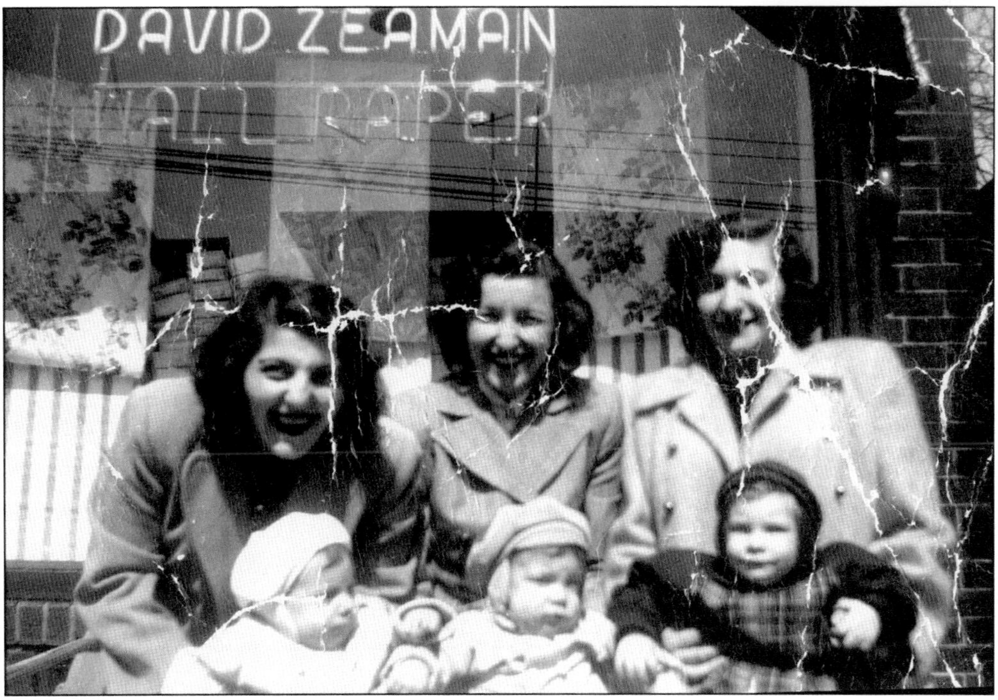

Mollie and David Zeaman, both from Berezdin, Russia, came to America to find each other and settled in the Frankford section. The couple's children, pictured in 1948 on Orthodox Street in front of the family's wallpaper business, from left to right are Faye, with her daughter Susan; Anne, with her son Barry; and Miriam, with her son Beryll. (Courtesy of Faye Zeaman Stern.)

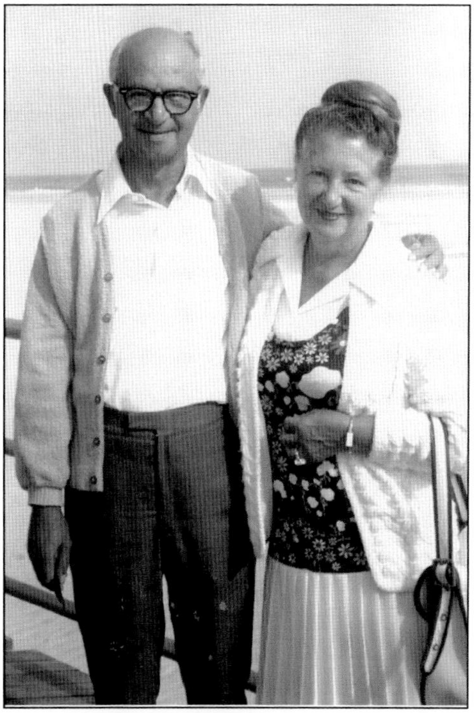

"My sweetheart forever" is the theme of many couples, but for owners of a corner drugstore, it is a working partnership. Vacation time is very much appreciated by people like Meyer and Yetta Bennett, who devoted their waking hours to running the pharmacy at 156 West Huntingdon Street, in the Kensington section. At the beginning of July, they closed their business and headed to Ventnor, New Jersey, on the shore, where they enjoyed sea breezes and strolls along the boardwalk. (Courtesy of Irv Bennett.)

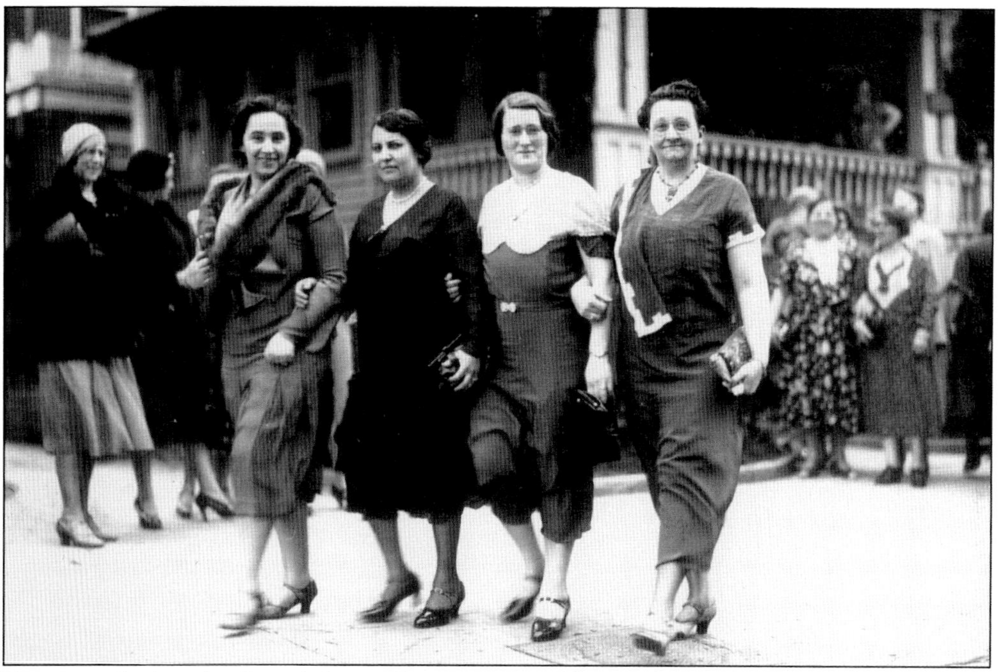

For many, the boardwalk in Atlantic City meant wealth. People loved to walk three, four, five abreast late into the evening hours. Everyone dressed up to "go down the shore," especially with mink stoles and ornate handbags. Sadie Levan (second from the right) and her friend Mrs. Joseph Stein of Stein's florist, on Front Street, stroll the boardwalk with other members of the Sterling Chapter of Hadassah in the 1930s. (Courtesy of Lawrence Levan.)

The power of family in a new land is more remarkable than it is in the old country. Reba Matless (center) married William, a shoemaker from Romania, and instilled in her child Tillie (right) the importance of having close relations with all of the extended family. Aunt Sarah (left) joined in family gatherings near the shoemaker's house and business, at F and Willard Streets in Kensington, to share old recipes. (Courtesy of Hope Matless.)

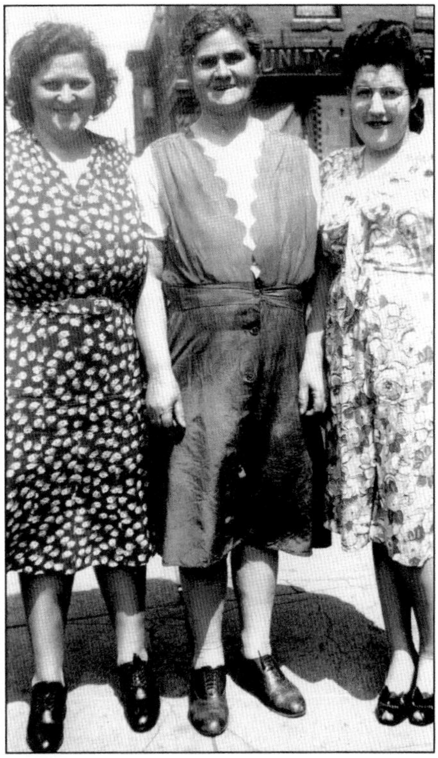

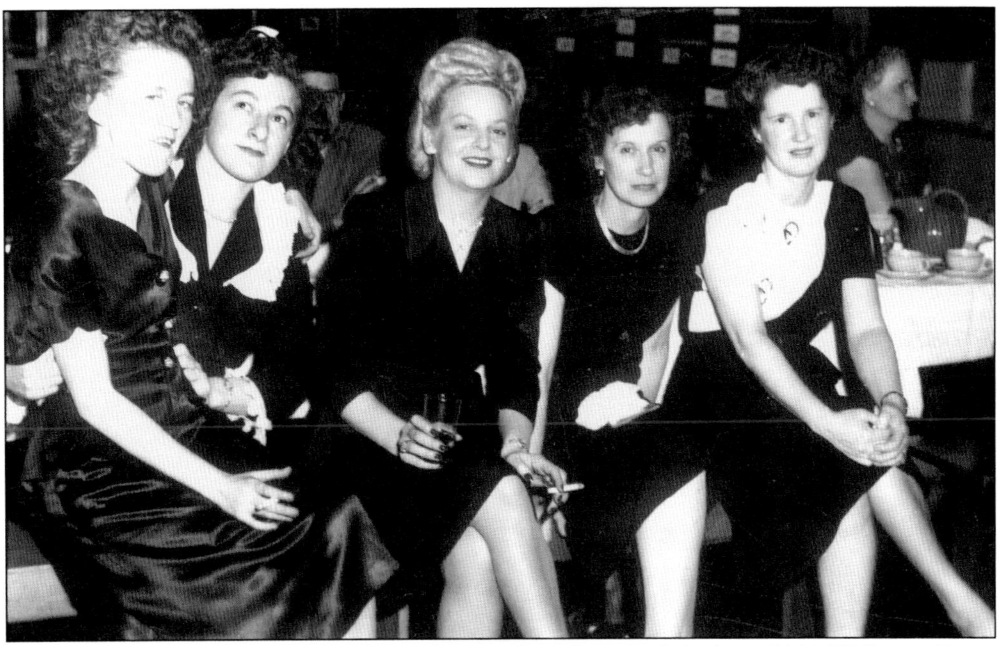

When women get together, they have fun. Leah Cohen (right), from 2100 Williams Street in Jewtown, had many friends whose parents were business owners, including the Plotnick toy people from Fifth and Lehigh Avenue and Elizabeth Allen (center), whose father had a doll shop on Frankford Avenue. The talk was about the type of faces they would paint on the Raggedy Ann and Kewpie dolls with pug noses after lunch. (Courtesy of Leah Cohen Karp.)

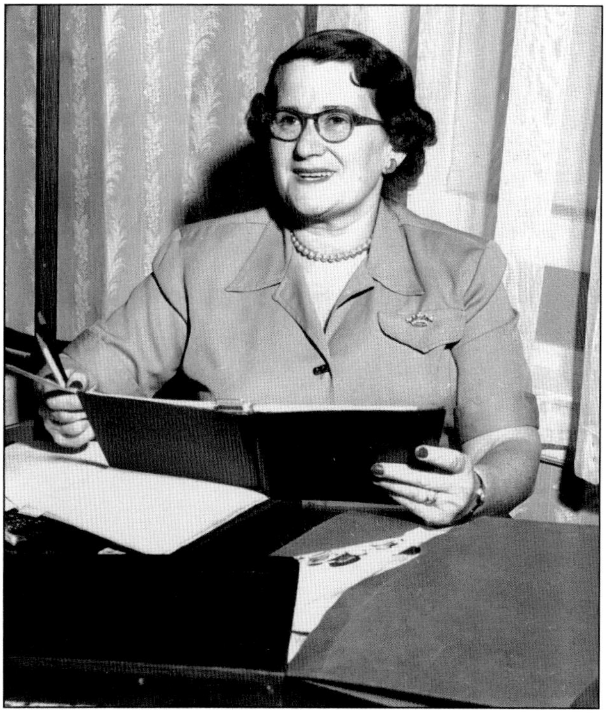

Business owners sometimes lead two distinctive lives. Sadie Levan, the wife of James Levan, toiled for many hours in the family's homemade chocolate business on Kensington Avenue under the Frankford El near Allegheny Avenue. Still, a creative mom, she found time to write and publish her poetry. Everyday activities and relationships worked their way into Sadie's penmanship, and she delivered her masterpieces on the radio in the evening. (Courtesy of Lawrence Levan.)

You and I

August 1941

Gentile or Jew,
The masses or few,
We all have the same things in common.

We hurry, we worry, we work and we play,
We wake in the morning to greet a new day,
We sleep through the night in just the same way,
We all have the same things in common.

When illness strikes
Or happiness reigns,
We laugh and we cry
And we feel the same pains.
Our joys and our woes
Follow as we go.
We all have the same things in common.

As for difference there is none,
Flesh and blood is all one,
So why think you're better than I?
Why not see the light
And admit that it's right:
We all have the same things in common.

As they get older, people remember their parents in different ways. Lawrence Levan is very proud of his mother, Sadie Levan, who shared her talent in two ways with Kensington, the community she loved. The ode to community fellowship and a sense of belonging is forever captured in her poem entitled "You and I," written in the summer of 1941. (Courtesy of Lawrence Levan.)

Seven

THE BUSINESS DISTRICTS

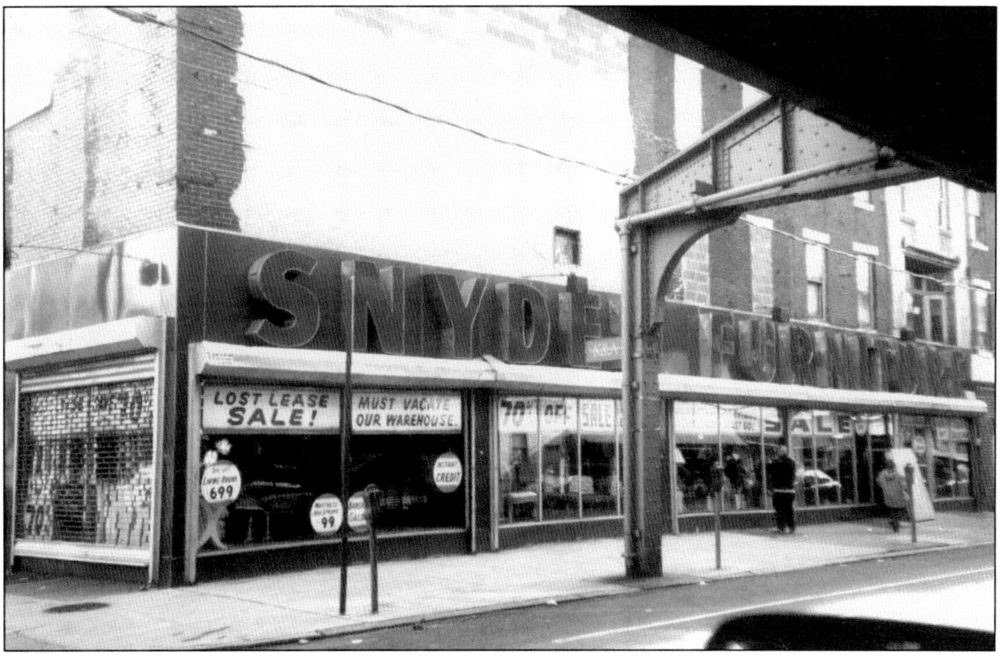

The upward mobility of the population with Jewish roots stems from the days of peddling that progressed to pushcarts and finally to the renting private residences for businesses of all kinds. Jews lived with their businesses above and behind their rented quarters while tending to their trade with no set hours of operation, accepting customers into the late evening hours. The hard work of the individual man and wife, plus their children as a team, yielded ownership of the properties they initially rented, as they anchored their communities on Kensington, Front, Frankford, and Richmond Streets and Torresdale Avenue. These hardy souls contributed to the Jewish community and their neighborhoods at large through the businessmen's associations they formed to advance civic activities and communal projects. Arnold Snyderman, a third-generation furniture dealer, continues to run the business that his family started more than 84 years ago in the 3300 block of Kensington Avenue under the Frankford El. (Courtesy of Allen Meyers.)

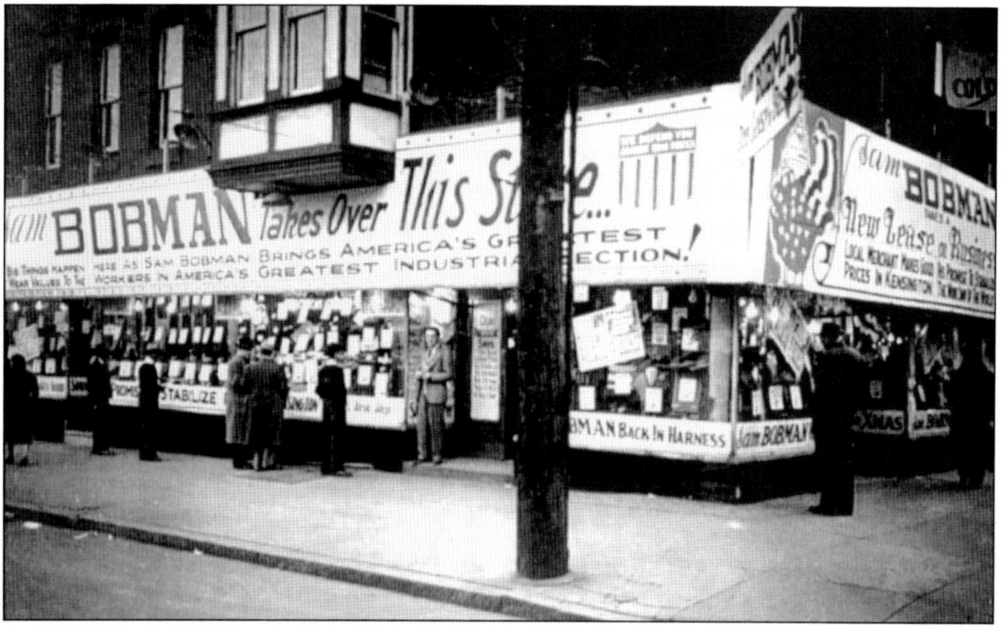

Up and down Kensington and Frankford Avenues, the Bobman family name dates back to the 1920s and is well recognized. Sam Bobman lived with his family above the store at Kensington Avenue and Cambria Street. The Bobman name meant true value for the working-class customer, as the store outfitted generations of people with daily work clothes. The lines of clothes changed with the times, but the promotional ideas remained fresh and eye appealing to all that shopped under the EL. (Courtesy of Herb Bobman.)

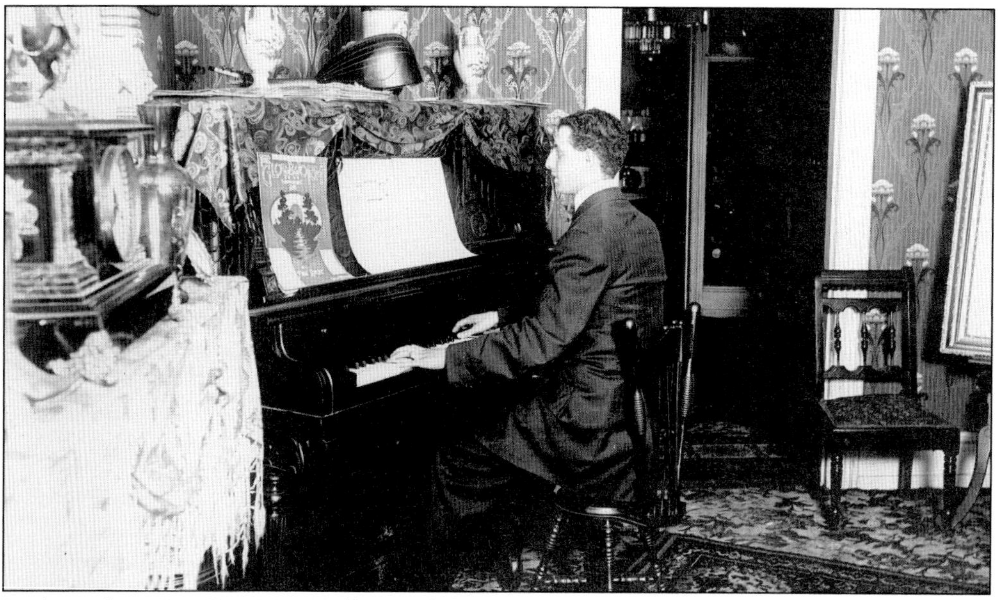

In the early 1900s, Doc Max Heller tended a pharmacy by day and in the evening played his piano with its secret pedal for the whole neighborhood to hear. Heller stepped on the fortissimo pedal to amplify the sound of the popular music of John Phillips Sousa, the conductor well-known from the Willow Grove amusement park. The whole community enjoyed the music that wafted from Heller's home, at 908 North Fourth Street. (Courtesy of Lois Heller Sataloff.)

Irwin Bennett, from 156 West Huntington and Howard Streets in Kensington, followed in the footsteps of his father, Meyer Bennett, by learning the pharmacy business. Father and son often took time off on Sundays to take in a baseball game at Shibe Park, where the Phillies played major-league ball. In the 1950s, the trip to the stadium, at Twenty-second and Lehigh Avenues, via the Route No. 57 and Route No. 54 trolley cars was much more fun than mixing cough syrup. (Courtesy of Irwin Bennett.)

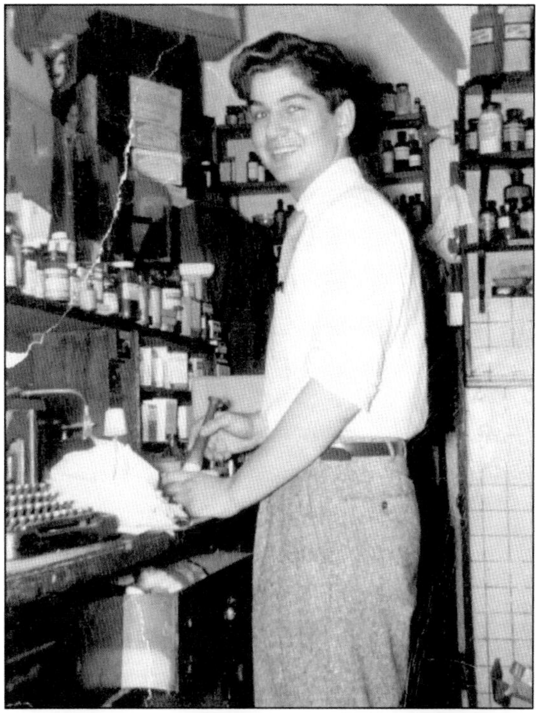

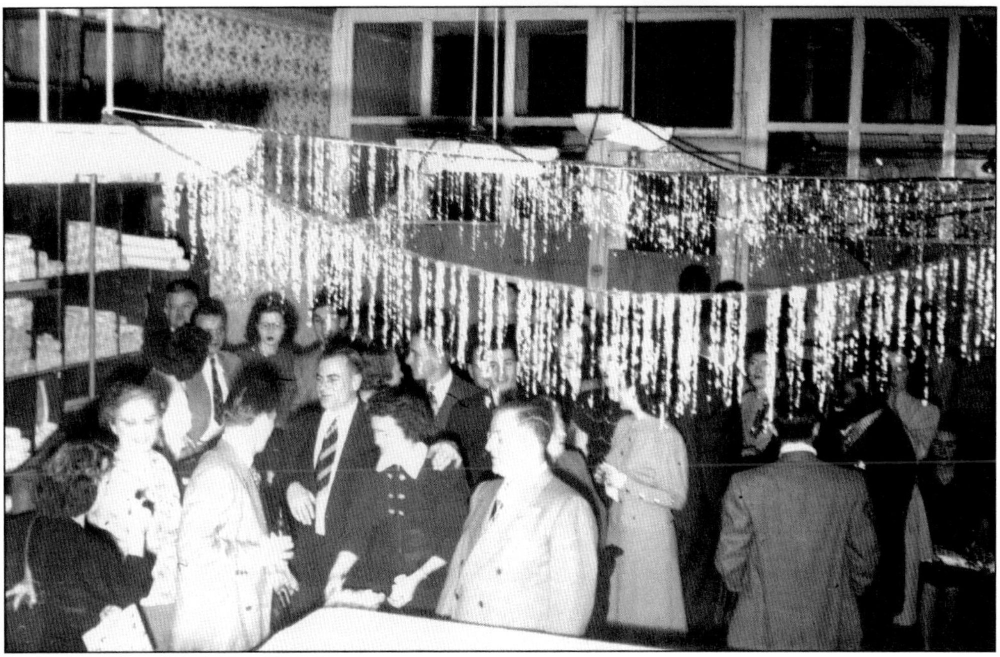

Marvin Spiro married Lillian Schultz in 1944, when they both lived in the Kensington community along the 2100–2300 blocks of North Front Street. The Schultz family ran a wallpaper supply business at 2102–2104 North Front Street, and the Spiros operated a dress shop at 2308 North Front Street. Every year, the combined families celebrated Chanukah with a gigantic party at the dress shop, where the merchandise was pushed back to the walls and the aisles were opened for fun, food, and dancing. (Courtesy of Marvin Spiro.)

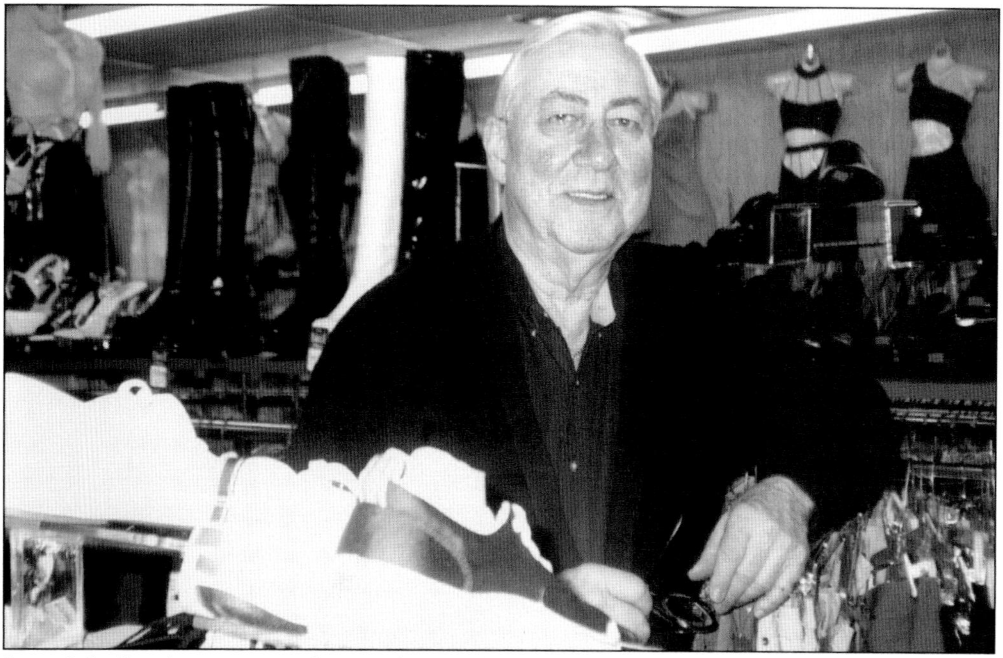

Jerry Schaff, a longtime resident and second-generation businessman of Kensington, knows all about the community he has called home for more than 70 years. His three stores carry women's wear and are located at 2912 North Fifth at Cambria Street, 3251 North Front Street above Allegheny Avenue, and along North Front Street under the York-Dauphin stop of the Frankford El.

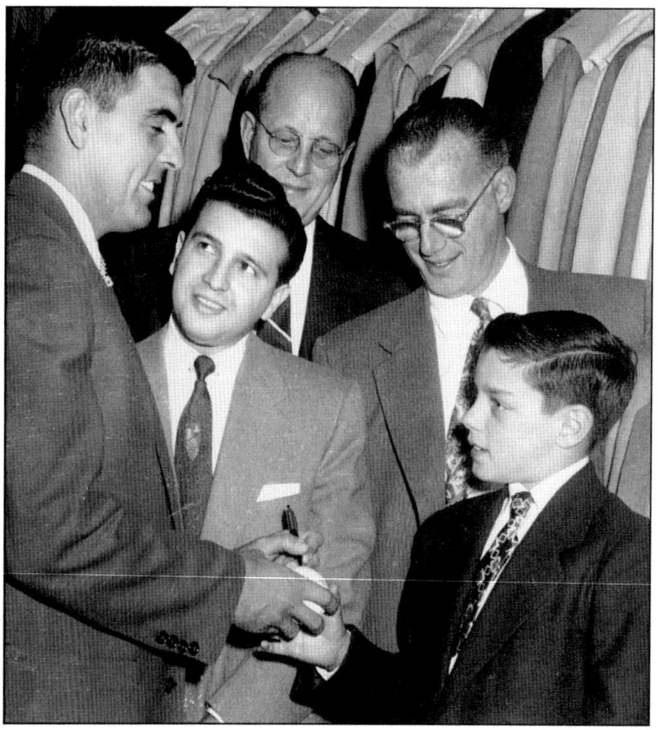

The shopping district under the Frankford El where Front Street meets Kensington Avenue was made up of men's wear shops and many other stores and was anchored by the Kent movie theatre. The Berg brothers, originally from Market Street, moved their store to Kensington shortly after 1910 in anticipation of more customers. Stan Berg and his son Dan share a moment with Phillies star pitcher Curt Simmons (left) in the 1970s. (Courtesy of Josie Rosenthal.)

Husband-and-wife teams portrayed the essence of Kensington and Frankford. If the store shared a corner with other businesses, it was called a mom-and-pop store, but on any avenue it was recognized as a full entity. When this picture was taken in 1992, Seymour and Claudia Wolf had been running their clothing department store for more than four decades (Courtesy of Allen Meyers.)

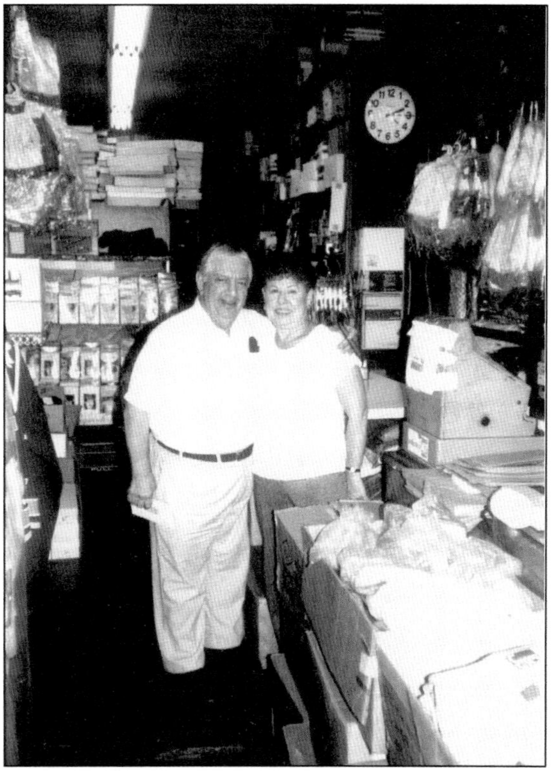

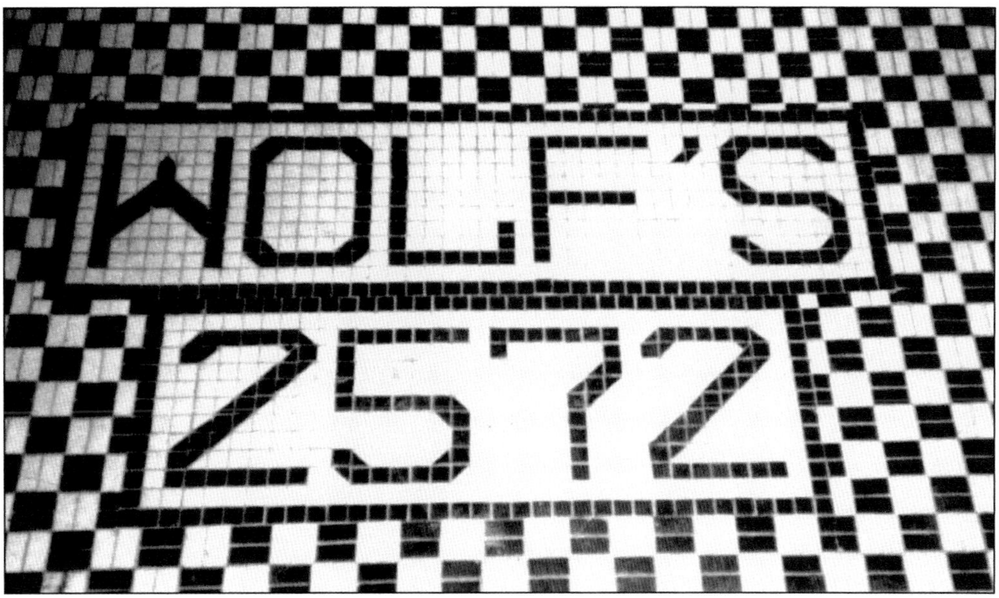

Ownership of a property became a lifelong dream for many Jewish merchants. Wolf's proudly displayed its name in black-and-white mosaic tiles in the entranceway to the store, at 2572 Frankford Avenue. Children's clothes were wrapped with clear, heavy plastic overlays on a wooden hanger for potential buyers to browse through or look over more closely. Before Easter and Christmas, shoppers arrived to buy outfits for their children and to leave their footprints at Wolf's. (Courtesy Allen Meyers.)

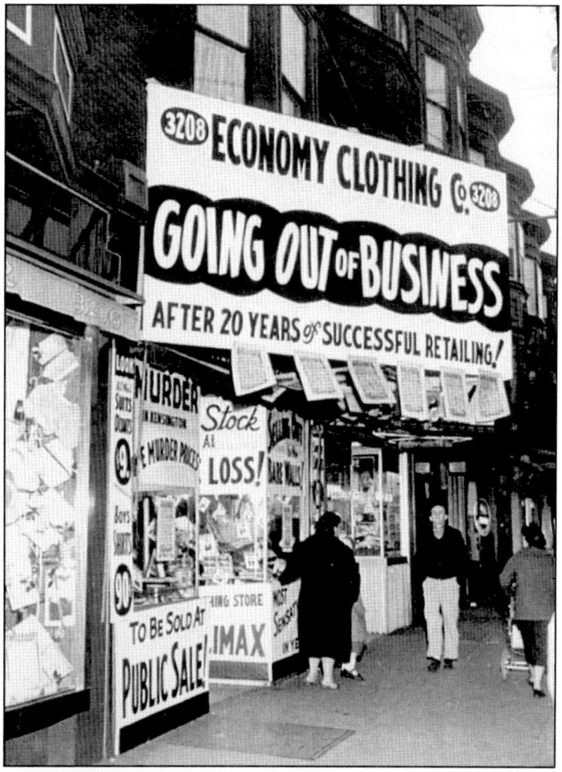

Every business had a gimmick to entice more customers to venture into the narrow aisles of its long and deep store along the famous shopping districts. A favorite promotion was the going-out-of-business sale, which drew hundreds of customers. The Bobman stores featured lines of merchandise that were being discontinued. Shown is a sale at one of Bobman's five locations, with the promise of deep discounts as merchandise was liquidated in a hurry. (Courtesy of Herb Bobman.)

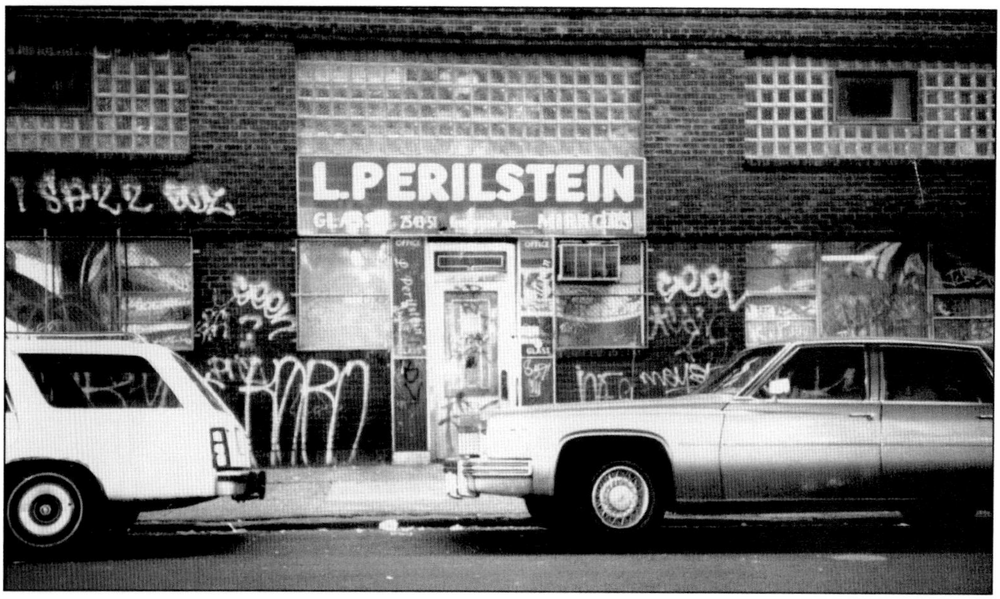

With the passage of time and changing neighborhoods, even once-thriving businesses leave their best days behind them. L. Perilstein glass, on Kensington Avenue below Lehigh Avenue, waned in the late 1970s, and the owners managed to survive only for a short period until the neighborhood became unproductive for business. The scourge of graffiti spread along the Frankford El corridor on a daily basis, unabated until the city hired people to remove the graffiti under the El and at all its stations. (Courtesy of Allen Meyers.)

The last relics of a bygone era can be found in Jewtown near Williams Avenue and Tulip Street, where Jewish life once abounded. People flocked to Friedman Shoes inside a private residence converted by a storefront façade. The four brothers as bachelors carried on the business long after their mother, who drove the business, passed away. The success of the business and its assets were passed on to the Jewish community in the way of a gift to name a wing at the Jewish hospital at Broad Street and Olney Avenue in the 1970s. (Courtesy of Carl Nathans.)

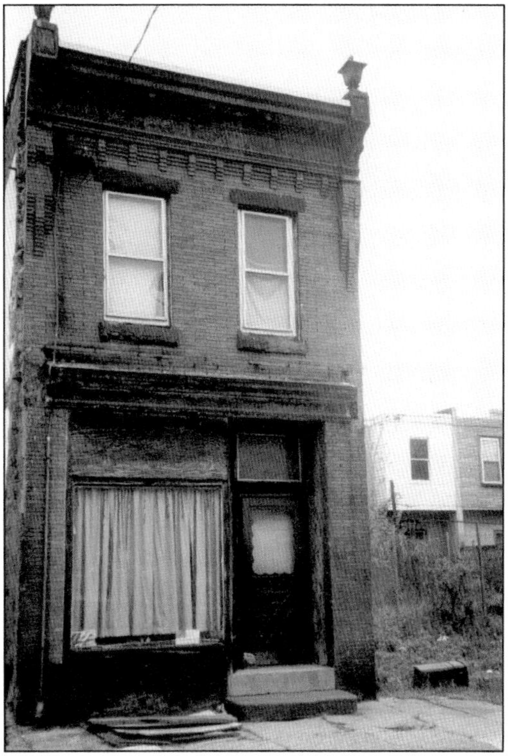

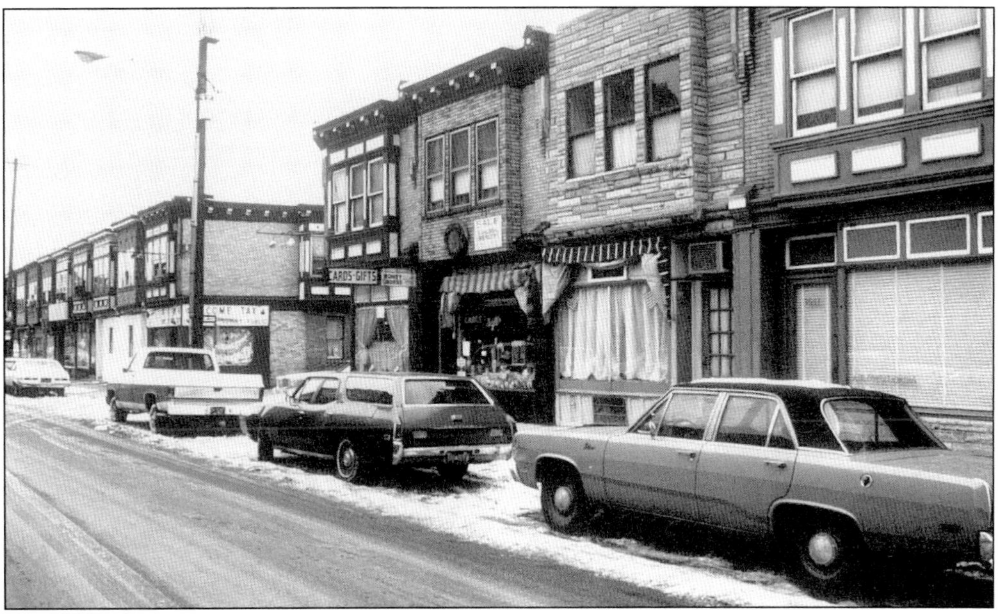

Migration of families from Jewtown took place in the 1920s, some 50 years after the founding of the settlement with a small-town environment that made the place so unique. Family values came along with the people who spread out to surrounding business districts to make a living. Barney Nathans opened a dry goods store at 3549 Frankford Avenue and gave shelter to Sidney, Esther, and Adele until the children were adults and could seek a life of their own. (Courtesy of Carl Nathans.)

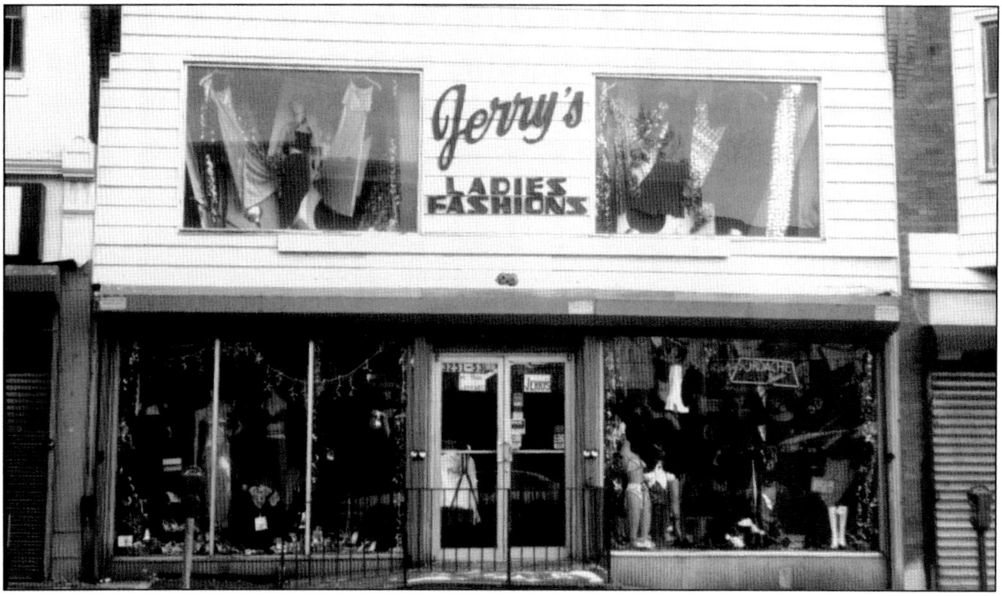

The Front Street and Allegheny Avenue shopping district catered to a separate enclave of working-class people in the western section of Kensington. The large intersection dominated by trolley car Routes No. 60 and No. 57 made it a perfect place to set up business. That is exactly what Jerry Schaff, the son of a Jewish merchant from Fifth and Cambria Street, did in the 1950s. (Courtesy of Allen Meyers.)

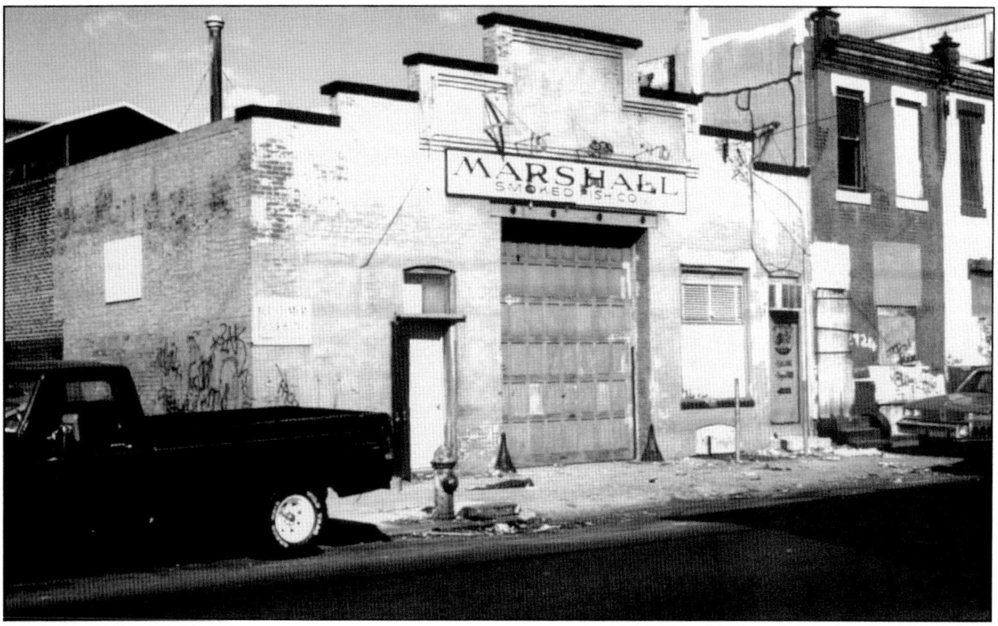

Every Jewish person in the city loved a good piece of smoked fish, especially nova lox on a bagel with fresh cream cheese and several rings of crisp white onions each Sunday morning. The ritual was almost a commandment. The Marshall Smoked Fish company (no relation to Marshall Street itself) produced the delicacies right on the premises, at Second and Lehigh Avenues into the 20th century. (Courtesy of Allen Meyers.)

Kensington Avenue near Allegheny Avenue, better known as K&A, supported scores of stores, especially on the east side under the Frankford El. Moe and Gussie Obod operated a linen shop at 3051 Kensington Avenue from the 1920s until the 1980s. The Obods managed to save enough money to move into their own home around the corner at 635 East Allegheny Avenue in the mid-1950s. Other merchants moved out of the community but continued to own their businesses. (Courtesy of Ray Obod.)

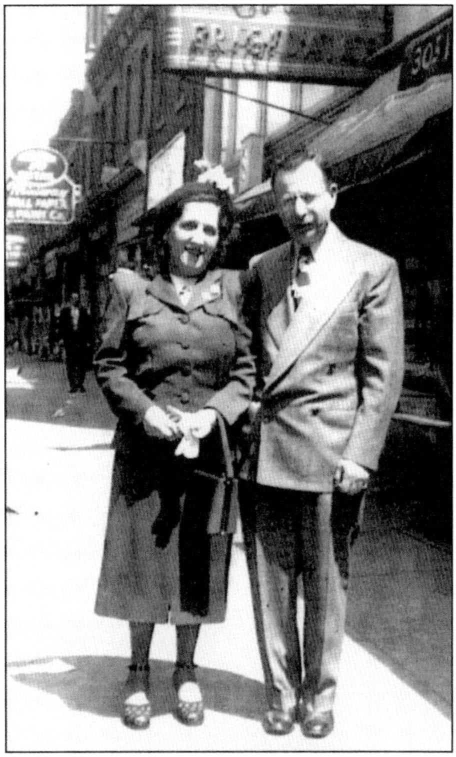

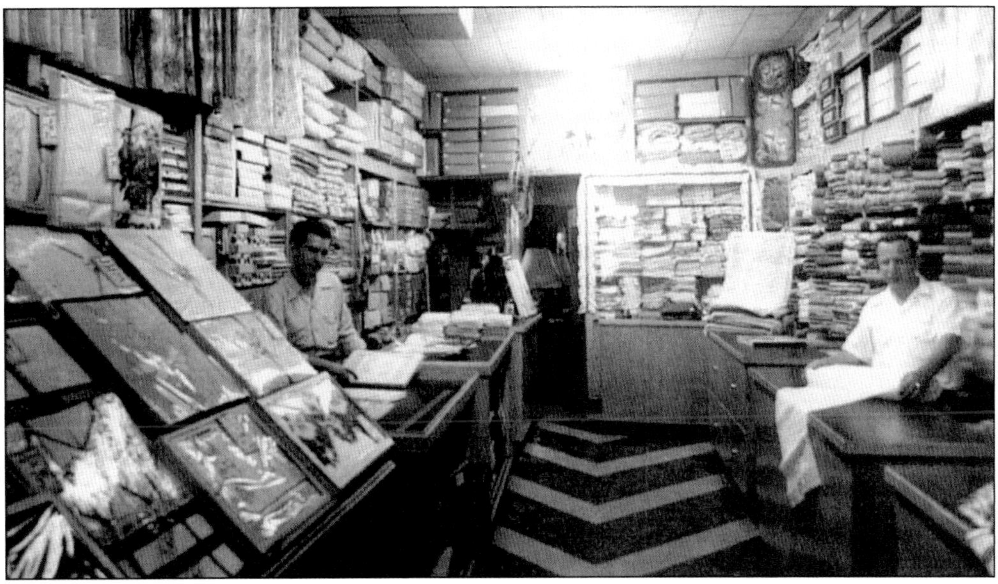

Ray Obod, son of Moe and Gussie, recalls the many experiences he had in his parents' narrow and long store, with merchandise piled high to the ceiling in the late 1940s. He cultivated his people skills and made friends with the children of nearby merchants, such as Bernie Spain and Harry Pasternack, and businesses France Jewelry, Zwickel tailor, Ruttenberg printers, Allen Grobman, and the Love brothers. He loved to visit his paternal grandparents, Joseph and Ida Obod, at their dry goods store, in the 2600 block of Kensington Avenue, especially during the Jewish holidays. (Courtesy of Ray Obod.)

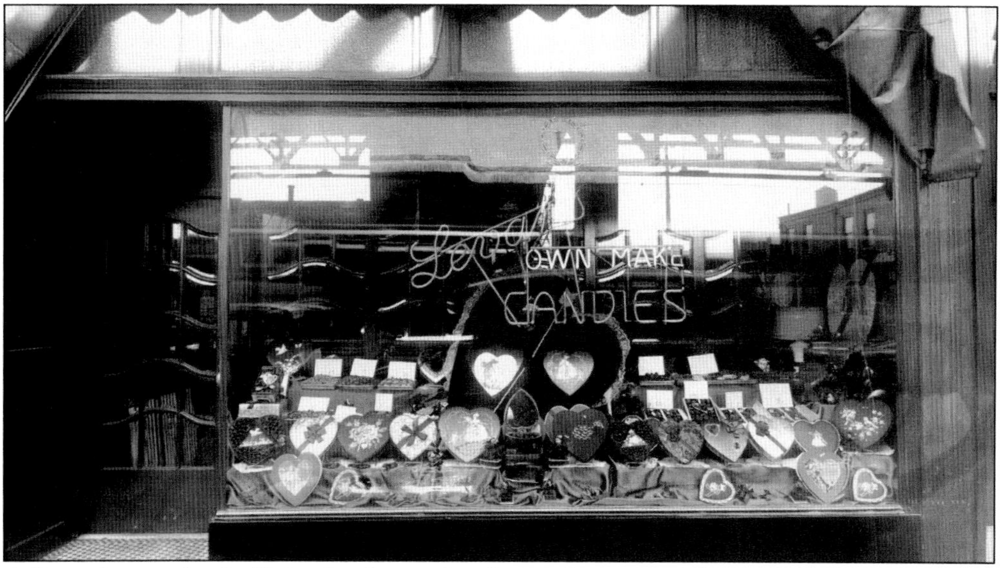

A "sweetheart of a deal" for the Levan family was leaving one business district (Fifth and Olney) and assuming a new business at 3230 Kensington Avenue in 1925. James and Sadie Levan, with ancestors in Russia and England, were delighted with making candy and raising a family. Neatness and perfection made for a brand second to none in the area and around the city. (Courtesy of Lawrence Levan.)

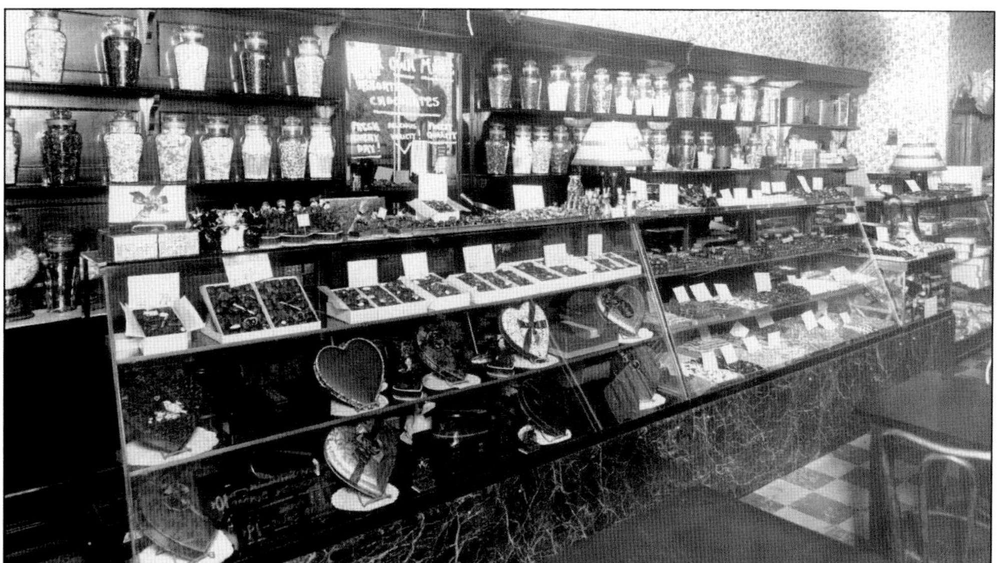

Henry and Lawrence Levan assisted their parents in the 1930s, while growing up with chocolate on the brain for breakfast, lunch, and dinner. Yet, they never tired of the work or the aroma. During the Depression, the children invited friends over to enjoy the wonderful world of chocolate that seemed to allow a person to stay young forever. It took extra effort to make and sell the candy delicacies during the intense candy seasons of Easter, Christmas, and Valentine's Day. The boys kept their promise to live up to father James Levan's motto: "Beautiful candy—too pretty to eat." (Courtesy of Lawrence Levan.)

Pride and joy went into everything Lawrence Levan did—including his special pose in front of the family business. The packing of the candy itself was an art, one that putting together silver boxes of chocolates (39¢) or gold boxes of chocolate-covered fruits and nuts (49¢). During the summer, the family made lemon stick, a treat to be inserted into sour lemons to make them turn sweet. (Courtesy of Lawrence Levan.)

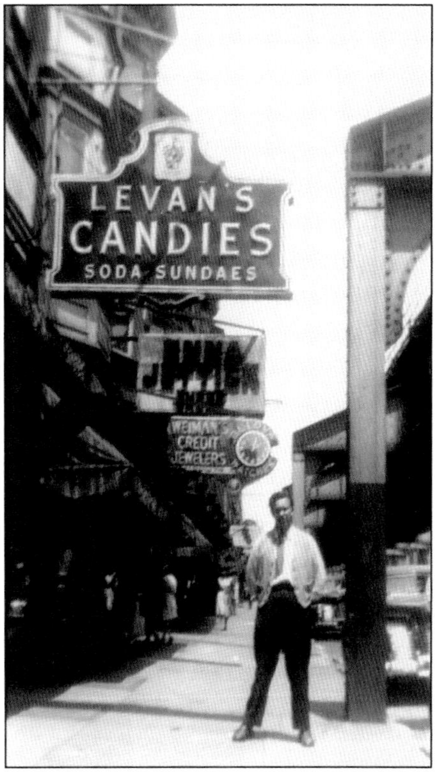

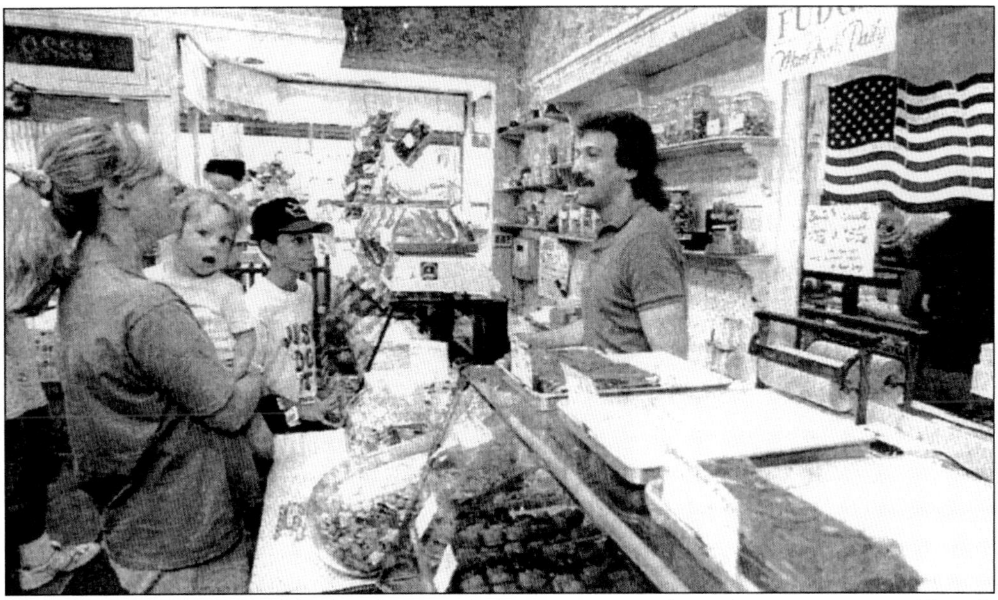

In the 1950s, Jewish neighborhoods around the city attracted another generation of Jewish people. The Levans retired and sold their property to Louis Ostroff's son Sol and his wife, Goldie, in 1953. Sol Ostroff strayed from his father's concentration on hard candies in South Philly to make his own chocolates and was best known for meltaways. Like father, like son—Brad Ostroff later took over the business in Kensington, serving countless customers. (Courtesy of Goldie Ostroff.)

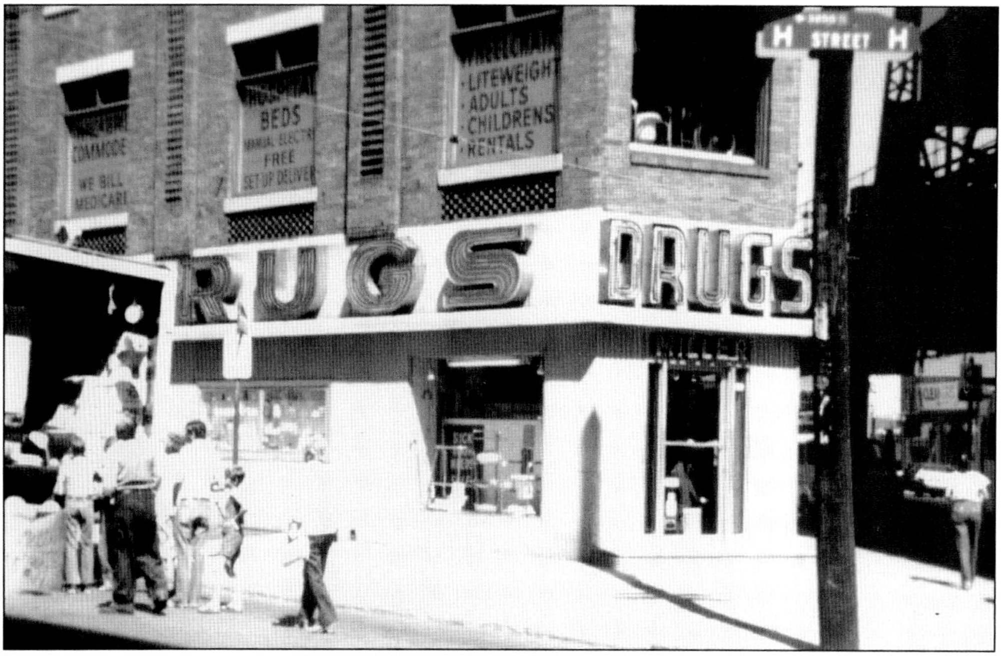

Independent druggists earned a great living throughout the city from the 1900s to the 1970s, if they could stand on their feet 12 to 14 hours a day. The plentiful supply of corner pharmacies provided a much-needed service and a way for many Jewish people to earn a living. Some of the drugstores in Kensington included Miller's, at H Street and Allegheny (shown); Samitz, at K Street off Allegheny; Gordons, at I Street and Kensington Avenue; and Russock's, at K Street and Tioga. (Courtesy of Hymen Kanoff.)

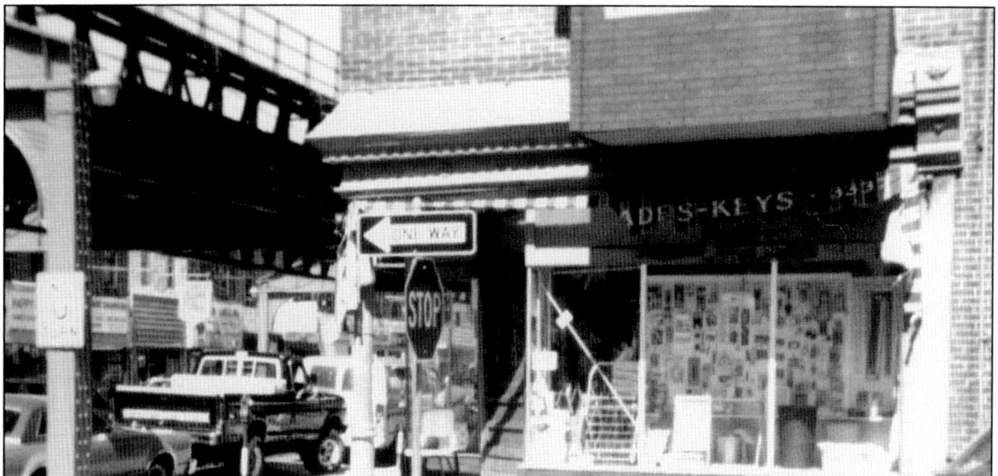

Kensington included small enclaves of Jewish merchants who operated stores on four corners of small intersections. The corner variety store, a tailor shop, a shoemaker, and a drugstore became the usual quartet and the basis for a mini Jewish community, with the owner and his family living upstairs. The Rosenbergs decided to open a drugstore off Kensington Avenue above Allegheny Avenue, and to serve more customers, they added cut-rate items and school supplies. The families, although spread out, had the Kensington Jewish Community Center in common. (Courtesy of Hymen Kanoff.)

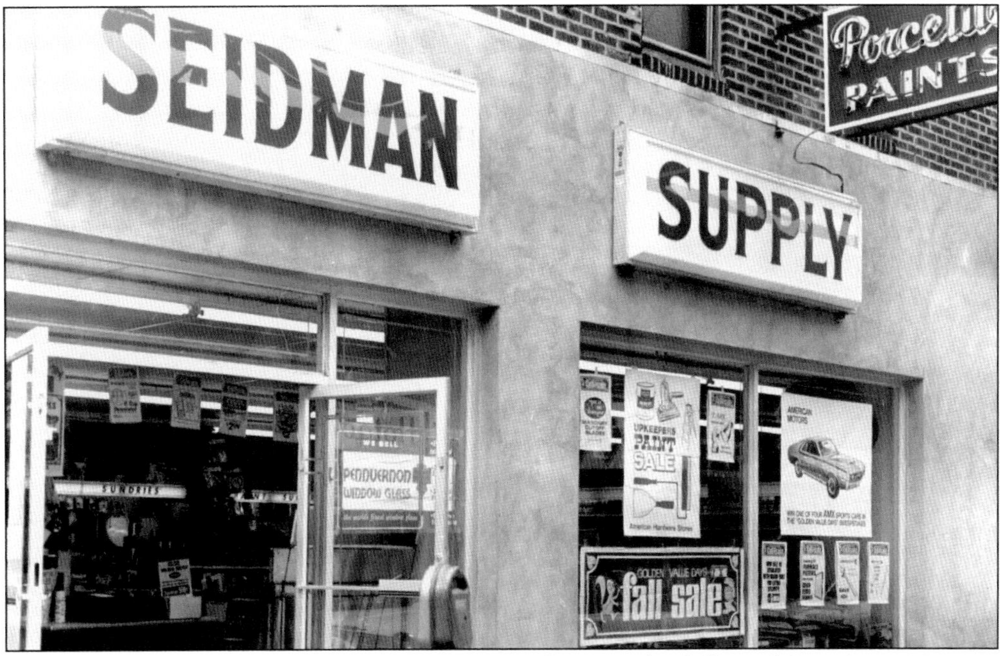

Izzy (Ed) and Edith Seidman came to Kensington from South Philly and Strawberry Mansion in 1946 as renters of a second-floor photography store. However, after Edith Seidman spotted a store for sale at 3368 Kensington Avenue, on the other side of the street, the couple abandoned their original plans. They bought the street-level property and ran it as a hardware store. They raised their children, Paul and Elliott, above their business and stayed for the next 50 years. (Courtesy of Edith Seidman.)

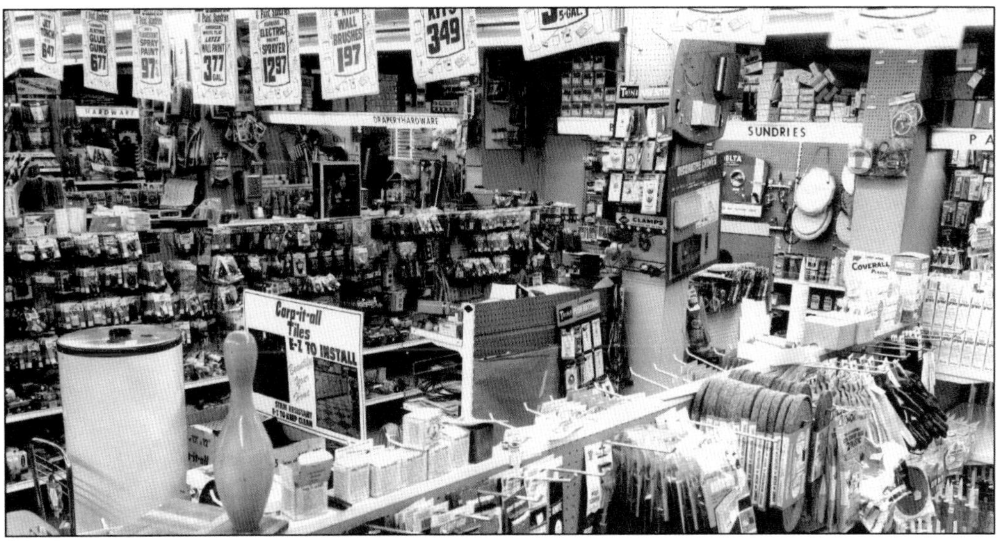

The Seidmans lived in the community along Kensington Avenue while expanding their business north of Allegheny Avenue. The decision to stay in Kensington came from a trusted financial adviser, K. Harold Smith, a former Sears and Roebuck manager, in the late 1960s, when many Jewish merchants were retiring, moving away, or abandoning their businesses. Izzy Seidman formed his own businessmen's association, Harrowgate, to address issues of merchants north of Allegheny Avenue. He passed away in November 2000. (Courtesy of Edith Seidman.)

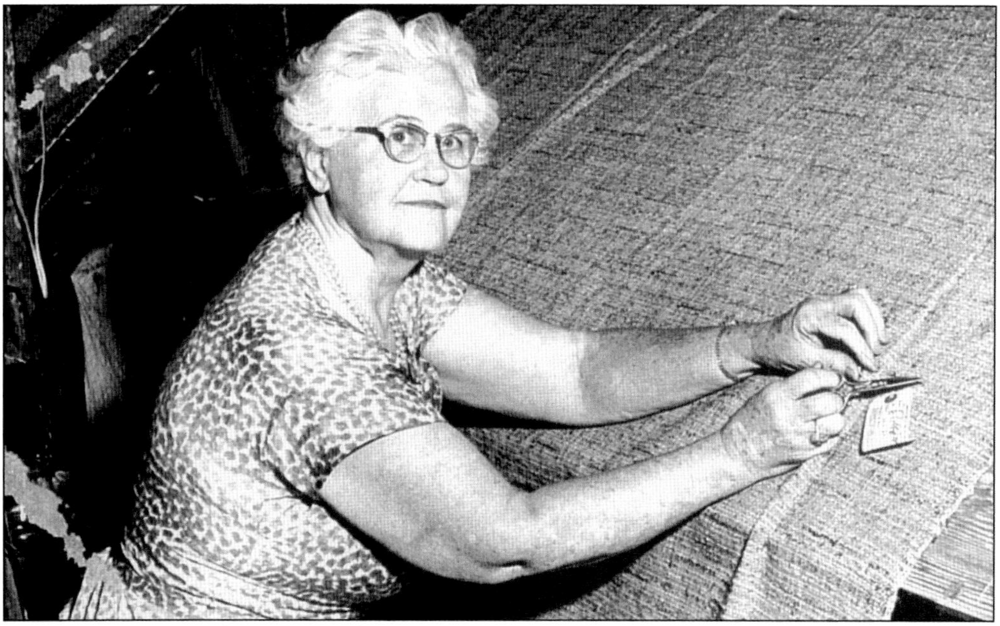

Janet and Herman Blum met at the Pioneer Suspender and Belt Company after 1910. Janet, a native of Carbondale, Pennsylvania, migrated to Kensington. Herman Blum, a Hungarian Jew, invented a belt buckle with removable initials, which he tried to patent, but his company bought his rights. He then bought the Craftex Textile mill and worked alongside his employees and his wife, who labored tediously on the looms, weaving many cloths. (Courtesy of Jean Seder.)

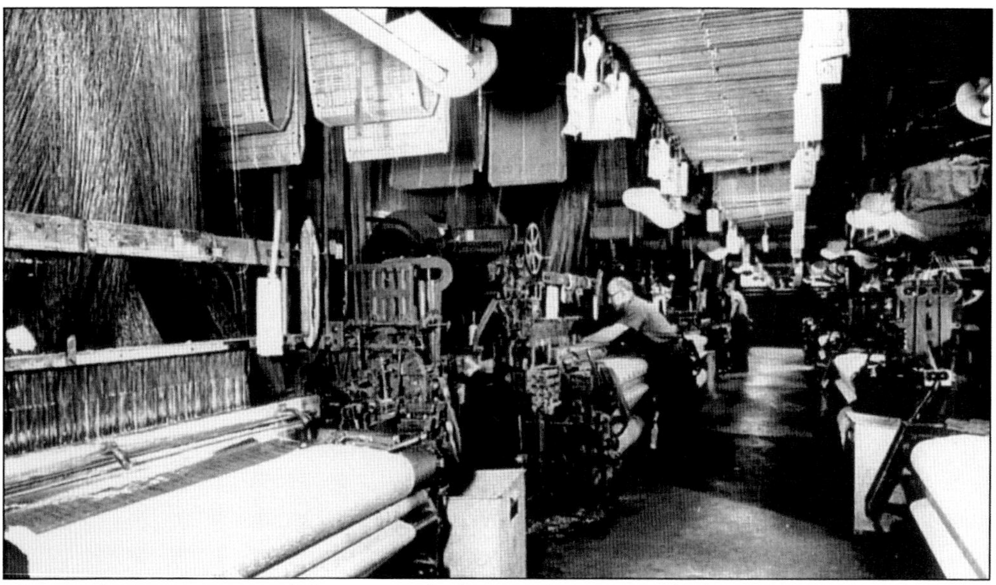

The textile factories created designs in clothing and carpets with the aid of a jacquard, a card cutter that served as the brain of the machine, with exacting loops and stitches. The large factories, sometimes taking up one city block in length, had hundreds of panes of glass to open for fresh air, although the interiors were usually dark and noisy from the constant hum of the machinery. (Courtesy of Jean Seder.)

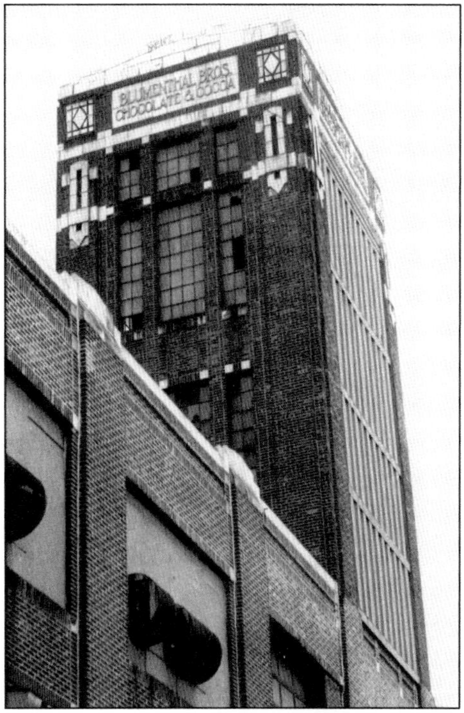

The aroma of roasting cocoa beans attracted many to the Blumenthal processing plant, off Wakeling and Aramingo Avenues in Frankford. Moses Blumenthal, a 1905 German-Jewish immigrant, started the company along with some family members, who included Joseph, Aaron, Jacob, Meyer, and Abe. The access of the plant to the nearby Reading Railroad and Frankford junction made it an ideal location. Blumenthal manufactured large quantities of chocolate for Nabisco (formula No. 2). (Courtesy of Larry Blumenthal.)

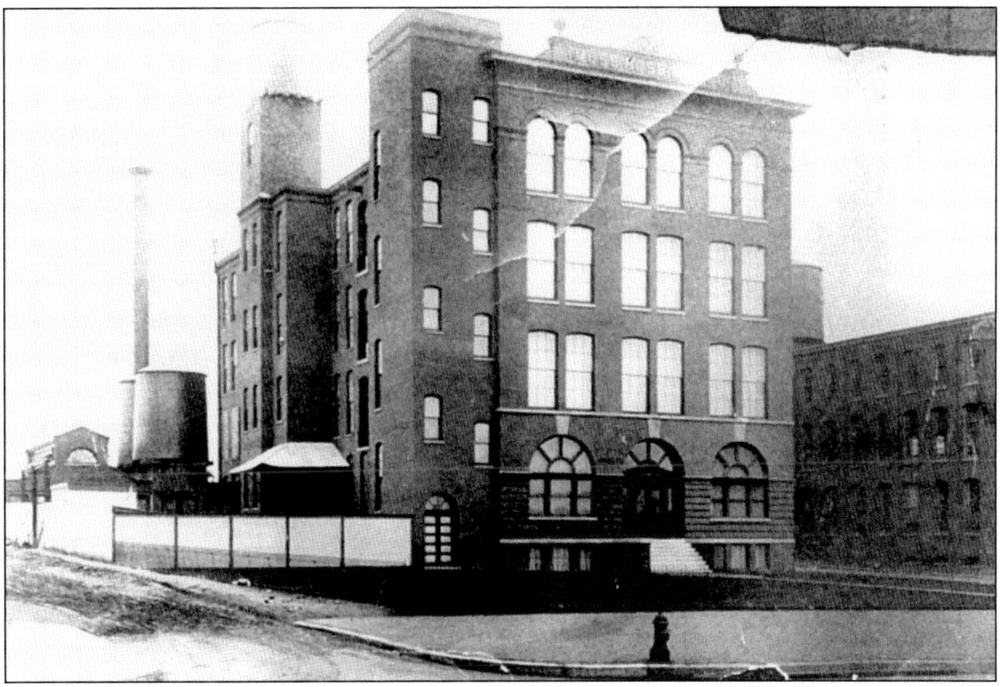

The Moss Rose Company, owned by Janet and Herman Blum, employed many types of workers, who included hosiery spinners, textile card cutters, textile winders, loom fixers, loom magazine fillers, textile burlers, and menders. The factory trademark, the huge water towers and tall smokestacks, could be seen into the 1960s, huffing and puffing in all directions on a cold winter day. (Courtesy of Jean Seder.)

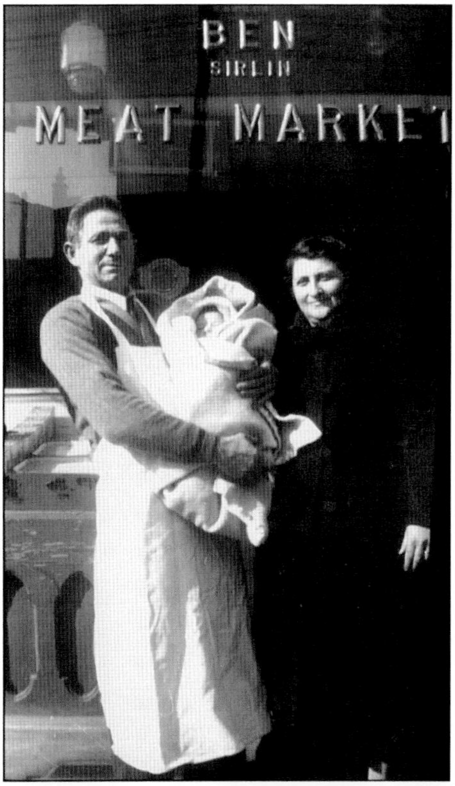

Ben Sirlin, a Jew from the Ukraine, and his wife, Bessie, came to live in Strawberry Mansion after World War I. Sirlin made a living as a Jewish butcher and moved his family to 3058 Richmond Street in the 1920s. The couple had many neighboring Jewish businesses, including Kanefsky Army & Navy, Rosencrantz grocery, Zilberg dry goods, Altman's drugstore, and Hahn's candy store. The neighbors spoke Polish, Yiddish, or Russian—all languages that the Sirlins knew. (Courtesy of Marilyn Sirlin Schwerin.)

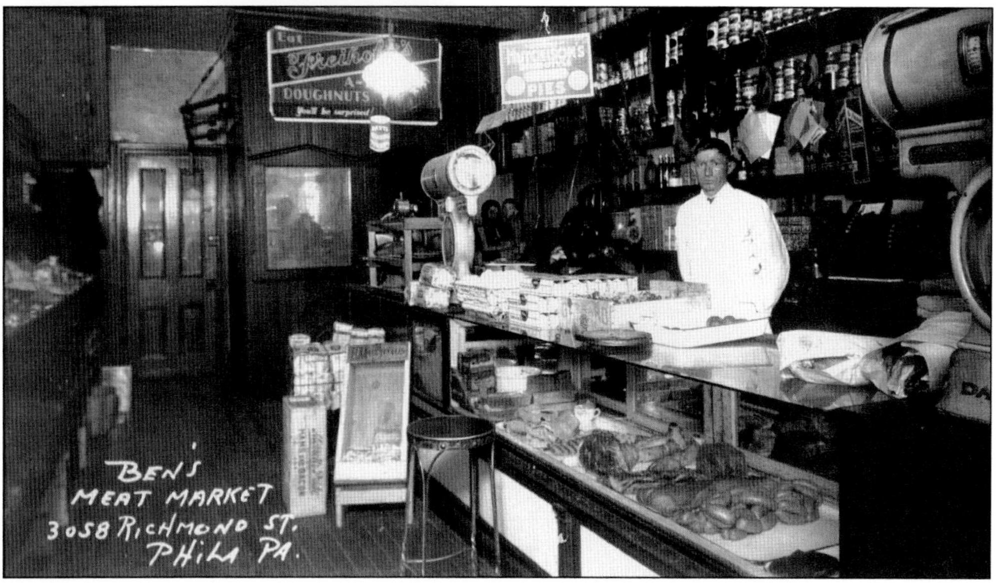

The Sirlins adapted to their home above the butcher shop. The store located was at 3058 Richmond Street, at the other end of the Strawberry Mansion Route No. 54 trolley car line, which allowed for long-distance relationships and weekly visits with other immigrants. The business fed many people during the Great Depression of 1929. Ben Sirlin provided for his immediate family and took in other relatives—a tradition from the old country. (Courtesy of Marliyn Sirlin Schwerin.)

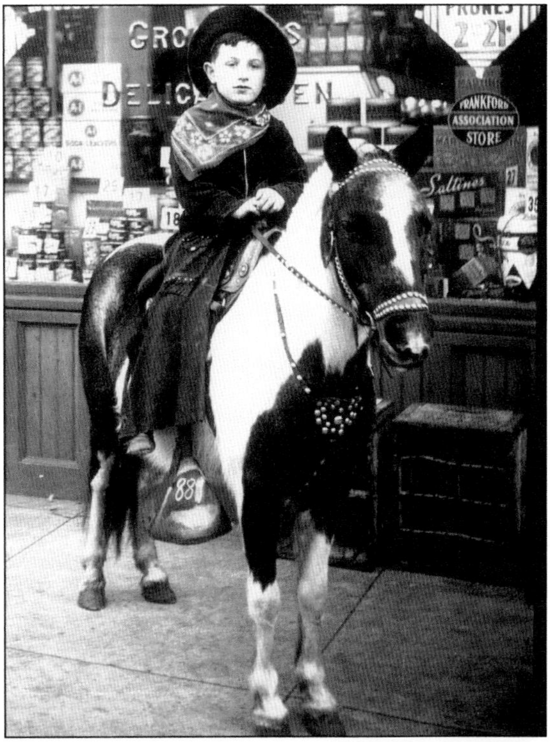

Morris Barren sits tall in the saddle in front of the family delicatessen and grocery store, at Memphis and Clearfield Streets. He and his parents, Dave and Freda Barren, moved from rented quarters on Erie Avenue near Venango Avenue to Richmond in 1935. The new neighborhood afforded Morris a chance to experience a melting pot, with items such as rye bread and Jewish pickles from Marshall Street for sale alongside Polish and American foods. (Courtesy of Morris Barren.)

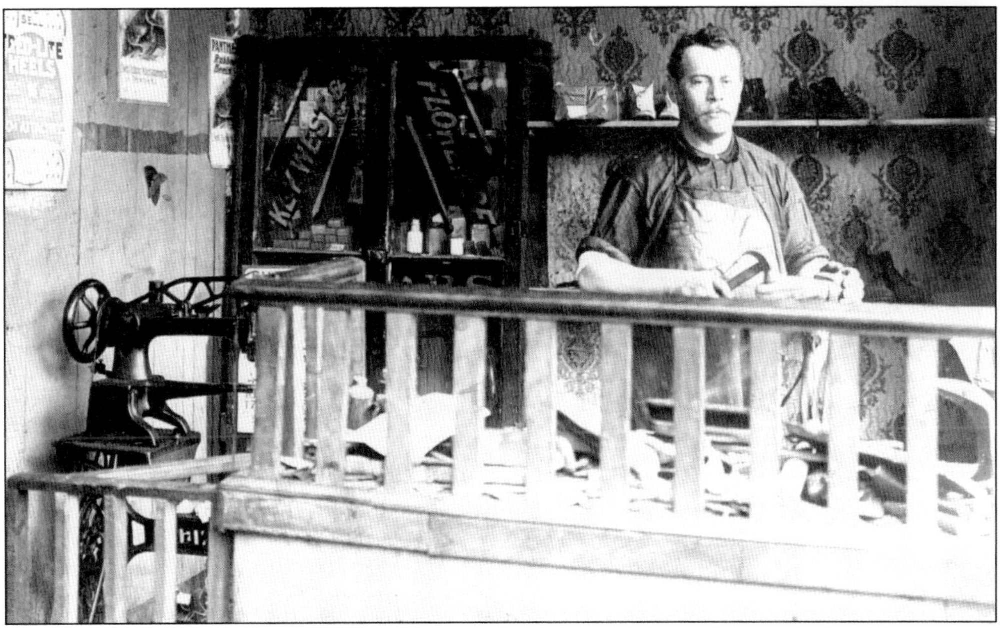

The corner properties on the small streets of Kensington provided excellent places from which to conduct a business. Craftsman and handyman William Matless, from Romania, settled in Kensington during 1903 with his wife, Reba, at F and Willard Streets. Matless built his living around the old Singer sewing machine and repaired and made new shoes. Everyone in the neighborhood was sure that the children (Sarah, Rae, Cecilia, Helen, and Abe) were from a rich family because they had new shoes every year. (Courtesy of Hope Matless.)

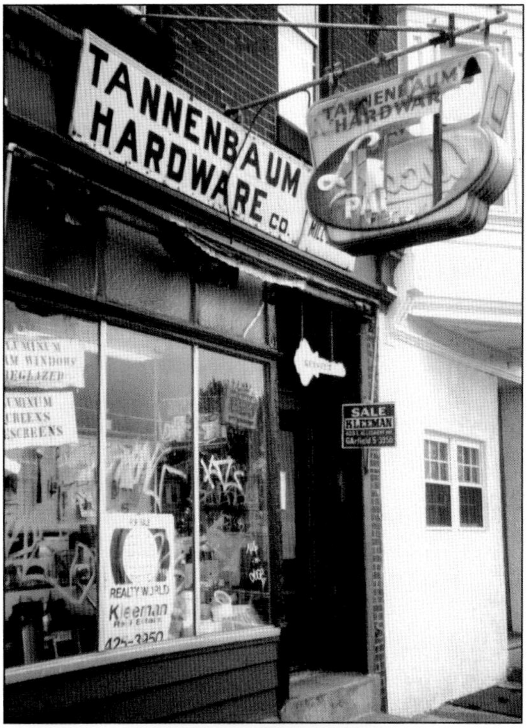

Abandoned stores in Philadelphia are a 20th-century phenomenon. More than 20 years ago while researching old Jewish neighborhoods in Philadelphia, author Allen Meyers stopped at Tannenbaum Hardware Company, in the 3500 block of Frankford Avenue, to talk with Mr. Tannenbaum. The business provided Tannenbaum with a good livelihood. Along with hardware, the store sold paint, made keys, and repaired screen doors. Today, the store is abandoned and for sale, with many of the old items still on the shelves.

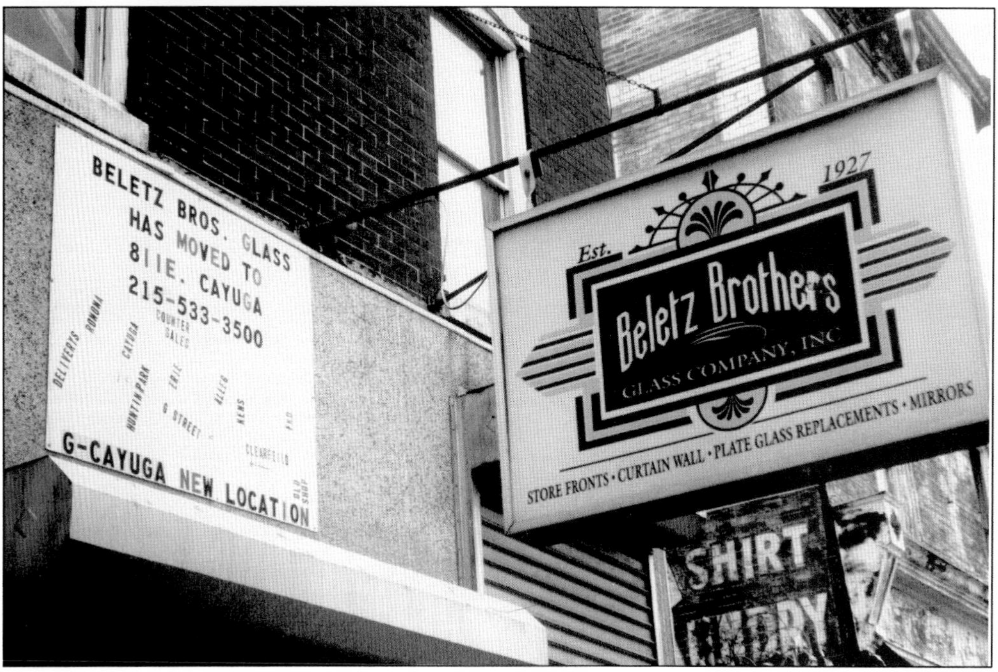

A trip down memory lane is difficult to take for many people, including author Allen Meyers, who attended Mastbaum Vocational High School in the late 1960s. The familiar Penn Fruit supermarket, across from the school, is long gone. The famous Geiger's bakery, on Clearfield Street, is only a memory. The latest abandonment is displayed with a sign notifying people that the Beletz Brothers Glass Company (established in 1927) has moved to 811 East Cayuga Street.

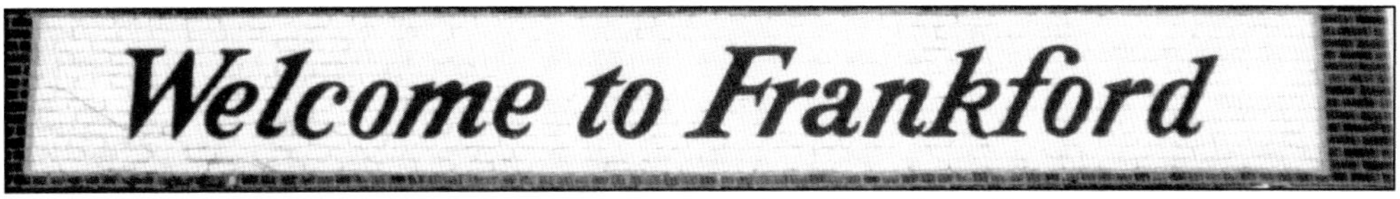

This recently photographed sign is located in a parking lot where Kensington Avenue merges into Frankford Avenue. It marks the start of Frankford's business district, where the Frankford El makes a sharp left turn high above the roofline. The park on the triangle, where the two streets merge, at one time had a huge water trough for animals, mostly horses.

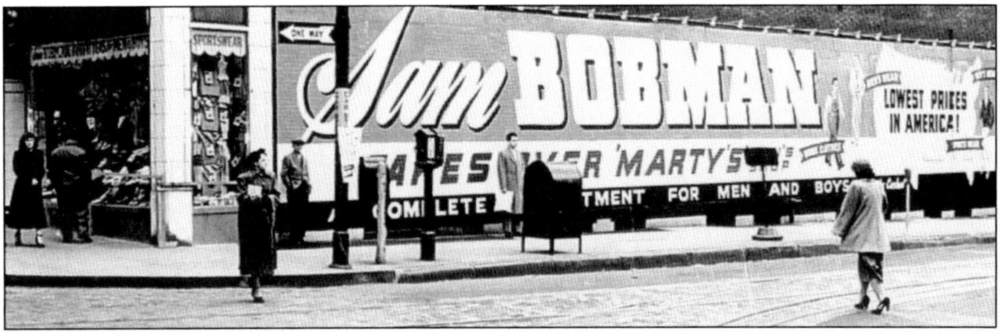

This famous corner under the Frankford El enticed shoppers walking the avenue who came off the El, the trolley car clientele getting off the Route No. 75 to make connections to the Oxford Circle in the northeast, and others travelers heading west to Feltonville or Logan. In those days, before 1950, Margaret Street was a two-way street. (Courtesy of Herb Bobman.)

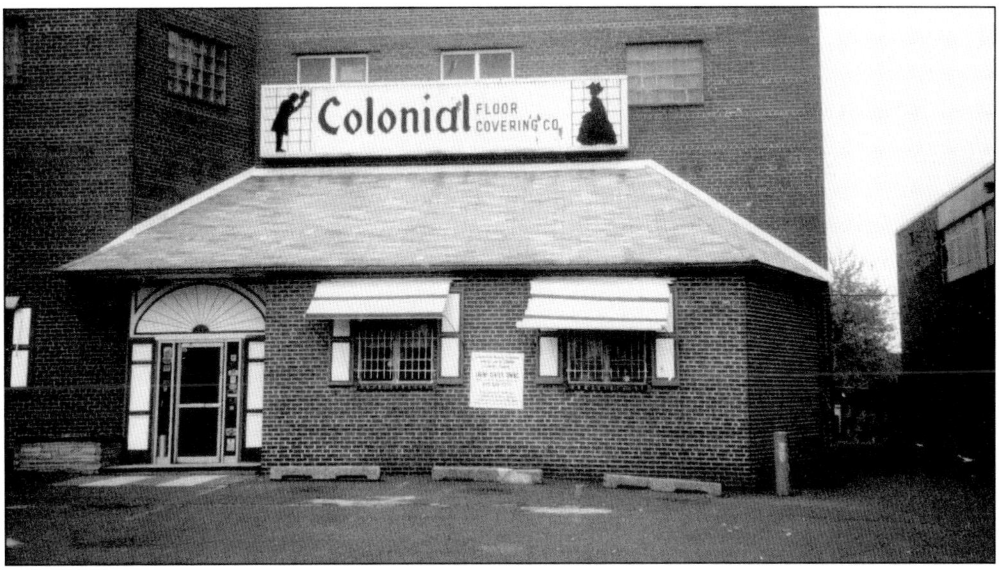

Frankford Avenue at one time had more than 100 shops from number 4300 to number 4700. Each store specialized in one or two items, and sometimes there were three or four stores that carried a similar product line. The avenue changed in the 1960s, and some viewed this as an opportunity. The Colonial Floor Covering Company, built with a free parking lot, enticed many do-it-yourselfers to drive right up to the front door and walk in. Today, you will still find Myron, the owner, at the front counter.

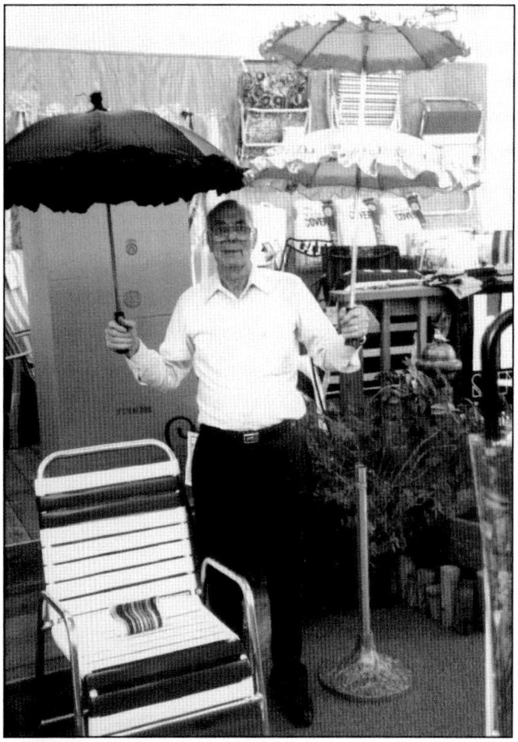

Izzy Frankford, the son of Austrian-Jewish immigrant Sam Frankford, took the El from his home in West Philly to work every day. He and his brother Martin Frankford ran several umbrella shops, including 3234 Kensington Avenue and 4349 Frankford Avenue from the 1940s to the 1980s. The motto of the stores, "an umbrella for all seasons," took on new meaning with the production of large beach umbrellas in later years after the local umbrella factories in Philadelphia all closed. (Courtesy of Izzy Frankford.)

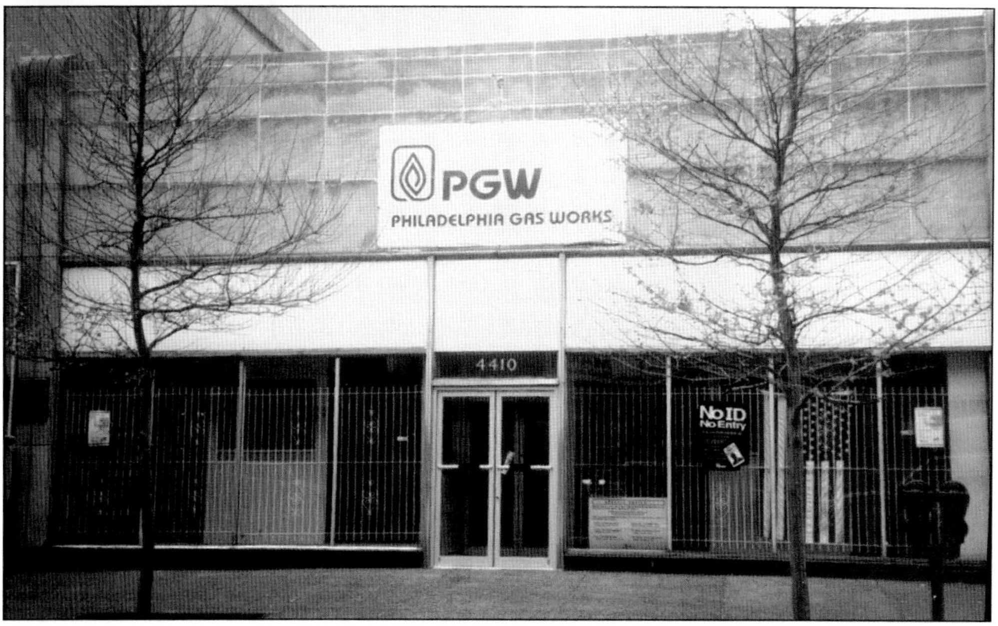

The Philadelphia Gas Works, in the 4400 block of Frankford Avenue, is a familiar sight. People for generations paid their gas bills, viewed new gas appliances, and attended meetings here. Browsing along the avenue was a favorite pastime. Sacks furniture, Mollie's Junk shop, Frankford Leather Company, Paramount Schultz wallpaper outlet, Kresege department store, Joseph's five and dime, Edco's husky men's clothing, delicatessens, and a whole array of shoe stores, such as Dial, Father & Sons, and Hardy's, were all neighbors of the gas company.

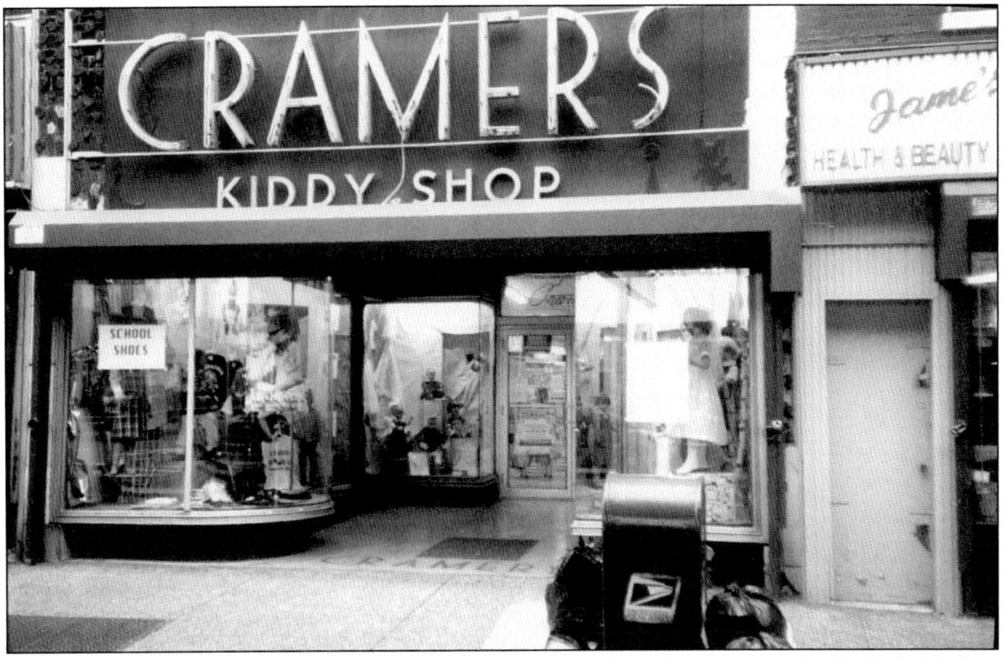

Charles and Fannie Cramer came from Russia after 1910 and settled in North Philadelphia, selling children's clothes. The move to Frankford Avenue below Orthodox Street took place in the next generation, with David Cramer and his wife, Marilyn, opening Cramers Kiddy Shop in the 1930s. Smaller businesses failed in the late 1980s, after the larger outfits did their own importing and people flocked to outlets. Yet, Cramers is still open today. (Courtesy of David and Warren Cramer.)

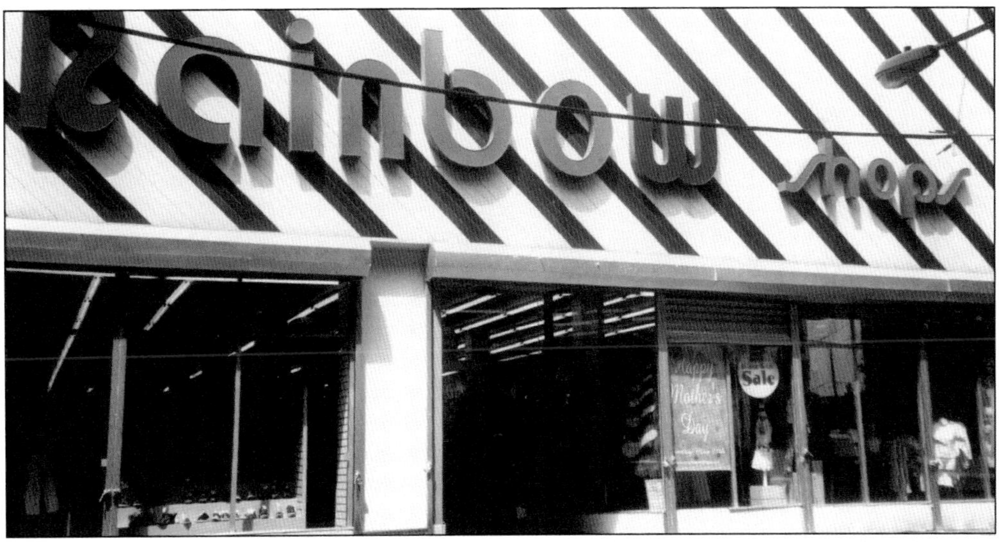

Frankford attracted many families every night of the week after World War II. The Charming Shoppe, a Frankford creation, went national in women's wear. The York Shop and the Kaiserman boys were also successful on Frankford Avenue, along with the American Pants Company and Krauss Brothers for men. The Rainbow shops and a new variety store, Value Plus, dominate Frankford Avenue today, along with a proliferation of well-known $1 stores and cellular phone franchises.

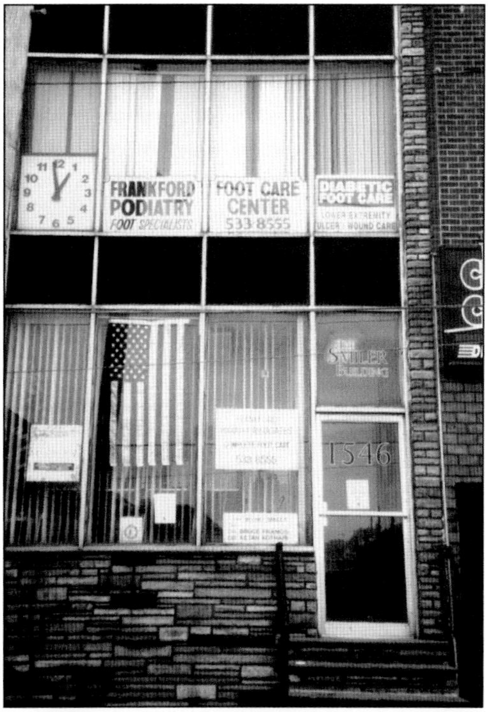

Irv Smiler, an untiring man and foot doctor by trade, led the Bridge-Pratt Professional Association. The group was formed to improve the community business, education, transportation, and arts. Author Allen Meyers served on the board while overseeing the operations of the McDonald's restaurant on Pratt Street in the 1990s. Smiler, a true community activist, advised local government on the new Frankford Transportation Center and its impact on business in Frankford. Sadly, he passed away recently.

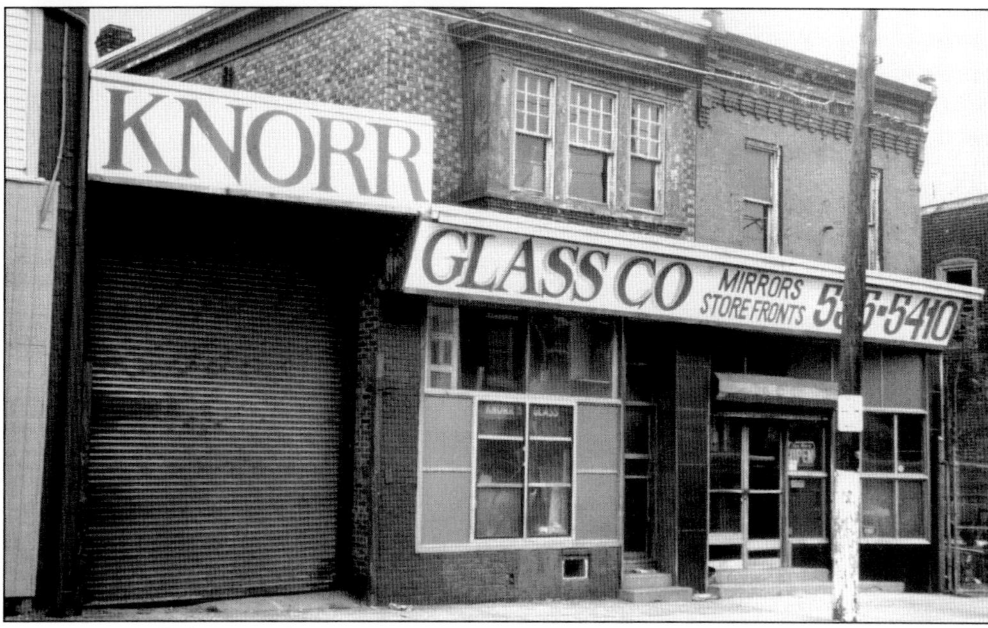

Businesses of all shapes and sizes existed in Frankford. The Knorr Glass Company, under the leadership of Rabbi Meles, from Young Israel of Oxford Circle, provided years of communal leadership along Orthodox Street. The hub of Frankford gave birth to another shopping district only blocks away at Orthodox and Torresdale Avenue. The small-town business district at the intersection of the J bus and Route No. 56 trolley car line served the community of Bridesburg and the workers of the huge Frankford Arsenal facility with banks, groceries, clothing stores, and shoe stores.

Eight

But I Am Not Jewish

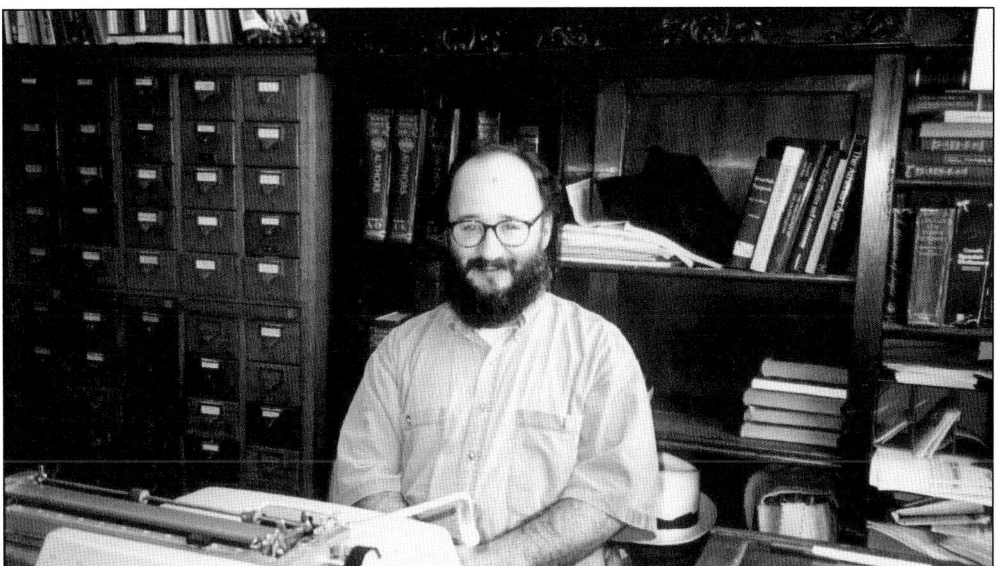

The happenings of Jewish life in Kensington, Fishtown, Richmond, and Frankford went on largely unnoticed by non-Jews, unless they had family or friends in those communities. Yet, many Jews found it conducive to set up a business in a non-Jewish area, especially with the completion of the Frankford El in the 1920s. This chapter is dedicated to the non-Jews who gave tolerance a new meaning and worked with Jews because they viewed them no differently and respected them for their traditions, such as closing their shops on Jewish holy days. Ken Milano is not Jewish, although he "looks the part." He is a historian and activist of the Kensington community and resides there today.

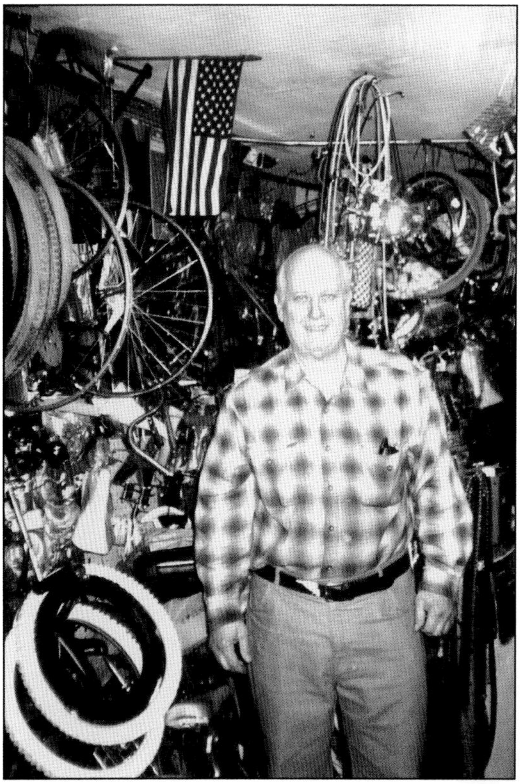

Richard Cannon has been repairing and selling all shapes and sizes of recreational equipment for more than 50 years at 2721 Kensington Avenue, just above Lehigh Avenue. Children, adults, police officers, and even nurses from nearby hospitals have relied on him to fix a flat tire or two. Bent rims are his specialty. Yet, most of all, the passage of time hurts, as he lost his sweetheart, Ann Mae, who made a big difference in his life for more than 40 years. (Courtesy of Richard Cannon.)

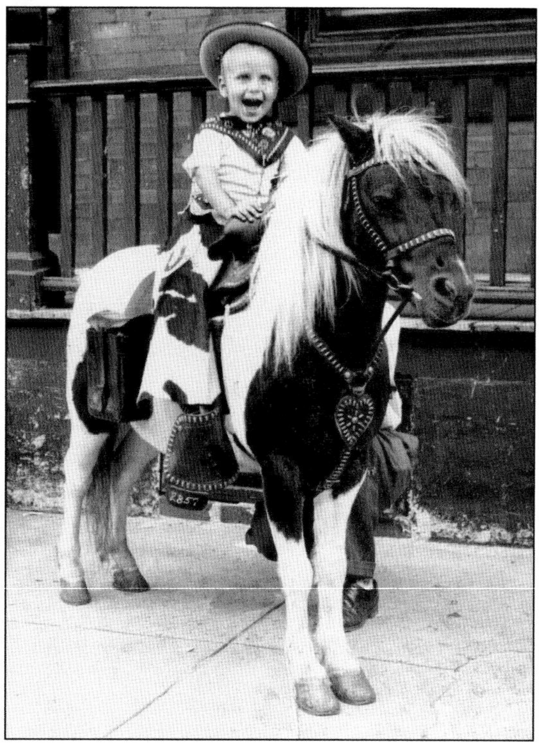

George Holmes saddled up on the pony that a local photographer brought around with cowboy outfits to 2140 East Stella Street. He mounted and later went to his mother, Margaret Holmes, to ask for a quarter to pay the photographer—one week later. Holmes is the author of *Philadephia's River Wards*, a photographic history published in 2003.

Francis Adler, a proud Kensingtonian, went off to World War II with the advantage of knowing the German language. Although he was not Jewish, the Germans captured him and accused him of being Jewish, which landed him in several concentration camps. He survived by squirreling away potato skins and fish eyes for his sustenance. Liberated by the Russians, Adler returned to Kensington as a decorated war hero.

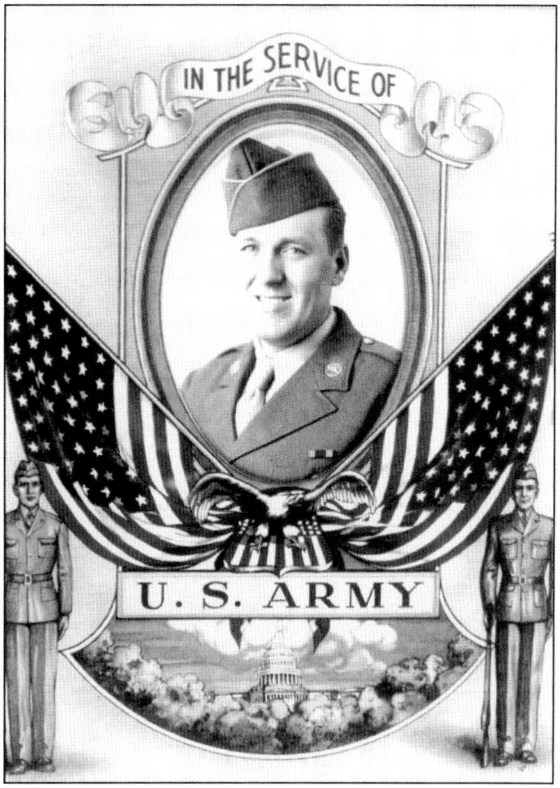

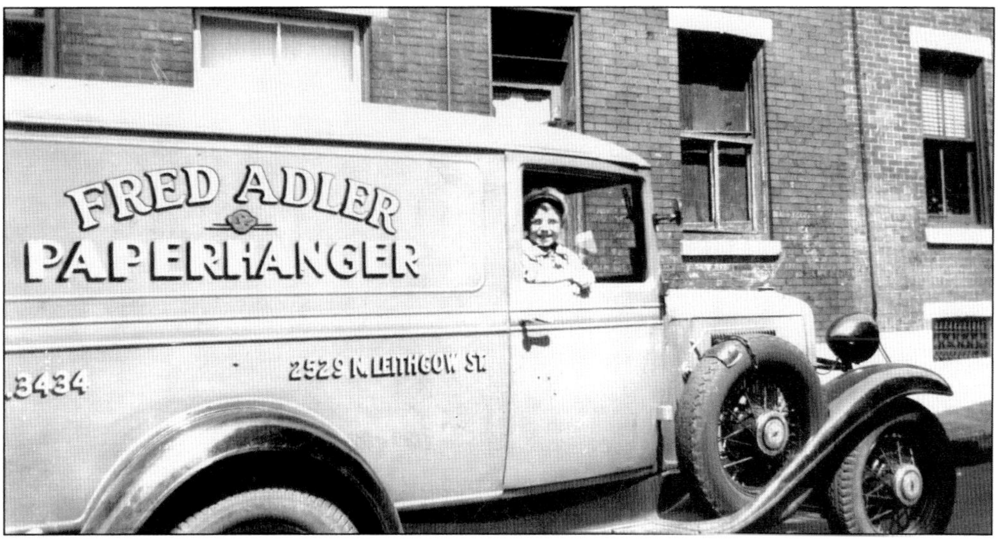

With a name like Adler, how could you not be Jewish? Adler's relative Frank Bender grew up in Kensington at 2520 North Leithgow Street, near Fourth Street off Lehigh Avenue, with his parents, Sarah and Francis Bender. The whole family lived in Kensington, including grandfather Fred, a wallpaperer, and grandmother Jennie, fixer of looms. Frank Bender went to fine arts school to learn sculpture. He is renowned throughout the world for his holocaust artwork. (Courtesy of Frank Bender.)

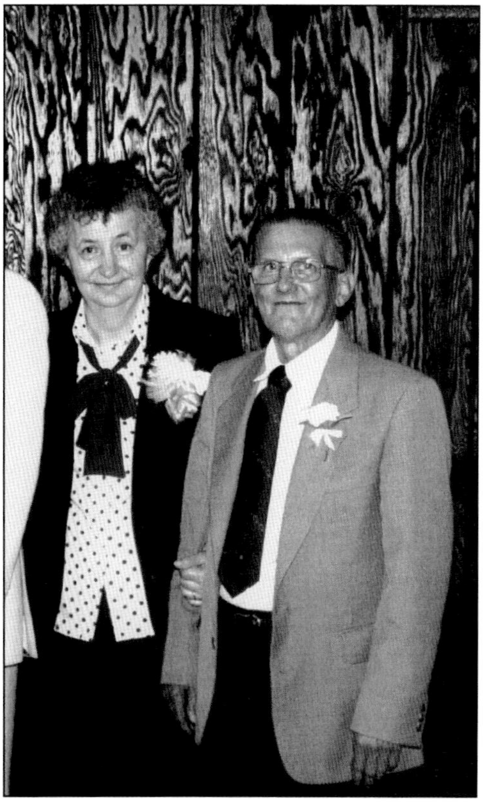

Helen and Gus Kirn were married in 1945, and the couple settled at 3446 North Water and Tioga Streets, off the business district and above Front and Allegheny. Helen Kirn was a native of Ottsville, Pennsylvania. Members of the Third Brethren Church, the Kirns led a good life and raising their five children, Lillian, Elizabeth, Nancy, Susanna, and Gus Jr. Gus Kirn supported the family by working as a wood-pattern maker. The convenience of the transportation system allowed the Kirns to remain in the community for more than 40 years until Gus passed away. (Courtesy of Helen Kirn and Tracy Bender.)

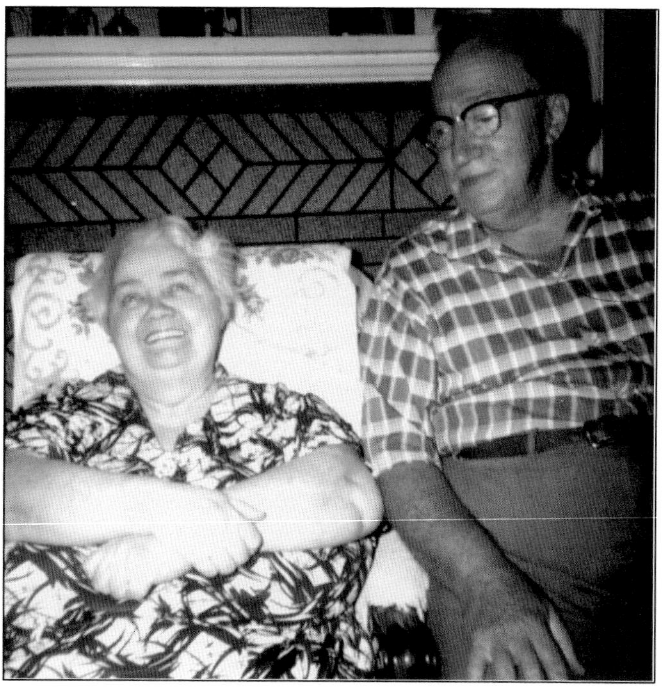

Kensington attracted many hardworking German and Irish immigrants to its community for many generations. The ancestors of Janice Rogg (left) migrated from Germany in the 1870s and gave birth to a new generation of children in Kensington at Belgrade and Dauphin Streets. The children included Janice Rogg's mother, Elsie. Her father, Alfred Rogg (right), was born in Northern Liberties. The success of assimilation worked in reverse for Janice Rogg: she grew up in Feltonville with many Jewish children whose parents were shopkeepers along Wyoming Avenue. (Courtesy of Janice Rogg.)

Nine

A Salute to Our Troops

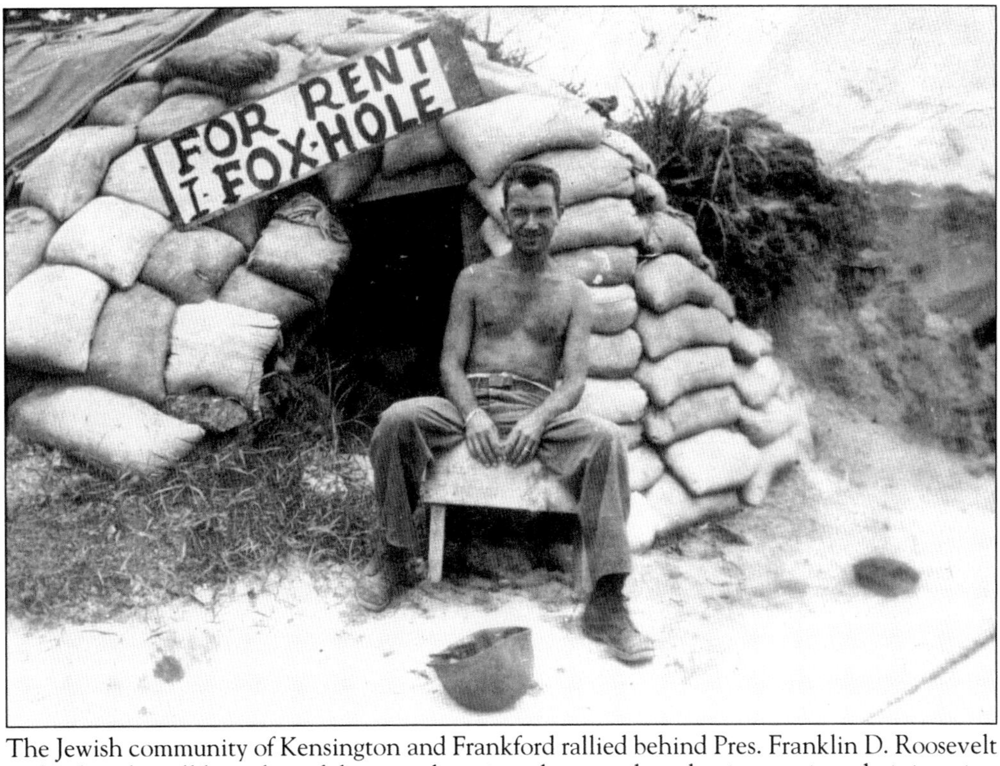

The Jewish community of Kensington and Frankford rallied behind Pres. Franklin D. Roosevelt and enlisted in all branches of the armed services down at the selective service administration offices, located at the convenient corner of Kensington and Allegheny Avenues from 1941 to 1946. The war took a toll on the Jewish community by hindering the ability of synagogues to conduct its services, which required 10 adult men to gather for a minyan and a call to communal prayer. The boys of the community, barely 18 years old, grew up very quickly as the draft drew in all able-bodied males for stateside and overseas duty and sent them off to war. Francis Bender, from Fifth and Lehigh Avenues, traveled to Germany and set up his new home (above) in 1942. (Courtesy of Frank Bender.)

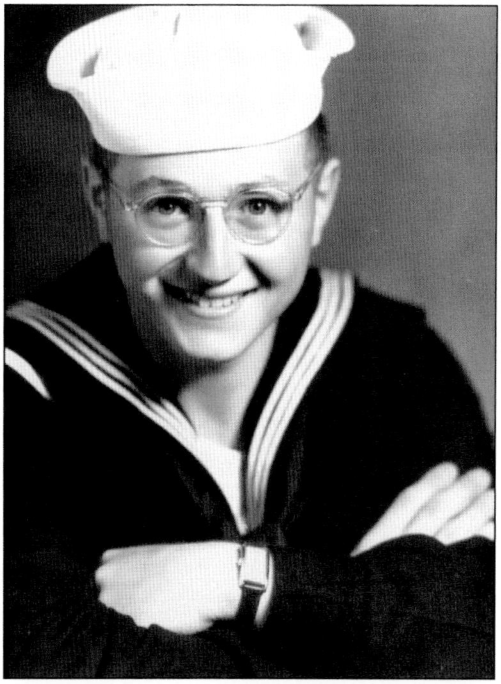

Service duties meant leaving the community and going somewhere foreign to help the war effort. Those in the service did not know their fate or even if they would ever return home. Yet, Marvin Levin put on a sailor uniform and a smile the size of Philadelphia as he joined the U.S. Navy and left his family for military service in the 1940s. (Courtesy of Marvin Levin.)

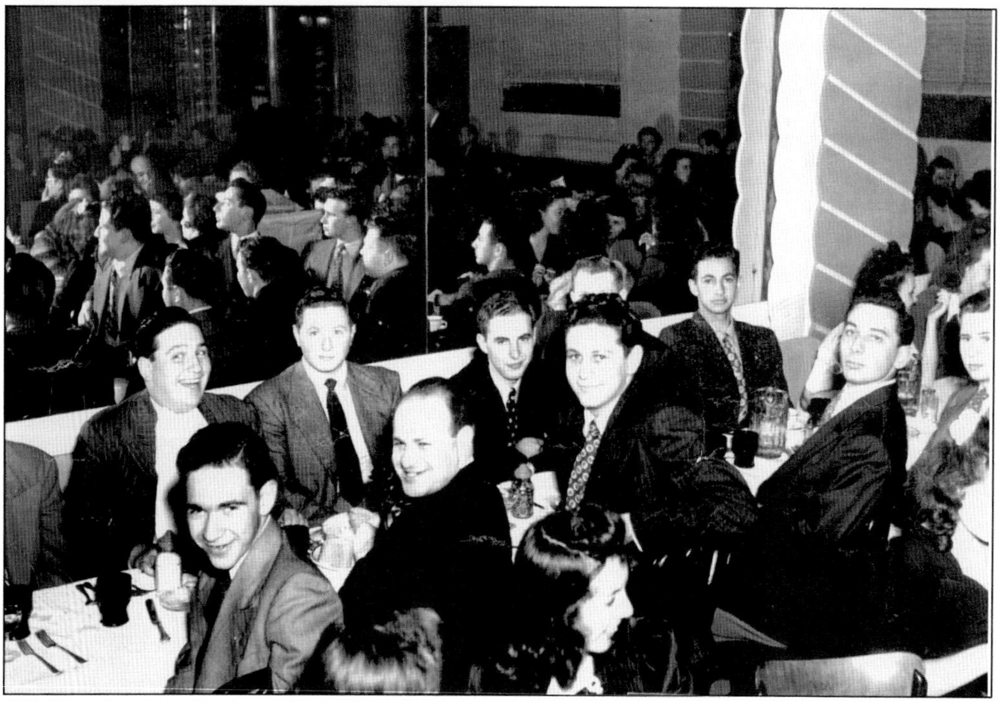

Soldiers assemble while on leave for a gathering at the famous Palumbo's Restaurant in South Philadelphia during 1943. The Boy Scout troop at the Kensington Jewish Community Center had prepared them for duty, and now they were grown up and ready. Among those pictured are Len Sokolove, Milt Sokolove, Ted Harris, Mort Friendly, Lawrence Levan, Izzy Goldberg, Mort Molotsky, Herky Kanefsky, and Ralph Denenberg. (Courtesy of Lawrence Levan.)

Service to one's country became the family's urgent plea. Many recently married young men put aside the future and enlisted. Patriotism in the Jewish community ran high, resulting in a large enlistment rate. Yet, the seriousness of the situation could be seen on the faces of the young men, including Leonard Sirlin, the son of Ben and Bessie Sirlin, from the 3000 block of Richmond Street, off Allegheny Avenue. (Courtesy of Marilyn Sirlin Schwerin.)

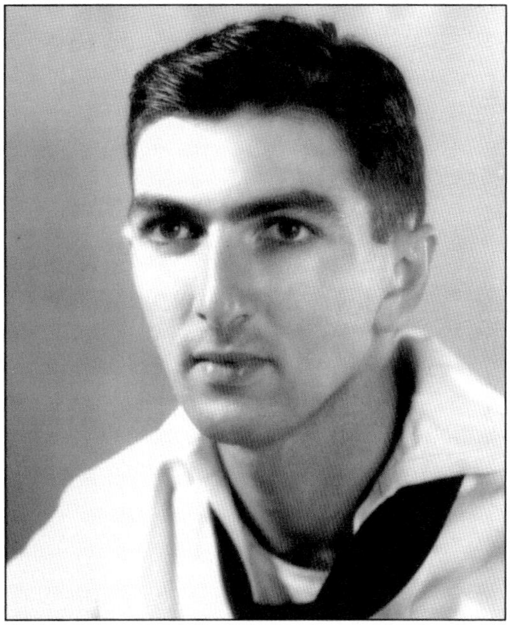

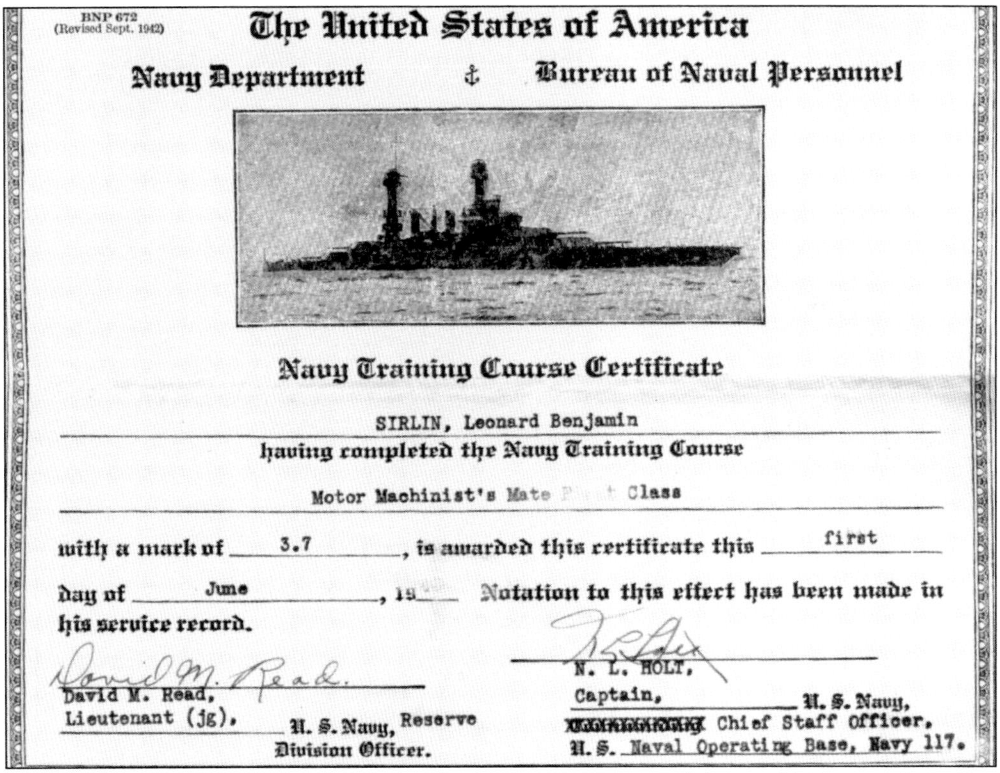

BNP 672
(Revised Sept. 1942)

The United States of America

Navy Department ⚓ Bureau of Naval Personnel

Navy Training Course Certificate

SIRLIN, Leonard Benjamin

having completed the Navy Training Course

Motor Machinist's Mate [illegible] Class

with a mark of 3.7, is awarded this certificate this first day of June, 19__. Notation to this effect has been made in his service record.

David M. Read,
Lieutenant (jg), U. S. Navy, Reserve
Division Officer.

N. L. HOLT,
Captain, U. S. Navy,
Chief Staff Officer,
U. S. Naval Operating Base, Navy 117.

Leonard Sirlin joined the U.S. Navy for the opportunity to travel the world. First, each trainee went through basic training, and since Philadelphia had its own shipyard with a great flotilla of ships, training took place in the local community. Sirlin received high marks (3.7), with a certificate of achievement for qualifying as a motor machinist's mate first class in 1943. (Courtesy of Marilyn Sirlin Schwerin.)

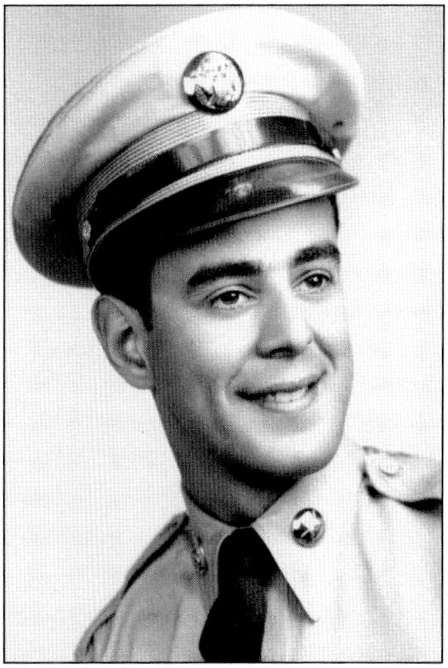

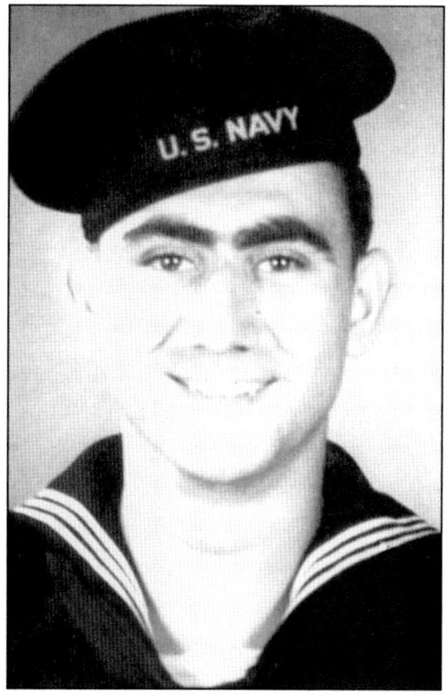

Members of the Jewish community joined the military effort to wipe out Nazism and fight the Japanese. Raymond Rosenblum (left), a cousin of Leah Karp, joined the U.S. Air Force. Harry Stern (right) lived with his grandparents in Woodbine, New Jersey, from age three to age eight. He worked as a mechanic for the Budd car chassis manufacturer before joining the U.S. Navy. (Left, courtesy of Leah Karp; right, courtesy of Harry Stern.)

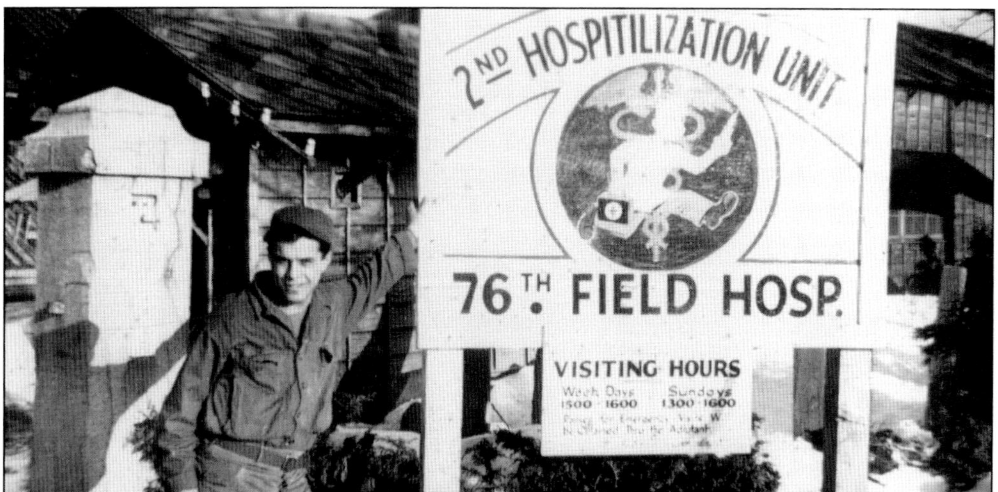

Sometimes one's upbringing lends itself to future appointments. Leo Prince, the son of David Prince, a Kensington druggist at 953 East Tioga Street, wanted to fill capsules and help sick people get better. That dream took shape in the military service; he was stationed at the 76th Field Hospital in Japan in 1946. Rebuilding Japan enabled him to practice his dream, but in a faraway place. (Courtesy of Lee Prince Waters.)

Looking the part is always key to success in life. Henry Merrill Levan, son of James Levan, from the famous chocolate candy store in Kensington, served his country in the last cavalry (2nd) division of the U.S. Army during World War II, with training at Fort Riley in Kansas City, Missouri, in 1942. (Courtesy of Lawrence Levan.)

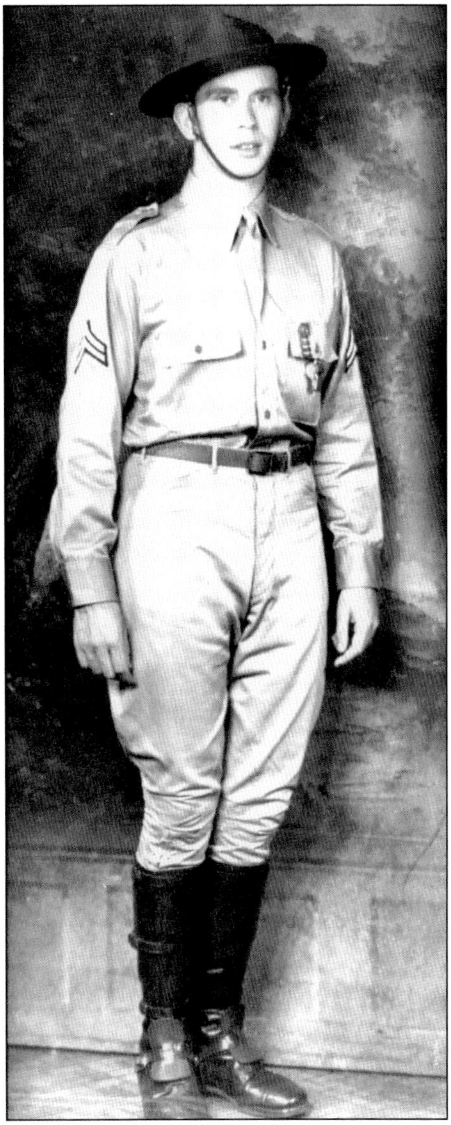

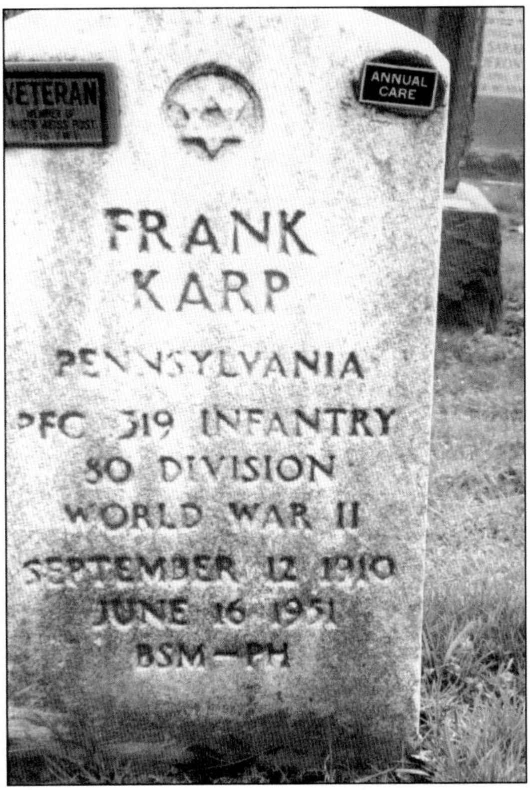

Jewish pride ran high in the community, and all the parents shuddered to think that their child might fall victim when events of war went awry, and the blue star in the front window would have to be changed to a gold star. Rebecca and Harry Karp knew that anguish when they received word that their son, Frank Karp, was killed in action during the Battle of the Bulge. (Courtesy of Al Karp.)

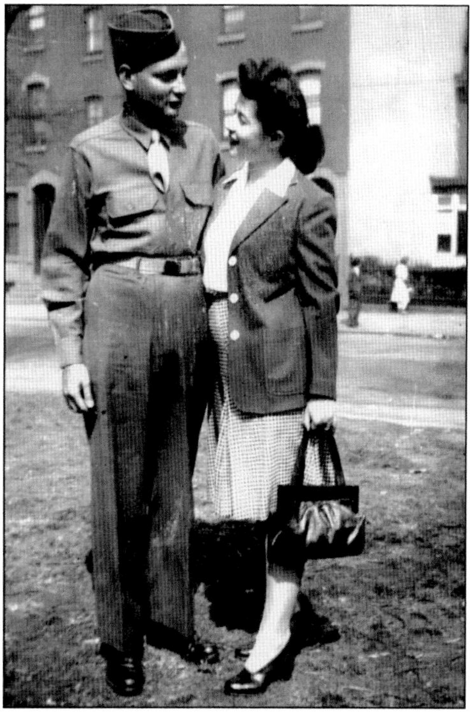

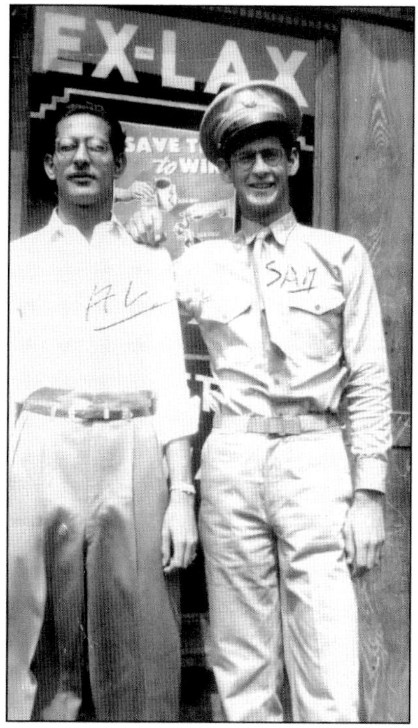

Marvin Spiro, a new recruit in the U.S. Army, and his wife, the former Lillian Schultz, share a brief moment (left) in Norris Square, near Front and Kensington Avenue, where their parents had businesses. Albert Karp (far right), from 2100 Williams Street, Jewtown, came home on leave to visit his brother Sam in front of Finklestein's drugstore. Neighbors came over to wish him well, too, including the Fishers, Lyons, Colemans, Gordons, and Rubins. (Left, courtesy of Marv Spiro; right, courtesy of Al Karp.)

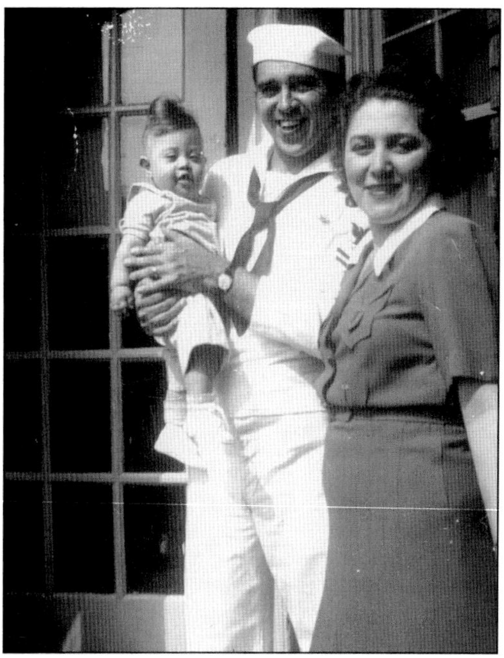

Proud parents themselves, Herbert Baker and his wife, the former Freda Rosner, from Strawberry Mansion, are pictured with their newborn child. Baker, a draftee, reported to the West Philadelphia Armory, at Thirty-second and Lancaster Avenue, where he was promptly asked, "What branch of the service do you want to serve?" He spent the next three weeks in the army before transferring over to the navy. (Courtesy of Herb Baker.)

Ten

Oy Vey, the Gang Is All Here

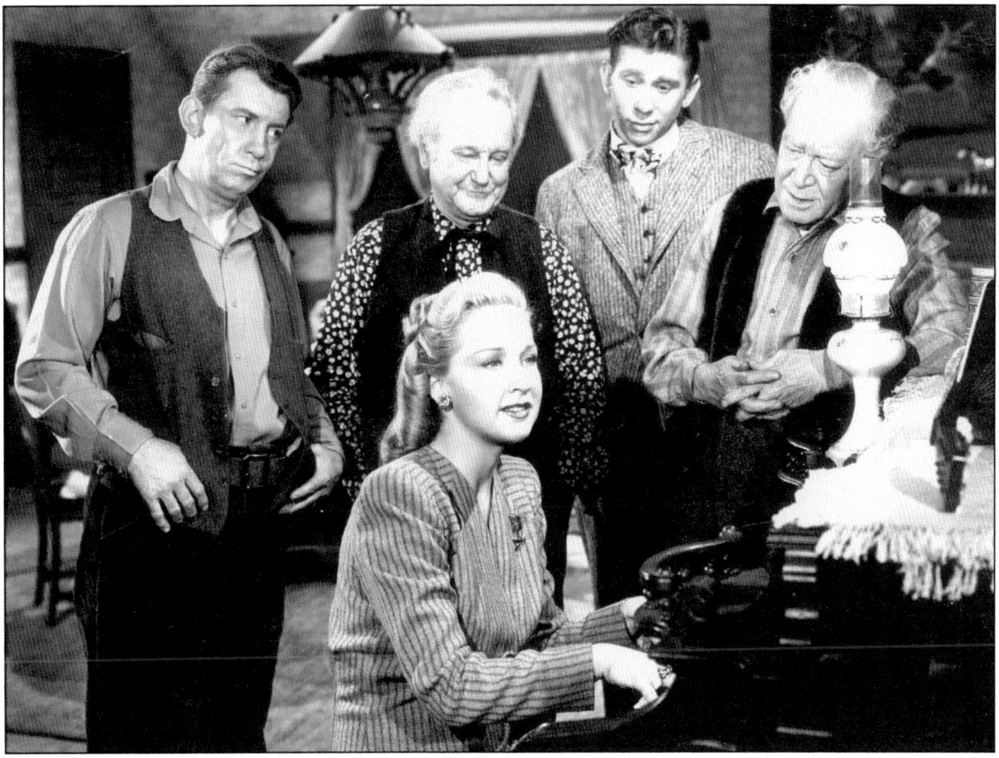

The absence of television allowed extended families to meet and have fun on many an occasion. This chapter reflects that camaraderie. The settings were hotel banquet rooms, catering halls, and anyplace into which 20 or more people could fit that had plenty of soda water and good food. By the late 1960s, those days had passed and individuals could lead their lives outside of the family circle with no pressure from the matriarchs or others who insisted on family gatherings. Groups at work soon took the place of family, as in the above photograph, which shows Bob Merrill (second from the right)—the son of James Levan, owner of the chocolate candy store in Kensington—during a production in Hollywood. Bob Merrill made the big times, and yet he continued to call and write home. (Courtesy of Lawrence Levan.)

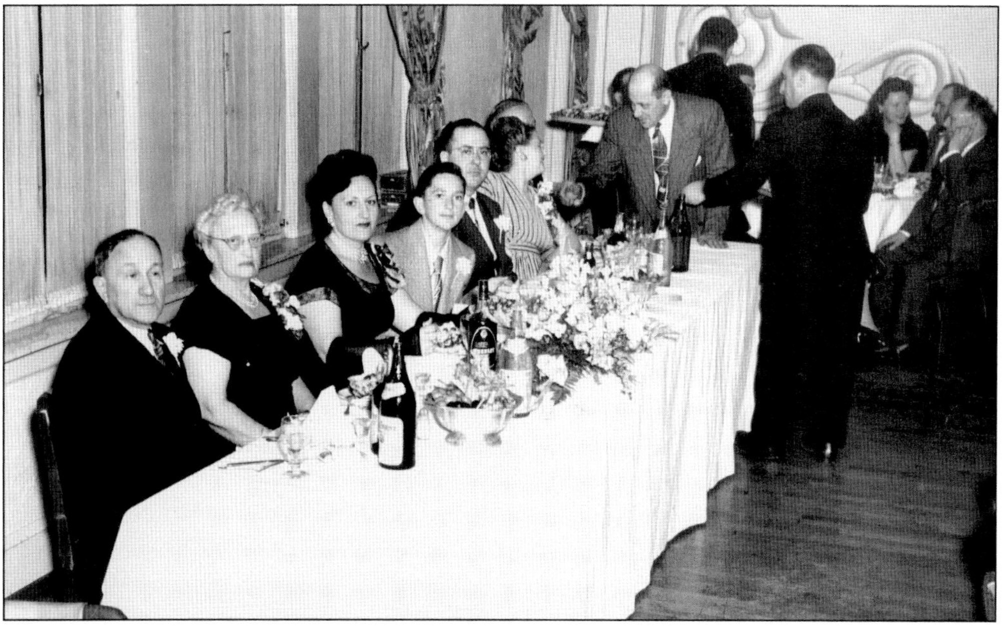

The Barney Gross family migrated from Russia in the 1920s. The pickle business grew from an idea in 1938 to collect fresh produce in New Jersey and process the cucumbers into pickles. Once packaged, two pickles for 49¢ later grew into a factory operation in Kensington at 1758–1764 North Front Street. Richard Gross's bar mitzvah at the Savoy catering hall, owned by Bob and Al Cohen in 1947, allowed the family to gather, with Barney and Dorothy Gross, Abe and Sarah Gross, and George and Bertha Parris in attendance. (Courtesy of Richard Gross.)

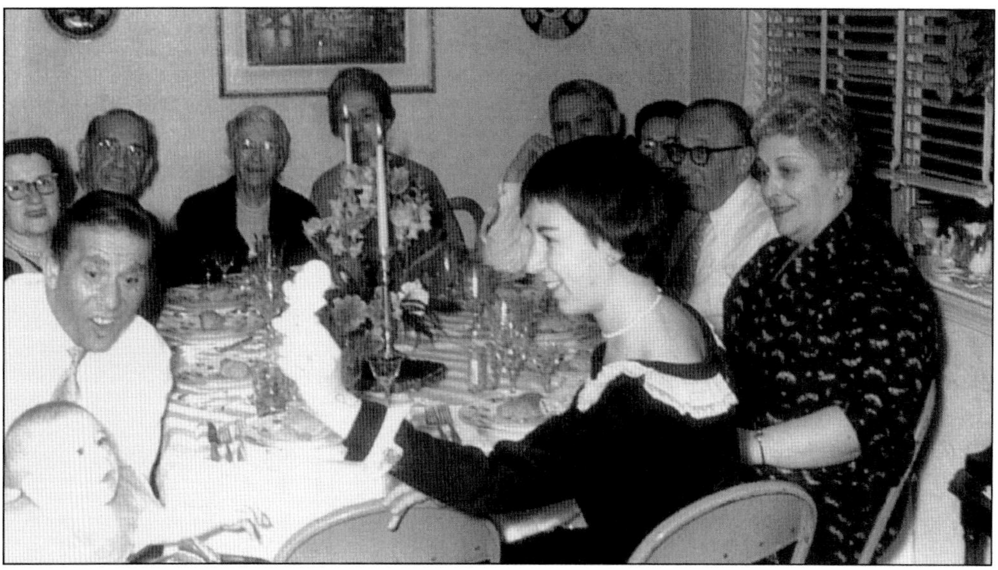

Henry Levan (left, behind the baby) took the stage name of Bob Merrill when he went west and made it big in Hollywood. The famous songwriter, known for "How Much Is That Doggy in the Window," never forgot his Kensington roots. He traveled back east to a Passover Seder in 1958 to visit with his parents, James and Sadie Levan, brother Lawrence, Nana Zimmerman, Char Zimmerman, Joseph and Mary Kall, and Michael and Eleanor Linden. (Courtesy of Lawrence Levan.)

Ben and Bessie Sirlin married off their daughter Marilyn to Norman Schwerin in the best manner possible, with great detail given to the maids of honor, right down to the exact number of flowers in each bouquet. The cost of the wedding for a Jewish couple traditionally fell on the shoulders of the young woman's family. (Courtesy of Marilyn Sirlin Schwerin.)

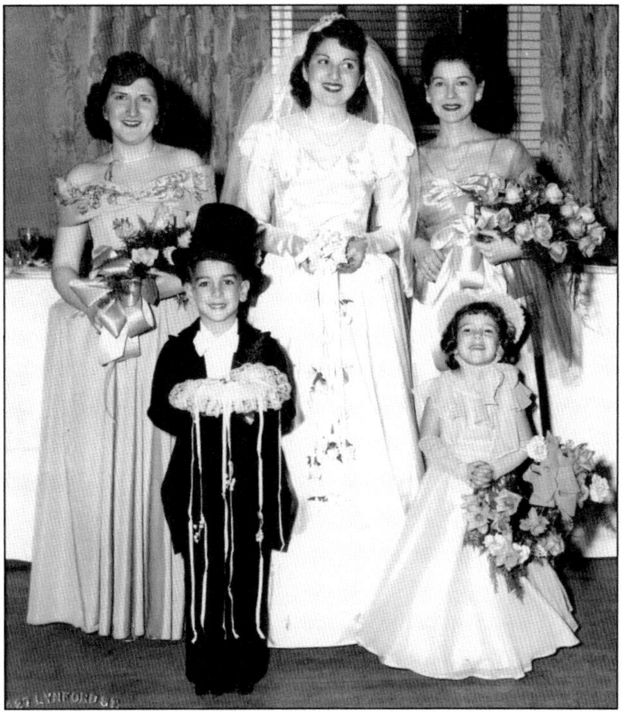

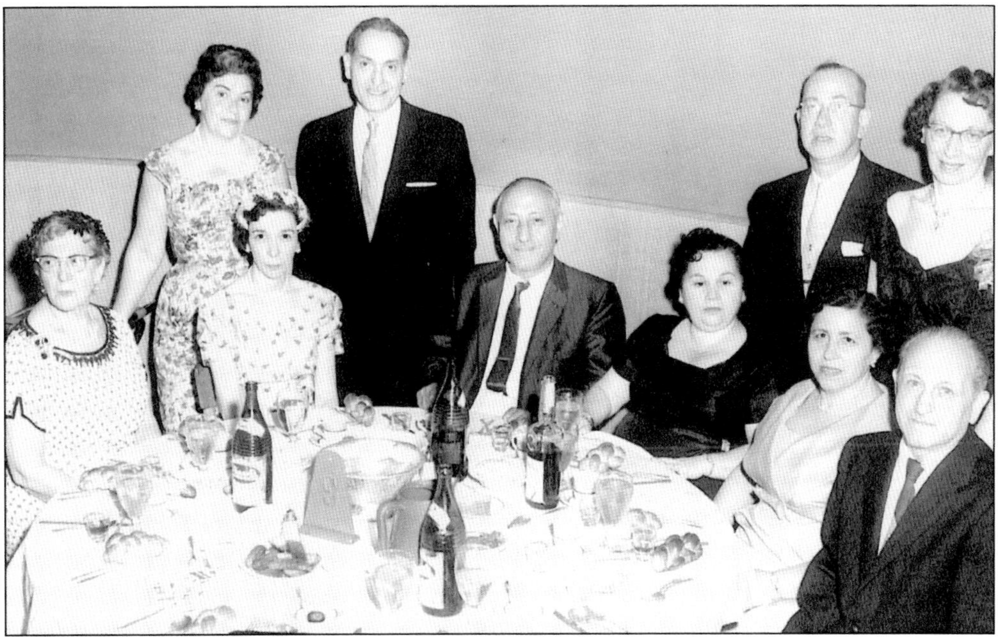

If it is, Franks—Thanks. The secret to long life included the dispensing of Franks soda water from South Philadelphia in big two-quart bottles. The Jewish introduction party became more than an event, since both sides of the family joined in. From left to right are the following: (seated) Edna and Doris Woodside, David and Ann Schatz, and Bessie and Leon Schatz (who introduced Martin to Janice); (standing) Gert and Irv Sablosky and Norman and Yetta Ruberg. (Courtesy of Janice Kleinman Spivack.)

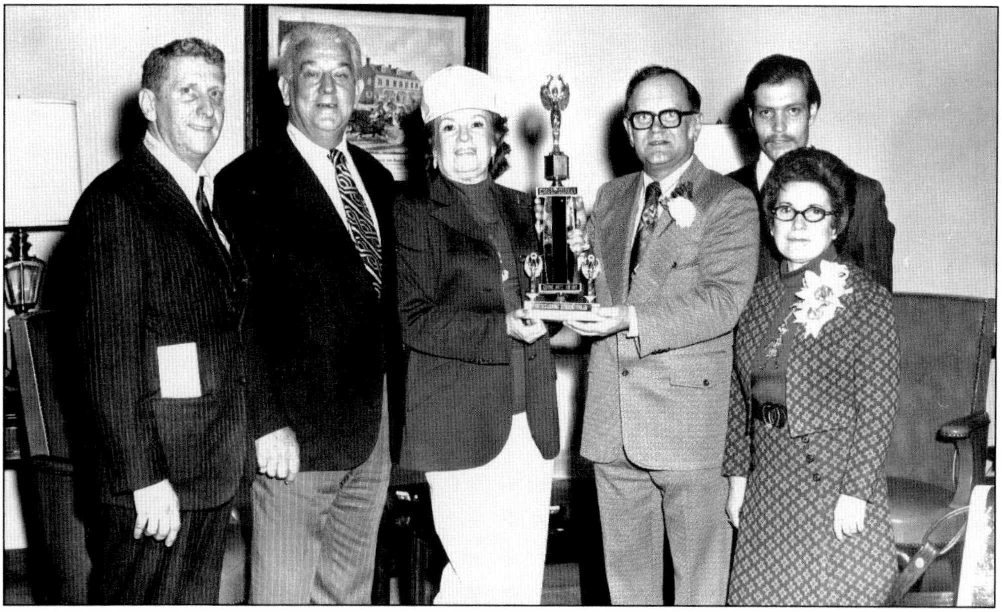

"So proud to be from Kensington" is what Edith Seidman tells everyone she comes in contact with about her adopted home. Ed Seidman was awarded the outstanding Kensingtonian honor in 1972 by the *Guide* newspaper for the community. In this picture, the award is being presented by Dorothy Mitosky and Matt Mc Kinney. Ed Seidman always gave back to the community, especially when fire raced through 10 homes on Schiller Street, leaving many homeless. A fund started by the new Harrowgate businessmen association saved the day. (Courtesy of Edith Seidman.)

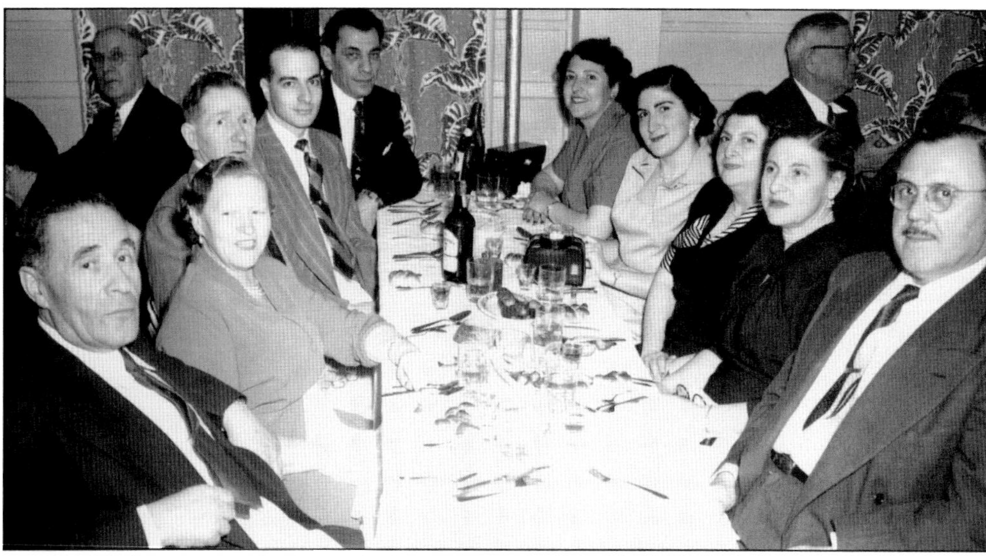

A catered affair was part and parcel of growing up in a Jewish household during the 1940s until the 1970s. The long and narrow rows of wonderfully decorated tables made Uhr's Rumanian Restaurant, at Fifth and South Streets, a good venue for any affair, especially that of family and friends. The nearness of the invited guests in close quarters was entertaining and eliminated the need to shout across the room. (Courtesy of Marilyn Schwerin.)

In 2000, various youth groups made up of children from the merchants along Kensington Avenue held a reunion for the people who once played Ping-Pong, put on skits, and played ball via the efforts of the Kensington Synagogue and its auxiliary community center building, only a few doors away. Held at the Bala Country Club, the reunion was a huge success. (Courtesy of Gladis Gimpel.)

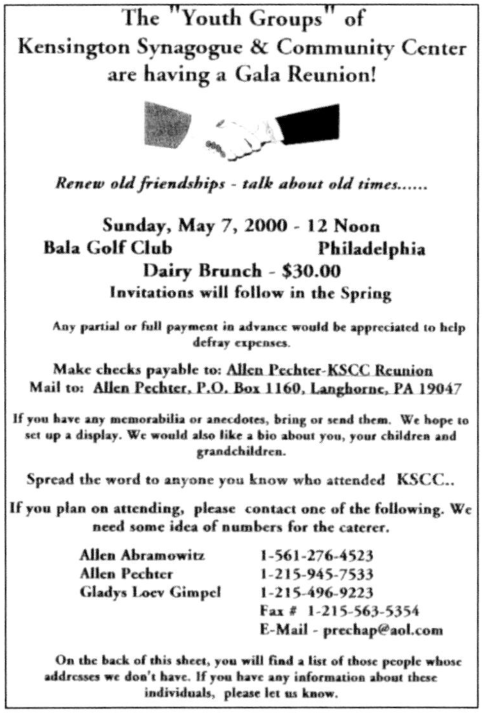

The "Youth Groups" of
Kensington Synagogue & Community Center
are having a Gala Reunion!

Renew old friendships - talk about old times......

Sunday, May 7, 2000 - 12 Noon
Bala Golf Club Philadelphia
Dairy Brunch - $30.00
Invitations will follow in the Spring

Any partial or full payment in advance would be appreciated to help defray expenses.

Make checks payable to: Allen Pechter-KSCC Reunion
Mail to: Allen Pechter, P.O. Box 1160, Langhorne, PA 19047

If you have any memorabilia or anecdotes, bring or send them. We hope to set up a display. We would also like a bio about you, your children and grandchildren.

Spread the word to anyone you know who attended KSCC..

If you plan on attending, please contact one of the following. We need some idea of numbers for the caterer.

Allen Abramowitz	1-561-276-4523
Allen Pechter	1-215-945-7533
Gladys Loev Gimpel	1-215-496-9223
	Fax # 1-215-563-5354
	E-Mail - prechap@aol.com

On the back of this sheet, you will find a list of those people whose addresses we don't have. If you have any information about these individuals, please let us know.

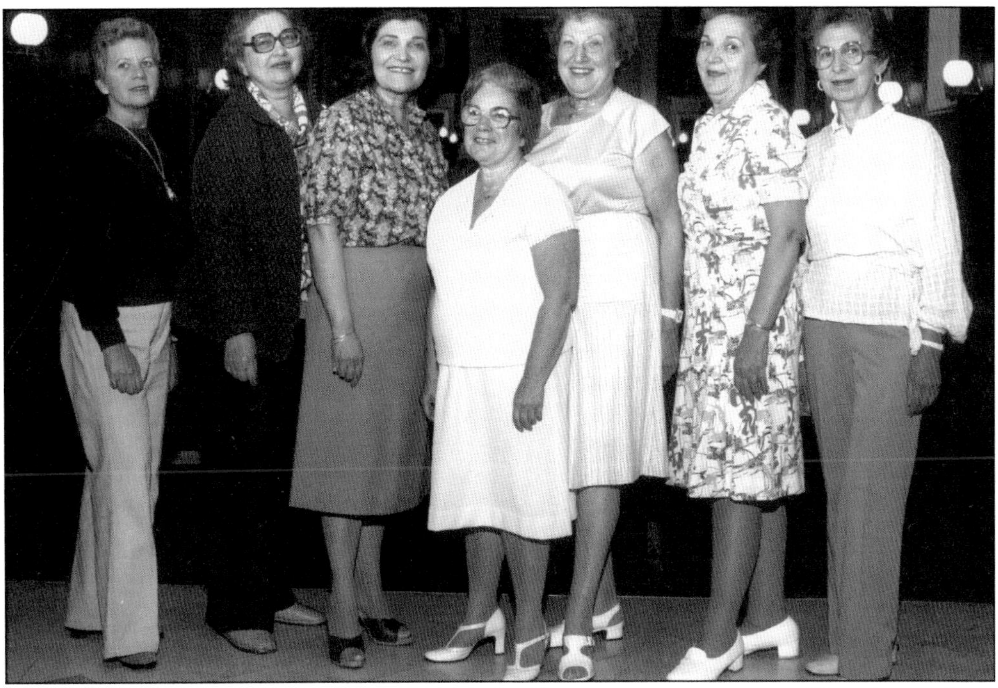

We were once young and up-and-coming in the Kensington community of Jewish merchant families. Kensington was never going to change, right? The parents did get older, and yet we celebrated our heritage as we always did, with photographs, of course. From left to right are Zena Forman, Goldie Ostroff, Marilyn Shuben, Edith Seidman, Frances Bogdanoff, Belle Friedman, and Yetta Gold. (Courtesy of Edith Seidman.)

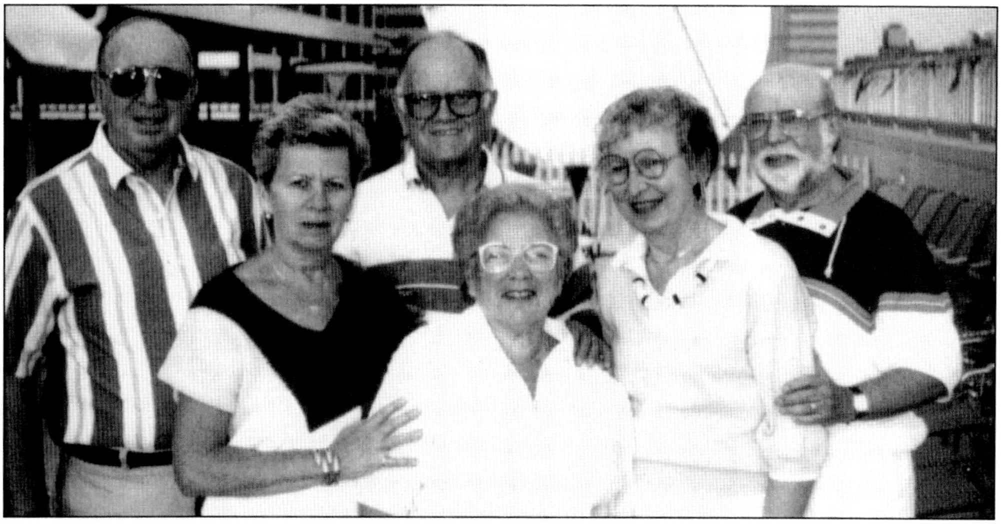

Some years later, a group of friends, now couples, met down the shore in their casual clothes to kibitz and pass away the time, just like in the old days. Friends forever include Charlie and Marilyn Shuben, Edith and Izzy Seidman, and Yetta and Len Gold. It seemed like only yesterday when the whole crew put on the skit *Fiddler on the Roof* at the synagogue on Allegheny Avenue. One thing has remained constant: having fun as a group. (Courtesy of Len Gold.)

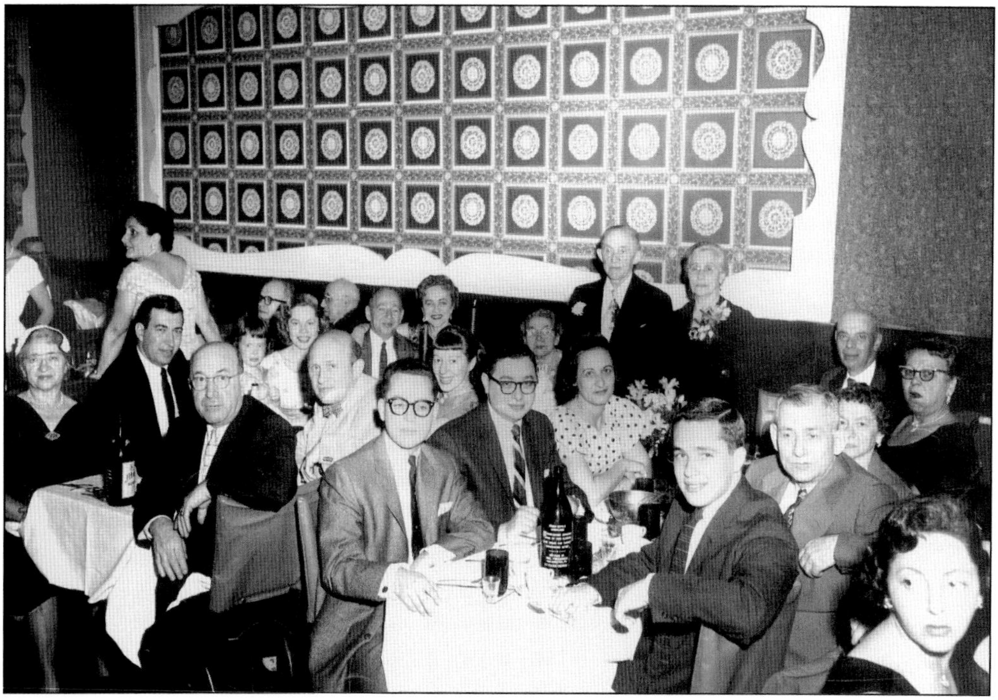

During World War II, Philadelphians led very precarious lives. The day-to-day rationing of food and the trek to food stores with ration stamps in hand did not make for joyous times. Yet many families celebrated the power of family when an anniversary came with much pomp and fanfare. The 50th wedding anniversary of Alan Remstein's grandparents attracted a large gathering. (Courtesy of Alan Remstein.)

Eleven

FAMILIAR FACES

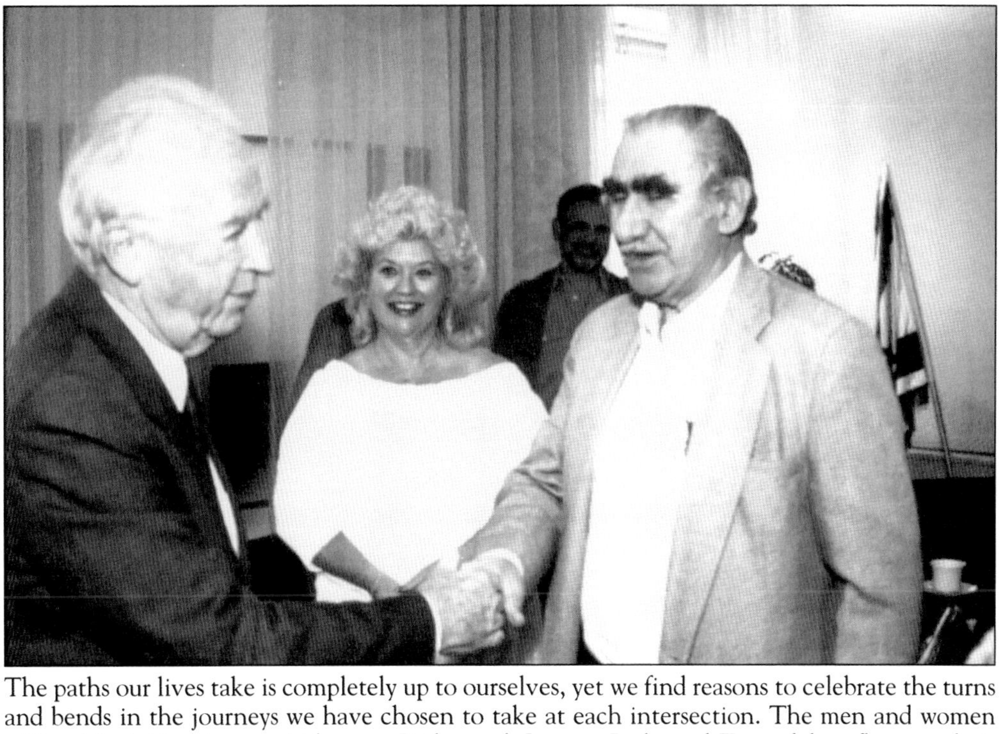

The paths our lives take is completely up to ourselves, yet we find reasons to celebrate the turns and bends in the journeys we have chosen to take at each intersection. The men and women of Frankford, Kensington, Fishtown, Richmond, Juanita Park, and Torresdale reflect on their choices 40, 50, 60, and even more years later. We have met friends, maintained family ties of utmost importance, and have given thanks for our parents who allowed us to pass through these neighborhoods years ago and for what it has meant to us today, half a century later. Harry Stern (right), a builder of the future with his many business dealings (Action Manufacturing, Frankford), fulfilled the age-old concept of giving back to the Jewish community. The generosity of this great man is widely known throughout Philadelphia. With him is then prime minister of Israel Yitzhak Rabin. (Courtesy of Harry Stern and Carl Nathans.)

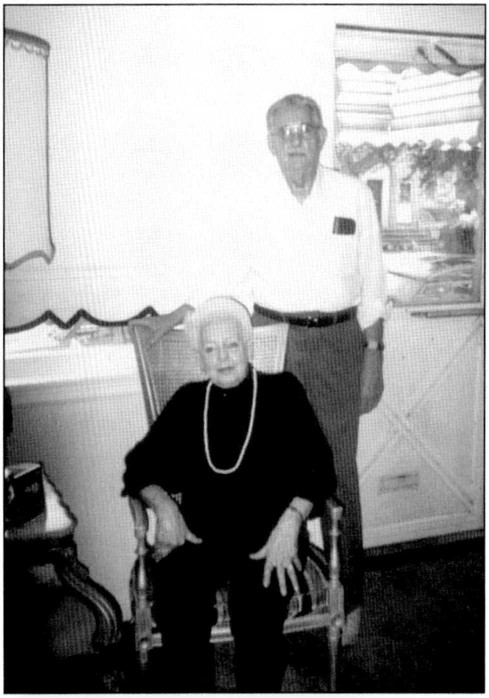

Through all the years, many Jewish couples remain strong and loyal to one another. Albert Karp and the former Leah Cohen, both from the Jewtown neighborhood near Williams Street, have honored the Bible belief of one partner for one lifetime. Married by Rabbi Brenner from the community in 1947, the Karps continue to respect and honor each other in old age. (Courtesy of David and Stacy Silver.)

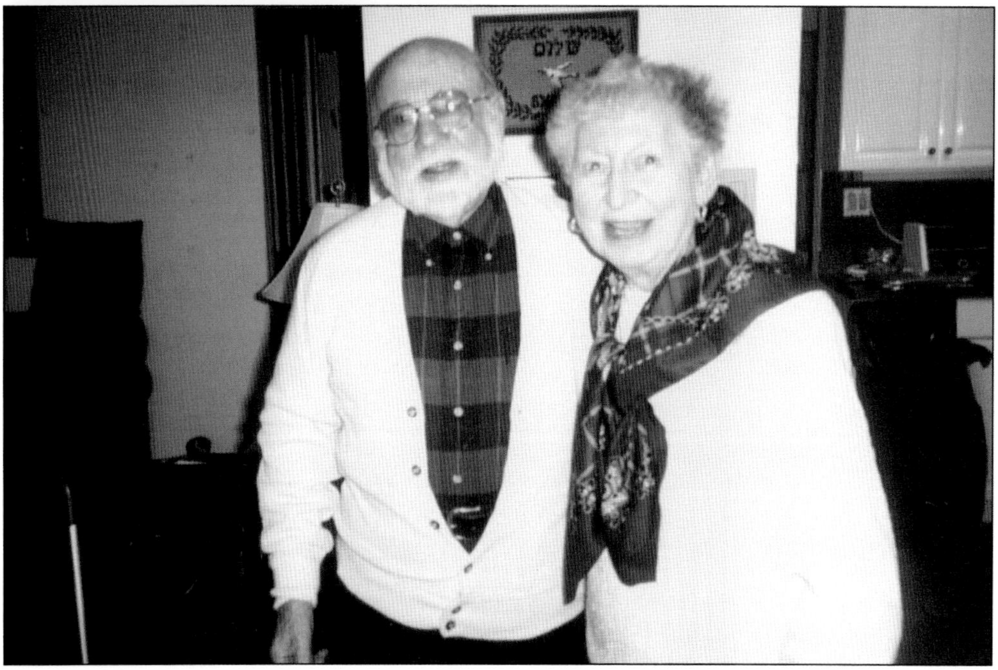

The final phase for most married couples is when they can enjoy their golden years as Zayde and Bubbie. That is where Len and Yetta Gold are today. Yetta Berman Gold grew up at Twenty-third and Jefferson Streets. She recalls her childhood in Philadelphia as one of freedom—when she could travel any place in the city with a nickel in hand for a trolley-car ride. Len Gold's parents, Michael and Mary Gold, met at Finklestein's summer retreat in Collegeville, Pennsylvania, and lived at 2975 Frankford Avenue. (Courtesy of the Golds.)

Food and a great place for conversation make for an opportune time to snap a family photograph. The Kleinman family, from 2732 East Cambria Street, lived at the end of the Route No. 54 trolley car line. David Kleinman took a job as a machinist while his wife, Eva Kleinman, managed a fruit and produce store. (Courtesy of Janice Kleinman Spivack.)

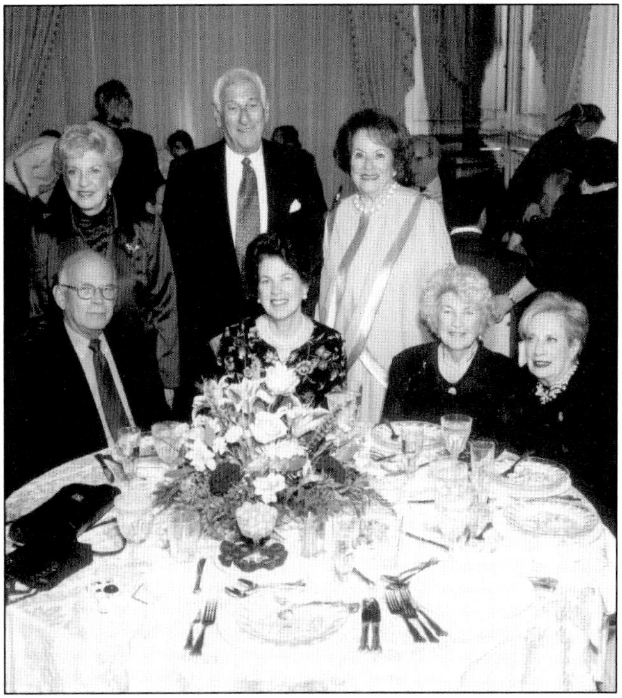

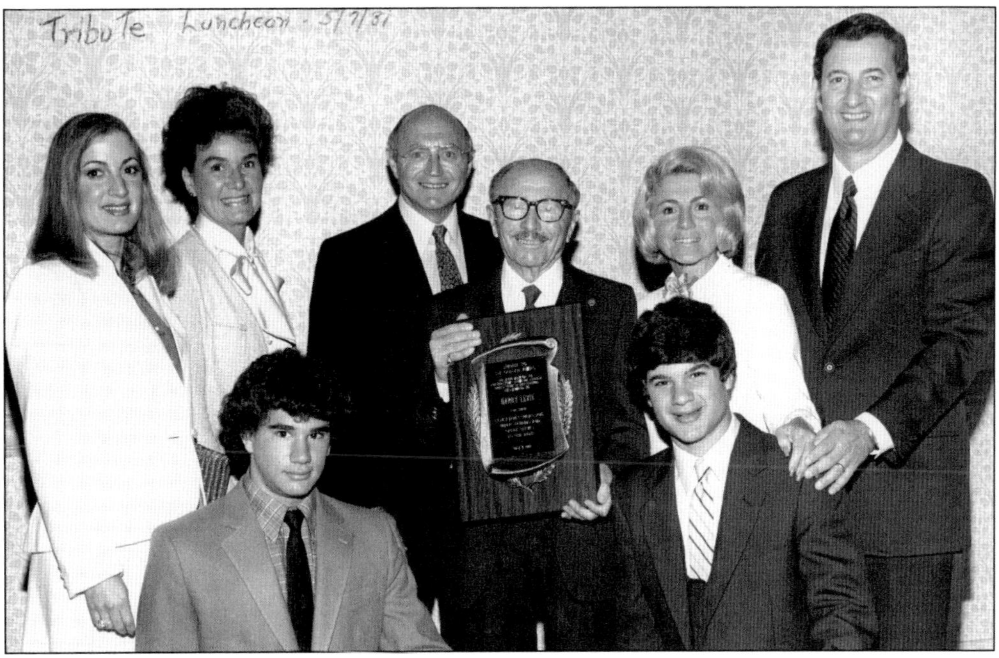

Honor thy mother and father is another Judaic concept that is ageless. The time to do so is while your parents are still alive. No matter how the community perceives the individual, it is the family that surrounds and supports each other with love, compassion, and respect. Harry Levin, a longtime merchant on Kensington Avenue, is honored for his work in conjunction with the Philadelphia Geriatric Center located in Logan. The Levin and Vizak families joined forces to honor Harry Levin at a tribute luncheon in 1981. (Courtesy of Marvin Levin.)

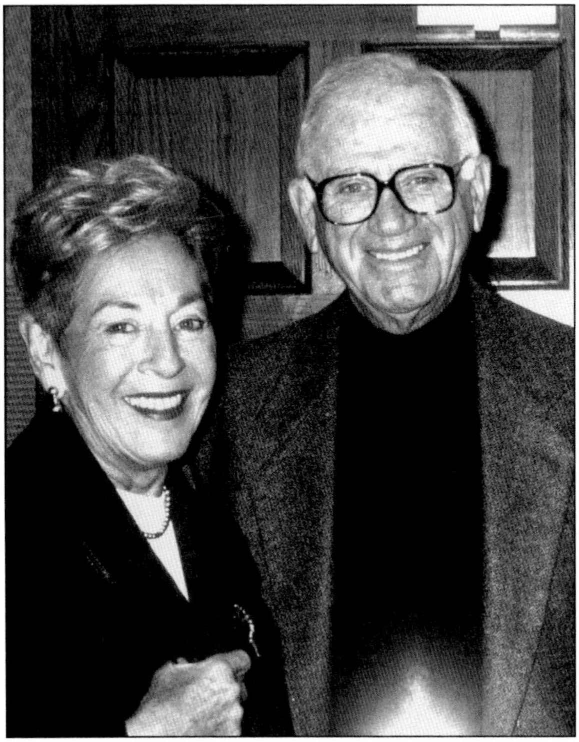

Stan Rooklin, from 2910 Richmond Street, enjoyed his childhood and owed a lot to his parents, Ben and Anna Rooklin, who provided him with a neighborhood where he was able to enjoy the meadows along the Delaware River and catch fish. He was friends with the children of the merchants in the area, including the Glousteins, Sterns, Loves, Freidmans, and Pearlmans. He and his wife, Leah Toplin, who grew up at 3441 G Street in Kensington, have been married for many years and have retired only recently to Martins Run in Broomall. (Courtesy of the Rooklins.)

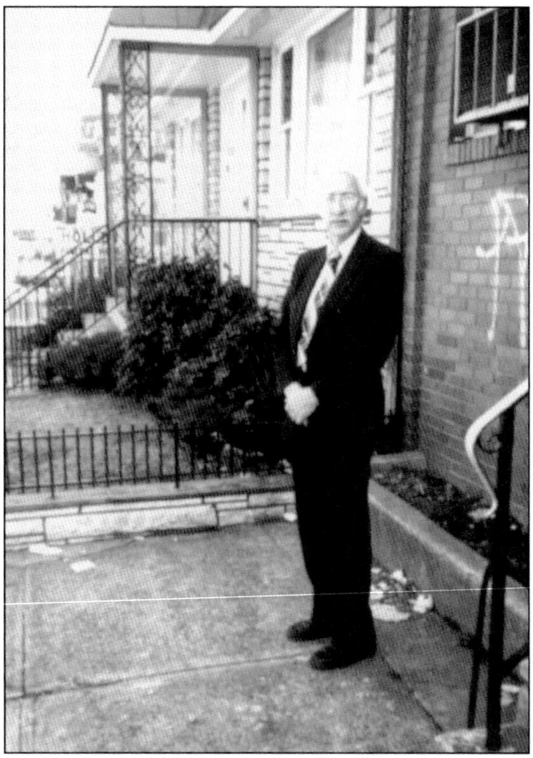

Dr. Hymen Kanoff set up his practice at 724 East Allegheny Avenue, off Kensington Avenue, in the 1950s. Visiting one's old neighborhood is an inspirational experience for many Philadelphians, and Kanoff did his tour of the old homestead in 1986. Doctors and professionals were plentiful and included Dr. Soltroff, Dr. Joe Bogdanoff, Dr. Ginsberg, Dr. Krausner, and Dr.Promerantz—all of whom enjoyed going to Kensington Avenue for a great delicatessen sandwich. (Courtesy of Hymen Kanoff.)

Jean Seder, the daughter of Herman and Janet Blum, lived at 4651 Leiper Street as a child, while her parents owned the Crafttex and Moss Rose (C Street and Indiana) textile mills in Kensington. Kensington had the work ethic of a small town. Jean Seder personally captured the factory workers' experience with a collection of vignettes published as the *Voices of Kensington* in 1982. Her contribution to history is now preserved for future generations to read. (Courtesy of Allen Meyers.)

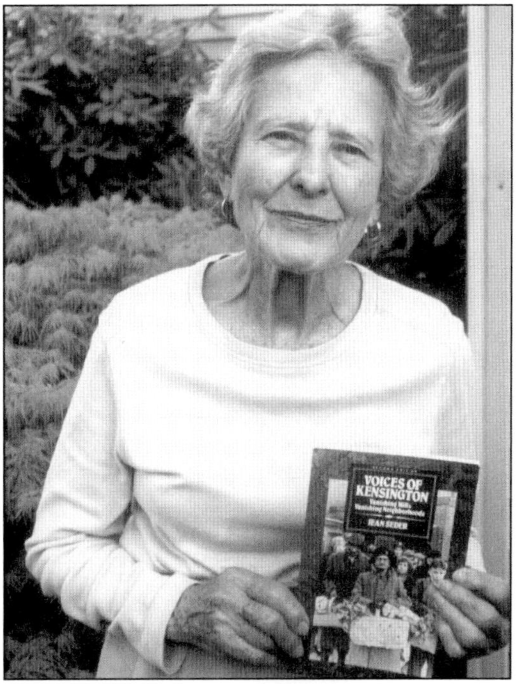

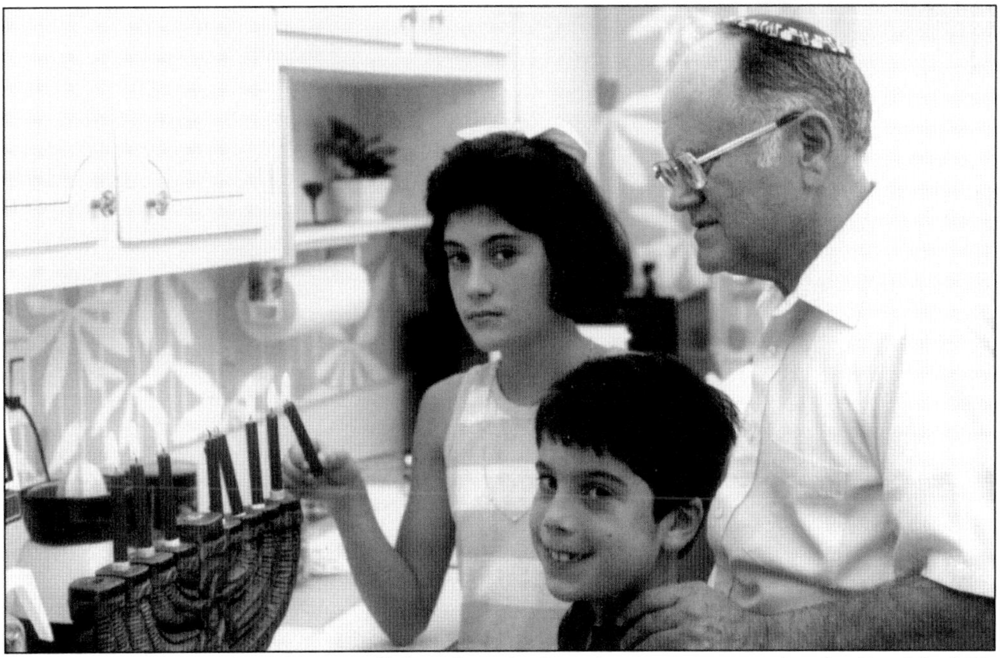

Culture, heritage, and history are all found in the Jewish community under the Frankford El. The Jewish people of these neighborhoods did not live in a predominantly Jewish area, yet they banded together to form a united community. Very few Jewish people married out of their religion due to a high level of support by other Jewish people who practiced their religion in public by closing their stores for the Jewish holidays. In this photograph, Izzy Seidman lights the Chanukah menorah with his grandchildren, as his grandparents did years ago. (Courtesy of Edith Seidman.)

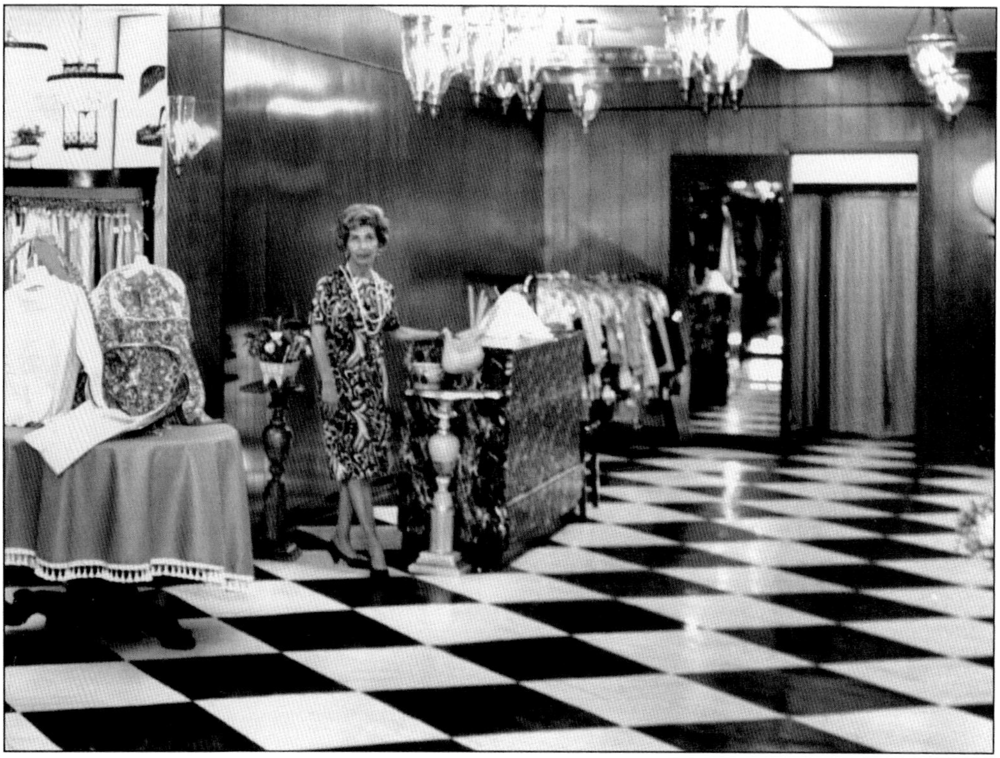

Helen Rowen and her husband, Emil, escaped Nazi Germany in 1932 and settled in Paris, France. The couple's stay lasted until 1942, when the Rowens fled to Switzerland. In 1946, they migrated to America, settling in South Philadelphia, where they started a hosiery business. The couple later opened a store in Kensington, where stockings were sold three for $1. After Helen Rowen added clothing, they needed larger quarters. They moved to 3079 Kensington Avenue, where a double store (the Fair Lady) did fantastically well from 1960 until 1975. Their store included a second floor where "knits," or three-piece suits, were sold. They carried the Ellen Tracy line of women's clothes until the passing of Emil Rowen in 1976 and the store's closing.

AFTERWORD

How specific photographs make it into books about old Jewish neighborhoods by Allen Meyers is a story all by itself and could take many hours to tell. This particular story is about survival of a physical, spiritual, and long-lasting variety. The Rowens survived the Nazis, and this photograph (rescued by Carl Nathans) was destined to survive, too. Marion Rowen Miller is joined by the grandchildren of the Rowens, Daniel, Gail, Deborah, and Judith, in paying tribute to the life of their Helen Rowen. May she always be thought of as a survivor and an inspiration to those who have had the privilege to know her. She passed away on Sunday, June 22, 2003.

The research and compilation of the history and preservation of the Kensington and Frankford Jewish communities will continue with your help. To share information and materials, please contact Allen Meyers at 856-582-0432, 610-212-4548, ameyers@net-gate.com, or 11 Ark Court, Sewell, NJ, 08080. His Web site is www.JewishPhillyNeighbors.com.